Televising Chineseness

CHINA UNDERSTANDINGS TODAY

Series Editors: Mary Gallagher and Emily Wilcox

China Understandings Today is dedicated to the study of contemporary China and seeks to present the latest and most innovative scholarship in social sciences and the humanities to the academic community as well as the general public. The series is sponsored by the Lieberthal-Rogel Center for Chinese Studies at the University of Michigan.

A complete list of titles in the series can be found at www.press.umich.edu

Televising Chineseness

GENDER, NATION, AND SUBJECTIVITY

Geng Song

University of Michigan Press
Ann Arbor

For questions or permissions, please contact um.press.perms@umich.edu

Published in the United States of America by the
University of Michigan Press
Printed and bound by CPI Group (UK) Ltd, Croydon, CR0 4YY
First published May 2022

A CIP catalog record for this book is available from the British Library.

Library of Congress Cataloging-in-Publication data has been applied for.

ISBN 978-0-472-07529-4 (hardcover: alk. paper)
ISBN 978-0-472-05529-6 (paper: alk. paper)
ISBN 978-0-472-22004-5 (e-book)

Library of Congress Control Number: 2022933390

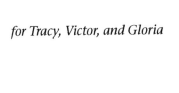

for Tracy, Victor, and Gloria

Contents

Digital materials related to this title can be found on the Fulcrum platform via the following citable URL: https://doi.org/10.3998/mpub.12221862

Acknowledgments

Working on an academic book is a process of ongoing dialogues with other scholars, both in real life and in metaphorical terms. This book would not have been possible without the benefit of the excellent work of my fellow scholars. In the process of working on the project, numerous scholars, in the capacity of mentors, friends, students, colleagues, conference coparticipants, editors, and manuscript reviewers, have provided helpful insights and advice. I feel deeply indebted to all of them. A far from exhaustive list includes Rey Chow, Sheldon Lu, Shu-mei Shih, Ying Zhu, Michael Keane, Chris Berry, Michel Hockx, Wanning Sun, Shuyu Kong, Ruoyun Bai, Peter Jackson, Hui Xiao, Hongwei Bao, Jamie J. Zhao, Travis Kong, Qian Gong, Lauren Gorfinkel, Roald Maliangkay, Yu Zhang, Haomin Gong, Xin Yang, Yongmei Wu, Stefan Harvey, and Xuying Yu. I feel privileged for the many fruitful conversations I have had with Kam Louie, Louise Edwards, Jiwei Ci, and Xiaoying Wang—my lifelong mentors and friends—over the years. With funding from the Hong Kong University Faculty of Arts, Stephanie Donald, in the capacity of a "critical friend," read the entire book in draft form and provided suggestions that have significantly improved it.

The book has also benefited from the feedback I received while giving talks on the interim results of my research during my visits to various institutions. I am thankful to the colleagues who invited me and hosted my visits: Shuge Wei of the Australian Center on China in the World, the Australian National University; Wenhong Chen of the Department of Radio-Television-Film, University of Texas at Austin; Derek Hird of Lancaster University; Binghan Zheng of Durham University; Margaret Hillenbrand of the China Center, University of Oxford; Xi Liu of the Department of China Studies at Xi'an Jiaotong-Liverpool University; Ling Yang of Xiamen University; and Cheng Guangwei of Renmin University in Beijing.

Particular thanks go to my research assistants and fieldwork helpers for their invaluable contributions: Magdalena Wong assisted me professionally with the focus group discussions with TV viewers; Jun Wang helped me with data collection on female images in Chinese television; and Leyuan Ma translated a number of online texts and interview transcripts from Chinese into English. I am also greatly indebted to Erika Hebblethwaite for her excellent copy editing service.

I am grateful to colleagues in the Faculty of Arts and School of Chinese at the University of Hong Kong for their moral support and collegiality, especially to Derek Collins, Cuncun Wu, John Carrol, Stephen Yiu-wai Chu, Guoqi Xu, Joseph Poon, and Richard Van Ness Simmons for their continuing guidance and help. I also wish to express my heartfelt thanks to my students for many fruitful discussions of the issues raised herein. They have much to teach me when it comes to the trends of popular culture and youth culture.

I owe a debt of gratitude to all the TV viewers who participated in the focus group discussions, as well as to the government officials and industry practitioners whom I interviewed, Zhou Jihong, Yang Ji, and Hu Ya in particular. My parents, Song Bainian and Niu Guoling, are both big fans of Chinese TV dramas and were my first and most loyal informants. Some of the ideas in the book came into being after long telephone conversations with them at night.

I wish to thank Emily Wilcox and Mary Gallagher for their interest in publishing the book as part of their "China Understandings Today" series. I benefited enormously from the helpful comments and suggestions made by the three readers appointed by the University of Michigan Press. I am also grateful to the acquisition editors: Christopher Dreyer for his confidence in the book project and Sara Cohen for her extraordinary efficiency, enthusiasm, and professionalism.

The book resulted from a research project supported by a General Research Fund grant from the Research Grants Council of the Hong Kong Special Administrative Region (Project No. 17609516). I would also like to acknowledge the support of the Louis Cha Fund for my fieldwork trips to mainland China.

Parts of this book have appeared in earlier forms, although they have since changed substantially. Chapter 1 (one section): "Cosmopolitanism with Chinese Characteristics: Transnational Male Images in Chinese TV Dramas," in *The Cosmopolitan Dream: Transnational Chinese Masculinities in a Global Age*, edited by Derek Hird and Geng Song (Hong Kong: Hong Kong

University Press, 2018); Chapter 3: "Consuming the Anti-Japanese War on the TV Screen in China: State Ideology, Market and Audience," *Journal of Oriental Studies* 49 (2) (2017); and "All Dogs Deserve to Be Beaten: Negotiating Manhood and Nationhood in Chinese TV Dramas," in *Changing Chinese Masculinities: From Imperial Pillars of State to Global Real Men*, edited by Kam Louie (Hong Kong: Hong Kong University Press, 2016); Chapter 5: "Imagining the Other: Foreigners on the Chinese TV Screen," in *Chinese Television in the Twenty-First Century: Entertaining the Nation*, edited by Ruoyun Bai and Geng Song (London: Routledge, 2015); Chapter 6: "Little Fresh Meat: The Politics of Sissiness and Sissyphobia in Contemporary China," *Men and Masculinities* May 2021, https://doi.org/10.1177/1097184X211014939.

CHAPTER I

Introduction

Gendering Chinese Nationalism

ON SEPTEMBER 1, 2018, the Chinese state broadcaster, China Central Television (CCTV), in collaboration with the Ministry of Education, broadcast the latest installment of *The First School Class*, an annual back-to-school program in which celebrities are invited to deliver lectures to primary and secondary school students. Schools across the country asked their students to watch the program. Considerable controversy ensued, however, when that year's guest celebrities turned out to be a girlish boy band known as New F4. The band's name is borrowed from the TV drama series *Meteor Garden* (*Liuxing huayuan*, 2018), an adaptation of the Japanese manga *Boys Over Flowers* (*Hana yori dango*), which features a group of four beautiful young men known as F4. The members of New F4 represent the new fashion of embodied masculinity—characterized by a trim physique, flawless skin, stylish haircut, and attractive facial features, sometimes enhanced by makeup—appearing not only in popular culture and commercial media, but also in the everyday life of urban youths in China. Their appearance on *The First School Class* generated heated debate over male effeminacy and its alleged harmfulness for the younger generation. Angry parents condemned the band's "sissy" image (*niangpao*) as representative of a "morbid culture" and a bad example for young boys. Both social media and such state media outlets as the *People's Daily* and *China Women's Daily* soon joined the fray, heatedly debating the proper standard of masculinity and its impact on the virility of the nation. Critics of the *niangpao* aesthetic trend warned that the "effeminacy of young men today means an effeminate China tomorrow" (J. Zheng 2018; L. Zhou 2018), while its defenders described it as "a more modern, less rigid form of masculinity" that is the result of China's opening up to the world and rise in the twenty-first century (H. Gao 2019, par. 4). As a consequence of the incident, however, a group of "sissy" male stars were blacklisted by state media, and the Ministry of Education even issued a directive in February 2021 calling on schools to strengthen their physical education curriculum to prevent the "feminization of male adolescents."[1]

This event exemplifies a conspicuous paradox in the gendered images in Chinese popular culture today: the increasing diversity of gender presentations, such as the proliferation of queer and nonmainstream images, goes hand in hand with conservative gender policing and a revival of patriarchy. This paradox, and its associated generational divide on gender issues, reflects both the changing political economy of the Chinese media and the tensions between neoliberal globalization and state-sanctioned ideology, nationalist politics in particular. It is notable that both camps in the aforementioned debate expressed their arguments in nationalist terms. Gender dynamics, as an important site of power negotiation, are thus both constructing and reflecting the paradoxical affective structure of confidence and anxiety associated with China's rise.

A variety of gender-related relationships—between sexism and nationalism; women, the body, and the nation; kinship and the nation—have emerged in popular entertainment, revealing an interesting yet little explored side of Chinese nationalism in the contemporary context. Nationalism, some scholars argue, reflects an essentially masculinist world view characterized by the dualistic construction of "a self in opposition to another who threatens one's very being" (Hartsock 1985, 241). With women and feminine virtue being depicted as the vulnerable embodiment of the land—to be protected by the masculine nation—gender normativity legitimizes nationalism and the social order associated with it. In addition, gender is not just about identity; it is also about "properly" nurturing the next generation, both physically and intellectually. Gender is thus central to reproduction of the nation. The rhetoric and norms of masculinity and femininity are closely linked with kinship and family, which in turn constitute the foundation of the nation. In this regard, few would disagree that television—by which I mean a multiplatform, consumerist culture of entertainment and knowledge production that grew out of the traditional TV channels—is currently the most powerful and influential mode of storytelling in fabricating both gender and national identities.

With a one-billion-plus domestic audience and growing transnational influence and accessibility, Chinese television has become a new symbol and carrier of China's soft power in an era of increasing global connectivity, and it is also playing a prominent role in cultural governance within the country. Yet compared with Chinese film studies, Chinese television studies remains an underdeveloped, albeit fast-growing, field. Echoing recent interest in the interplay between subjectivity and communication in the context of contemporary China (Schneider 2012; S. Kong 2014; H. Lee 2014), this book regards television and online drama as an effective and dynamic medium of communication and explores the roles it has played in the formation of postsocialist Chinese subjects, gendered subjects in particular. In doing so, it offers a new angle on and critical reading of a selection of Chinese TV programs, mostly TV dramas, that have proved overwhelmingly popular nationwide in recent years (most of them have aired since 2015). It also investigates how a state-sanctioned, globally negotiated version of "Chineseness" is being articulated through gender and how gender politics relates to "government of the self," to borrow Michel Foucault's term, by and through television in contemporary China.

To examine Chineseness as an affectively mediated notion, the book combines textual analysis of select TV drama series with ethnographic research of TV audiences and producers. The audience study component of the book, informed by the "active audience" concept (Morley 1992; Ang 1991), explores the multiplicity of ways in which the texts are given meaning by viewers. Firsthand data collected through interviews and focus group discussions with audiences comprising viewers of different ages, genders, and educational backgrounds shed light on how television culture relates to the power mechanisms and truth regimes by which people are shaped and shape themselves as gendered subjects in postsocialist China. This interdisciplinary approach constitutes one of the distinctive features of the book.

POWER, KNOWLEDGE, AND SUBJECTIVITY

Television is not only a medium of information and communication, but, more importantly, a routine escape from reality. The heterotopic space of TV accommodates audience fantasies about what is lacking in their lives, as well as projections of their various desires. Embedded in the multiple discourses of everyday life, television is a "profound and basic substrate for the conduct of everyday life" in high-modern or postmodern society (Silverstone 1994, 87). Through its moral and political regulation of everyday life, television functions as an important tool for cultural governance and produces the desirable subject in a given society.

According to Michel Foucault (1980b), a subject is discursively produced, "stripped of its creative role and analysed as a complex and variable function of discourse," and is an effect of power relations (138). Power functions only in the form of a chain, and individuals, including the many millions of TV viewers, are not only its "inert or consenting target," but also "the elements of its articulation" (Foucault 1980a, 98). In other words, individuals are the "vehicles of power, not its points of application" (98). This dynamic and productive notion of power helps us to understand the mechanism of knowledge production and what Foucault terms "government of the self" through mass media. The development of liberal society enables a new art of government in which the citizen has become a consumer who makes responsible choices. Through discourses on self-improvement and self-actualization, individuals are linked to society by acting as active agents in consumer form. In the process, media representation plays a central role in producing the knowledge associated with the desirable middle-class lifestyle. Power, knowledge, and subjectivity are thus interlinked in a circular way: power relations produce the knowledge needed to form and regulate the subject, which in turn reinforces power relations.

China provides a complex—and contested—case study of how the interrelationship among power, knowledge, and subjectivity operates in a nonliberal context. On the one hand, there is little doubt that the Chinese state has no intention of retreating from its people's lives, particularly in terms of cultural and intellectual control. Indeed, in his address to the 19th National Congress of the Chinese Communist Party (CCP), President Xi Jinping called for the party's renewed intrusion into almost every aspect of life, ranging from the economy to religion and morals. In the cultural arena, recent years have seen tightened control over and censorship of the media.

On the other hand, the privatization and marketization of state-owned enterprises in recent years have seen the state retreat from providing housing, health care, and social services to a significant extent, triggering a shift in governing strategies and modes of thinking. Concomitant with China's integration into global capitalism has been the party-state's increasing interest in and appropriation of a host of strategies and discourses that in many regards correspond to the "neoliberal" trend in the West to manage, control, and educate the Chinese population. As a result, the postsocialist Chinese state demonstrates a hybridity of political rationalities that combines authoritarianism with an attempt to govern at least a portion of the population through its own autonomy (Sigley 2006, 489). This significant shift from the old, repressive, cohesive form of power to "seemingly neoliberal strategies designed to govern through the desires of individuals" (Jeffreys and Sigley 2010, 7) has been pinpointed by Lisa Rofel (2007) as the center-piece of China's contingent, piece-by-piece reconfiguration of its relation-ship with the postsocialist world. The creation of such "desiring subjects" has taken place largely through people's engagement with and imagination through public culture. At the center of the discourses and strategies mobi-lized by the government during this process lies the formation of a "middle-class" society and a state-sanctioned notion of Chinese nationalism.

Inspired by the Foucauldian concept of governmentality, a critical ana-lytical tool for examining how power is exercised through the guidance of self-disciplined subjects,[2] recent scholarship on "Chinese governmental-ity" has fruitfully examined various rationalities, tactics, and discourses associated with governing through self-improvement and self-decision-making in China, the *suzhi* (moral, intellectual, and behavioral "quality") discourse in particular (see Ong and Zhang 2008; Jeffreys 2010; Wallis 2013a, 2013b). Without emphasizing rights or liberty, Chinese governmen-tality involves both a "facilitative" dimension, namely, free individuals pur-suing their own interests, and an "authoritarian" dimension, that is, the production of controllable citizens who are loyal to the party-state (Wallis 2013b, 10). Within China, think tanks and scholars have been arguing for a shift from government (*zhengfu*) to governance (*zhili*), that is, from the old, oppressive mode of the party-state apparatus to more dynamic governance that grants choice and autonomy to the middle class through consumerism and economic growth. Renowned Chinese political science scholar Yu Keping puts it this way:

> [The p]ower of government operates always from top-down to bottom-up pri-marily through orders, statues, bureaucracy and coercion while [the] power of governance operates mutually, interacting both from top-down to bot-tom-up and from bottom-up to top-down, primarily through collaboration, coordination, negotiation, social networking, neighbourhood, identity or consensus. (Cited in Sigley 2006, 503)

Television plays a central role in producing citizens who are "both loyal to the Party and useful for the market" (Martin and Lewis 2016, 24). For example, the Chinese subject is being interpellated through knowledge production associated with the discourse on historical national humiliation, followed by national rejuvenation under CCP leadership. The frequent TV images of the manly anti-Japanese heroes of the past and successful self-made entrepreneurs of today serve to embody and enhance this form of knowledge production. As will be discussed in the next chapter, talent shows, singing contests, and "idol" shows, most of them copycatted from Western or Korean programs, are becoming increasingly popular in China and are particularly favored by the commercially oriented provincial satellite channels. These programs demonstrate that ordinary people, be they farmers, migrant workers, single mothers, or even those with disabilities, can become celebrities overnight by dint of talent, hard work, persistence, and moral support from family and friends. The inspirational theme (*lizhi*) of such programs echoes the ethos of President Xi's Chinese Dream and is in line with "technologies" devised to foster middle-class subjecthood. A notable example is Dragon TV's *Mama Mia* (also known as *Super Diva China*), which is adapted from the Korean program *Super Diva*. In each episode, mothers, usually housewives who once cherished a dream of stardom, try hard to impress three judges and an onsite audience with their performing talent and moving life stories. Winners leave with a veritable fortune and appointments as advertising ambassadors. According to the *Mama Mia* webpage, the program helps ordinary women to attain happiness and self-confidence and project "positive energy" (*zheng nengliang*) by pursuing their dreams.

Although the government's hand is never invisible, the new images, motifs, and discourses that have emerged on the Chinese TV screen urge us to reflect on television's capacity as an effective device of the "technology of the self" for the postsocialist state, or, in other words, on the production of desirable selfhood through the relatively autonomous consumption of television. Centering on the dynamics of gender and notions of Chineseness, the subsequent chapters of this book lay bare the disciplinary elements of Chinese television culture, characterized by the self-improvement, self-discipline, and positive attitudes required by the socialist market economy. They also illustrate how these governing strategies and motives are negotiated in different ways by different cohorts of viewers and by capital, especially in terms of gender construction.

CHINESENESS AND CHINESE-STYLE COSMOPOLITANISM

While Chineseness in the Western context frequently operates as a "desired other" in an Orientalist manner (Wong 2018, 12), it takes on a different face in the context of contemporary mainland China. It connotes the unchanging essence of a "Chinese culture" and, in an exceptionalist way, highlights what makes China and Chinese culture unique in the world. The concept is closely related to the identities and subjectivities preferred by the state and produced for the nation. In this sense, Chineseness can be understood as cultural justification for political sovereignty.

The various knowledge production efforts exerted by the post-Mao, post-socialist state center predominantly around patriotism, which functions as an ideological pillar to legitimize and cement the leadership position of the CCP, build societal consensus, and create the subjects desired by the party-state. Patriotism is explicitly "the most profound, essential and eternal" constituent of the "core socialist values" advocated by the Xi administration.[3] The periodic outbursts of anti-Western, nativist, and nationalist sentiments by the Chinese populace (in both cyberspace and on the streets) witnessed in recent years have attracted growing concern in the West (e.g., Unger 1996; Y. Zheng 1999; Chang 2001; Gries 2004; S. Zhao 2004; Hughes 2006). Scholarly attention has also been paid to the various forms of "cultural nationalism," as Yingjie Guo (2004) terms it, expressed in China's media and culture sectors. In line with the state's nation-building agenda, such nationalism encompasses not only a desire for restoration of the nation's past pride and prestige and the struggle for the strong position rightfully due the country by dint of its population and size, but also a search for a national identity in the era of globalization. Although many scholars have pointed out the "incoherence and contradictions among the different expressions of Chinese nationalism" (Yu 2009, 56), most regard nationalist sentiment as the result of indoctrination and propaganda from the top rather than embedding it in a complex network of power negotiation and identity constructions. In fact, Chinese nationalism builds on a multifaceted imagination of national unity that in turn reflects a dynamic, comprehensive system of knowledge production that engenders a new vision of Chineseness defined as follows by Xudong Zhang (2008, 7).

[China] is mired in increasing imbalance, disparity, conflict, and contradictions as it becomes an awkward new player in the global economy and in global power relations. In this process, various components of what used to be imagined as part and parcel of a congruent, uniform sociogeographic and cultural-ideological space called China are now moving in different, sometimes opposite directions. At the same time, there are political, social, intellectual, and artistic forces that are mobilized to articulate and justify the new coherence, new rationale, and new meaningfulness of China's unity—as a nation, as an empire, as a "form of life," or as a sociopolitical order (as disorder).

Some scholars contend that Chineseness as an identity construction project involves contested political and economic forces, whereas Chineseness as a signifier works only within a Self/Other dichotomy framed by different contexts (Chun 1996; Chow 2000; A. Louie 2004; Wong 2018). For the Chinese government, and as reflected in most of the TV programs discussed in this book, Chineseness constitutes a form of cultural capital that can be used to legitimize and strengthen the state monopoly on discourse. Equating cultural tradition with membership in and loyalty to the nation-state, China is constructed as the common root of the worldwide Chinese population, and knowledge of "traditional" Chinese culture, the Confucian moral code in particular, as the embodiment of "orthodox" Chineseness. A pivotal device of this cultural engineering project is the cultivation of reliance on a national father, and hence a patriarchal gender order in popular sentiments. Chineseness is not only a parameter for identifying the Self and Other (as discussed in chapter 5), but is also a standard for making moral judgments about Chinese people at the margins, such as those in Hong Kong and Taiwan and in overseas Chinese communities. As revealed in chapter 4, the unmanly men depicted in TV dramas more often than not are intended to reify abnormity or inadequacy in terms of Chineseness.

Chineseness, however, is a notion of tension and contradiction, with alternative and competing discourses existing both inside and outside China. The state-sponsored discourse, which blurs the distinctions between race and nation and between culture and regime, has met with resistance from Taiwan, Hong Kong, and other Chinese-speaking communities, manifested in recent years by the rise of the notion of a decentralized Sinophone literature and culture. Within China, cyberspace as a public sphere has generated various forms of alternative Chineseness, including aggressive Han Chinese chauvinism, liberal nationalism, and Maoist nostalgia, among others. As we will see in chapter 7, TV dramas featuring a form of womanhood that is not in conformity with the official vision of Chineseness have been criticized or even banned by the authorities. Therefore, as Andrea Louie (2004) points out, "far from being produced in a vacuum, Chineseness is used as both an inclusive and exclusive concept, empowered as racial discourse, used to reinforce a sense of rootedness, or turned in[to] a commodity" (21). At the same time, in most of the TV programs under study herein, a keen desire to pursue a cosmopolitan identity paradoxically coexists with strident nationalist sentiment.

Although studies of Chinese transnationalism have largely focused on how transnational mobility has engendered the detachment of Chinese subjectivity from the state (Ong and Nonini 1997; Mayfair Yang 1999), investigations of younger and more recent Chinese immigrants in the West indicate that "nationalism has become part of a cosmopolitan Chinese youth identity in overseas locations" (Nyíri and Zhang 2010, 25). A China-centric view of cosmopolitanism represents what Lisa Rofel (2007) calls "cosmopolitanism with Chinese characteristics," namely, "a self-conscious transcendence of locality, posited as a universal transcendence, accomplished through the formation of a consumer identity; and a domestication of cosmopolitanism by way of renegotiating China's place in the world" (11). This ambivalent attitude toward the West has been referred to as "rooted cosmopolitanism" or "cosmopatriotism"—a paradoxical yet dialectical combination of cosmopolitanism and patriotism—in the context of East Asian popular culture (Jurriëns and de Kloet 2007). The phenomenon invites a new understanding of cosmopolitanism, the extant scholarship on which in the Euro-American context positions nationalism and cosmopolitanism as opposing forces (Gerard Delanty 2012).

The past two decades have witnessed the forward march of cosmopolitanism as a buzzword across the humanities and social sciences. Although different interpretations and applications of the term coexist, cosmopolitanism can be broadly defined as a "condition of openness to the world and entailing self and societal transformation in light of the encounter with the Other" (Delanty 2012, 41). Delanty (2012) also posits a four-level spectrum of cosmopolitan relations in late modernity, ranging from "cultural omnivorousness" to an orientation toward world consciousness that places nonnational interests above the national interest (44). Hence, "cosmopolitanism is not a zero-sum condition, present or absent, but is always a matter of degree" (Delanty 2012, 44).

Challenging the idea that cosmopolitans are necessarily members of the elite and that cosmopolitanism presupposes mobility, Haiyan Lee (2014) identifies a form of "vernacular cosmopolitanism" or "cosmopolitanism from . . . below" in discussing images of nannies and peasants in Chinese film and TV. She defines cosmopolitan subjectivity as a form of subjectivity that "honors the humanity of the stranger" (H. Lee 2014, 245). Enlightening as this theorization is, most of the male and female characters discussed in this book suggest that cosmopolitan identity is achieved primarily through consumption and is considered an important form of cultural capital in heterosexual romance. Cosmopolitanism is almost always coupled with a distinct class background and hierarchy, with cosmopolitan subjects often constructed in relation to the aforementioned *suzhi* discourse, which, in the words of Gary Sigley (2009, 539), "through a commoditization and dehumanization of the body, constructs a hierarchy of worthiness and utility." Therefore, instead of self-problematization and reflexivity, to which critique is integral, Chinese-style cosmopolitanism is more a confirmation of the self through claims of cosmopolitan subjectivity that transcend parochial identity. It is obvious that this version of cosmopolitanism ranks fairly low in Delanty's (2012) structure and is not necessarily in tension with nationalism. As a matter of fact, the inextricable entanglements between Chinese cosmopolitanism and nationalism can be traced back to at least the turn of the twentieth century; cosmopolitanism that emphasizes the formation of new subjects in a more open, stronger China is as much nationalism's supplement as its negation (Wang and Hu 2016).

Gender norms and stereotypes in Chinese television show both influences of global popular culture and deep-seated obsessions with a Chinese essence. In many of the TV programs under discussion, cosmopolitan qualities are depicted as indispensable elements of desirable masculinity and femininity alike, which provides an interesting lens through which to examine how China sees and hopes to be seen by the world. The gender stereotypes on the Chinese TV screen exhibit an anxiety about facing the West and imply "an unpleasant posture toward the putative provincial" (Appiah 2006, xiii). The white-collar employees of transnational corporations and returnees from overseas are depicted in a self-congratulatory manner as more connected with the world than their provincial counterparts, and thus as possessors of cosmopolitan cultural capital. Their sophistication is often illustrated through English proficiency and the practice of a Western lifestyle (characterized, for example, by the consumption of wine and coffee). As this book demonstrates, these images square with the state agenda to build a modern, cosmopolitan image of the country, its educated young elite in particular.

GENDER IDEOLOGY AND QUEERNESS IN CHINESE TELEVISION

The book also examines Chineseness as an affective impact created by gender imaginaries and, in particular, how a cosmopolitan imagination of queer modernity negotiates with cultural hegemony. As noted above, analysis of the male and female images in Chinese television introduces important gendered issues to contemporary discussions of globalization and Chinese nationalism in response to the limitations of existing studies on Chinese nationalism in the West. These studies focus primarily on the political dimension and understand such nationalism as a form of one-way indoctrination from the top rather than a "structure of feeling" arising from an array of complementary motivations. Through the lens of gender and sexuality, this book unravels the links between state agenda and popular imaginations/sentiments in the construction of a postsocialist Chinese subjectivity that serves as a mediator between nationalism and cosmopolitanism.

Gender constitutes a core sense of self. Feminist political theory highlights the analogy between nationalism and heterosexism, with the binaries of male-female bodies and masculine-feminine identities foundational to the symbolic ordering and discursive practice of nationalism, at the center of which lies the hierarchical dichotomy of selfhood and otherness (Peterson 1999). The conceptual ordering of masculine over feminine is inextricable from the political ordering imposed in state-making and reproduced through masculinist discourse that legitimizes the state's hierarchical relations. Central to this ideology is male entitlement to women, land, and sovereignty (Peterson 1999). Nationalism is thus inscribed in and through the body and how we live through our bodies as men and women.

Chinese nationalism has historically been interwoven with gender discourse, gender anxiety in particular, with femininity and masculinity functioning as important benchmarks for Chinese modernity and the construction of Chinese nationalist agency since the late nineteenth century (P. Zhu 2015). For one thing, Victorian-era discourses on sexual dimorphism and gender differences were appropriated as constituents of "colonial modernity" (Barlow 1997) and became dominant in Chinese society, particularly after the cultural modernization of the New Culture Movement in the early twentieth century. For another, Chinese intellectuals have resorted to gender discourses, such as the imagination of a revirilized Chinese masculinity or empowered femininity, to counter the "Western gaze that [tends] to associate China with an essentialized femininity of weakness, passivity and decadence" (P. Zhu 2015, 1). As spaces of negotiation, gender and sexuality have been closely intertwined with the tension and struggle between colonial power and nationalist resistance, laying the foundation for modern Chinese subjectivities. The discourse of national humiliation, including reference to the infamous term allegedly imposed on China by foreigners—"sick man of East Asia" (*Dongya bingfu*)—reflects the gender anxiety that is deeply ingrained in the structures of feeling of generations of Chinese people.

Contemporary Chinese television constructs and displays a variety of gender images and imaginaries that are essential for cultural governance. As discussed in this book, most of the stereotypical images and discourses on the TV screen pivot on a (hetero)gender binary and in one way or another legitimize and enhance male dominance in society, which in turn symbolically buttresses the patriarchal power of the state (Reeser 2010). As many critics have pointed out, images and leitmotifs giving expression to male fantasies about polygamy, concubinage, and Cinderella-type hypergamy, and thus subverting or reacting to Maoist discourse on women's liberation, now enjoy wide currency on the Chinese TV screen. This mainstreaming of patriarchy and the cult of the Chinese male are reflected in such popular images as the hypermasculine anti-Japanese hero (chapter 3) and the gloating businessman characterized by misogynist and sexist language and behavior, who have been dubbed by some netizens as sufferers of "straight man cancer" (chapter 4). In general, these images resonate more powerfully with middle-aged and older audiences, as well as those with a lower educational background.

At the heart of this "sexism with Chinese characteristics," which is discussed in greater detail in chapter 4, lies heteronormativity as an internalized norm. A significant consequence of TV censorship in China has been the banning of any types of sexuality or gender identity that are not in conformity with the state-approved, mainstream mode. Web series that explicitly represent homosexual relations have been proscribed or pushed offline owing to their supposedly "indecent content" (Lavin, Yang, and Zhao 2017, 1), leading Petrus Liu (2018) to summarize the mindset of gender policing in the context of (masculinist) nation building and modernization as follows.

> [B]efore China can assert its proper place in the family of respected, modern nations, it must first redefine its sexual culture, and in order to redefine its sexual culture, it must first re-imagine itself in some way as a continuation of Euro-American culture.

At the same time, however, in conjunction with the international #MeToo movement and with rising awareness of gender issues in China, recent years have witnessed the proliferation of feminist thinking and more diversified gender images on Chinese television. Independent, confident, and success-ful women are constructed as beneficiaries of social change, and noncon-forming gender images, such as androgynous "manly women" (*nü hanzi*) and effeminate males known as "little fresh meat" (*xiao xian rou*) or "sissy pants" (*niangpao*), have become increasingly popular (chapter 6). The trend is in keeping with the TV industry's efforts to reach out to the younger, better-educated portion of the population, in particular young female view-ers with enhanced purchasing power, along with the fast-paced develop-ment of online dramas. Yet instead of subverting the hegemonic gender dis-course, these new images are more often than not contained or even co-opted by the hegemonies. A salient example is the presence of a powerful "bossy CEO" who verges on being sexist in stories about inspirational successful women (chapter 7).

Indeed, queerness has long existed in Chinese TV and in its fan commu-nities and practices, albeit largely in ambivalent forms. Recent years have seen a proliferation of queer images and allusions to same-sex intimacy in variety shows, especially those streamed online.[4] Critics have also pointed out the potential queer interpretation of such popular images as the "neu-trosexual" singer Li Yuchun and effeminate skit actor Xiao Shenyang (Shen He).[5] The most famous transgender star in China, Jin Xing, frequently appears on talent shows as a celebrity host. As illustrated later in this book, however, same-sex desire and intimacy are more commonly seen on the TV screen in depictions of brotherhood (*ge'mer*) and sisterhood (*guimi*) in het-erosexual settings. These depictions can be traced back to the long-standing tradition of same-sex bonding in Chinese literature and culture and, at the same time, invite fruitful analysis in light of Eve Kosofsky Sedgwick's (1985) theory of "homosocial desire," that is, same-sex desire disguised through rivalry in heterosexual love. In Chinese TV, intimacy between characters of the same sex, both physically and emotionally, is noticeably more common and acceptable than in the West, demonstrating the relative absence of sen-sitivity to charges of homosexuality (see, e.g., Song 2010, 425–26). In addi-tion, the influence of the homoerotic BL (Boys' Love) and GL (Girls' Love) subcultures in East Asian popular culture can be discerned in the ambiguity of the androgynous images in Chinese TV (see Lavin, Yang, and Zhao 2017).

The queer elements in Chinese television culture, and the negotiation of meaning associated with them, should be considered in the broader context of the nuanced negotiation between nationalism and China's entangled obsession with cosmopolitanism discussed above. On the one hand, queer identities and culture have been imaginatively associated with Western culture, and in this context embody a type of cosmopolitan modernity (J. Zhao 2017, 72). On the other, the overarching homosocial framework and playfulness in nonnormative gendered expressions paradoxically reinforce rather than challenge heteronormativity, and ultimately maintain "a compulsory heterosexuality" (Butler 1990, 35).

A recent example is one of the plotlines in *The Story of Yanxi Palace* (*Yanxi gonglue*, 2018), a highly popular sweeping tale of palace intrigue during the Qing dynasty (1644–1912) produced by Huanyu Entertainment Company. In episode 16, the villain, Consort Gao, spreads rumors of intimacy between her two palace rivals, Empress Fucha and Consort Chun. Emperor Qianlong is angry and barges into the empress's chamber. The truth, however, is that the naked empress, who is sick, is receiving acupuncture treatment from Consort Chun. The audience also later finds out that Consort Chun had approached the empress because of her crush on the empress's handsome young brother. The queer sensationalism thus dissolves into a misunderstanding/joke, with heterosexuality reinforced as the norm. This "de-lesbianizing strategy," to borrow a term used by Jamie Zhao (2018), "produces and promotes queer images as attention-grabbing, profitable entertainment elements without seriously disturbing and menacing heteronormative structures in the real world" (3).

A more prominent form of queer expression, however, lies in the fantastically recreative activities of TV fans in online communities and social media. Influenced by Japanese fandom culture, the parodic practice known as *e'gao* (spoof, or *kuso* in Japanese) is becoming increasingly popular in cyberspace among younger TV fans, female fans in particular. In many cases, these fans are keen to identify potential gayness between TV characters and, in a carnivalesque manner, imagine and recreate a romance between them. Some of them even create videos of their imagined couples by professionally editing scenes from the original shows and posting them on such video platforms as bilibili.com and Sina Weibo. For instance, after the airing of the hit spy series *The Disguiser* (*Weizhuangzhe*, 2015), stories about and images of an imagined gay relationship between the characters Ming Lou (Jin Dong) and Ming Tai (Hu Ge) mushroomed on video streaming platforms. Both actors are handsome young men who enjoy widespread popularity among female audiences. "Bullet curtain" (*danmu*) comments, which viewers post while watching dramas streamed online, displayed euphoria over a scene in which Ming Lou, a communist-Guomindang double agent, spanks his adoptive brother, Ming Tai, with a stick while the camera lingers on the latter's ambiguous position and closes in on his buttocks (episode 26). Audiences have also formed self-entertaining communities through the communication of such queer interpretations and imaginations of TV characters. Most of these activities exhibit a playful attitude, and yet, significantly, they also give expression to various forms of repressed desire by transforming mainstream works for these fans' own cultural purposes. This practice exemplifies what Muñoz (1999) calls "disidentification," a key to negotiating identity in a majoritarian world.

To return to the question raised at the beginning of this chapter about the paradoxical coexistence of more diversified gender presentations and a postsocialist revival of patriarchy in Chinese television, how can we understand the tension between two poles that are also coterminous in cultural and social expressions of gender? The following chapters embed the phenomenon in the wider social and political context of China, including its shifting ideological landscape and demographic constitution in the past decade. Through close readings and a multifaceted analysis of a corpus of recent TV programs, the chapters unravel a variety of competing forces and elements—and of autonomy and heteronomy—that revolve around gender politics and subject making in Chinese television. They reflect engagement with both the global and discourses that are deeply rooted and embedded in the local sociopolitical context.

METHODOLOGY AND CHAPTER OUTLINE

This book constitutes a dialogical inquiry into televisual texts and their various readings. Most of the TV programs discussed herein are dramas, some of them broadcast on video streaming sites alone, although a number of popular reality shows and variety shows, such as the yearly Spring Festival Gala (*chunwan*), are also touched upon. For reasons of space, however, the book does not consider news, current affairs, documentary, education, sports, or children's programs, although such programs are without question also important constituents of the mechanism of knowledge production. In other words, the focus is on entertainment television alone. Program selection was based primarily on three criteria: (a) quantifiable widespread appeal (confirmed through ratings); (b) relevance to the themes and focus of the study; and (c) societal impact (as evidenced by online comments and discussions). Additional programs were identified during the process of audience research, as new programs mentioned by the informants were added to the discussion pool. The selection process was therefore iterative, resembling snowball sampling. Instead of collecting a representative sample of Chinese TV programs, I was more interested in collecting programs that have provoked debate in terms of gender, Chineseness, and subject making. Accordingly, the "texts" selected are by no means the most representative, nor has the corpus of subgenres under discussion been exhausted.

As noted above, the book's textual analysis of select TV programs is supported and supplemented by empirical study of the programs' production, consumption, and reception. That study is based on fieldwork carried out during trips to Beijing and Zhuhai in February 2015, July 2016, June–July 2017, and October 2019. These two cities were selected because, as the national capital and an economically robust new coastal city, respectively, they are representative of the demographic diversity of Chinese TV viewers. The participants in the focus group discussions comprised holders of both urban and rural household registrations. During my fieldwork, I also interviewed officials of the central government's National Radio and Television Administration and a number of TV production personnel, including directors and scriptwriters. Finally, I also interviewed (via WeChat and telephone) several mainland media practitioners who were introduced to me by friends about a variety of issues related to the production, circulation, and reception of TV programs.

I organized several focus group discussions with TV viewers to collect firsthand data on the topics under discussion, followed by in-depth and open-ended interviews with some of the informants (through phone calls, e-mails, and face-to-face communication). The first focus group discussions were conducted in Beijing in February 2015 with two groups of women (with an average age of sixty-two and twenty-two, respectively) to compare their reception of a hit TV drama series titled *Red* (chapter 3). The second round of discussions was then conducted in July 2016 with twenty-five undergraduate and postgraduate students (ten men and fifteen women), most of them from Renmin University and Beijing Foreign Studies University, to determine the impact of television's construction of gender ideals.

In Zhuhai, the informants were recruited through Qianmu Information and Consultation Company, a local survey agent. Focus group discussions were then held in July 2017 and October 2019 with a total of eighty-nine avid

TV viewers. They were divided into seven subgroups according to gender, age, occupation, and income level:

Group 1: Male university students aged eighteen to twenty-two
Group 2: Female university students aged eighteen to twenty-four
Group 3: Retirees (half men and half women) aged fifty to seventy-one
Group 4: Employed Zhuhai residents with a midlevel income (3,000–8,000 yuan per month), half male and half female, aged thirty to forty-five
Group 5: Employed Zhuhai residents with a high-level income (above 10,000 yuan per month), half male and half female, aged thirty-two to fifty-four
Group 6: Male migrant workers aged nineteen to twenty-eight with at least two years' working experience in Zhuhai and no family there
Group 7: Female migrant workers aged eighteen to twenty-eight with at least two years' working experience in Zhuhai and no family there

All the discussion group participants were self-proclaimed frequent viewers of domestic TV programs and web dramas, with an average viewing time of one and a half hours per day. The questions and discussions centered on (a) their responses to gendered images in TV programs, (b) comparison between representations and real-life enactments of gender, and (c) the link between gender and national discourses. Video clips were sometimes played during the discussions. To explore Chineseness as an affective impact, the focus group discussions and interviews were designed to tease out the ways in which the informants variously take up, draw close to, rework, adapt, ignore, or repudiate the depictions of men and women they encounter in Chinese television programs. Particular attention was paid to the informants' emotional and embodied engagements with the programs, particularly during the viewing sessions, to fully flesh out how those engagements affect the constitution, practice, and expectation of gender norms in their everyday lives.

Based on the research outlined above, the book is organized into seven chapters and one epilogue. The chapter division is made for convenience of discussion; it does not imply that the conceptual frameworks and questions herein can be neatly divided according to program genre and type. Rather, they are dynamically interconnected and (sometimes paradoxically) responsive to one another and thus constitute different aspects of the discursive space of Chineseness.

Chapter 2 provides a brief genealogy of the development of the TV industry in China from the 1980s as a symbol of modernity to the twenty-first century as a multiplatform, profit-driven entertainment complex. The distinctive mechanism of TV production and censorship in China makes this form of culture an important site for examining the tension and complicity between state intervention and global capitalism. That mechanism also gives rise to the distinctive features, both ideological and aesthetic, of Chinese television programs. The chapter also answers the question of why television is an important site for the study of cultural governance in China and how the vision of Chineseness has been influenced by recent technological developments affecting the medium.

Chapter 3 discusses a subgenre that can be regarded as the epitome of party-state nationalism: TV drama series depicting the atrocities committed and resistance faced by the Japanese imperial army during what is known in China as the Anti-Japanese War (1931–1945). Anyone turning on the TV in mainland China will quickly find ugly and brutal Japanese soldiers in the process of being defeated by the brave Chinese people under CCP leadership. Using an old enemy to support a new leadership, anti-Japanese dramas exemplify the exploitation of Chineseness for both state power and commercial expediency. Through critical analysis and audience study of several representative dramas, the chapter illustrates how nationalist heroism bespeaks a phallocentric preoccupation and how gender images are given different meanings by audiences of different generations.

Chapter 4 interrogates "sexism with Chinese characteristics" through an examination of "bossy CEO" and "straight-man cancer" dramas and audience reactions to them. The "bossy CEO" (*badao zongcai*), a domineering but devoted male lover, is a popular image in romantic stories between a young man of wealth and power and an ordinary girl of humble background. This class-based pattern of hypergamic love is commonly found in TV dramas adapted from web fiction that cater to the Cinderella fantasies of young female audiences. As gender discourse, the "bossy CEO" normalizes the male protagonists who patronize women and the female protagonists who organize their behaviors to ultimately be deserving of such patronage. "Straight-man cancer" (*zhinan ai*), a vogue term used by many of the informants during the interviews, reflects interesting issues within contemporary gender relations in China that can be fruitfully analyzed from a feminist perspective. The term, which carries an implication of helplessness on the sufferer's part, is jokingly used to refer to male anxiety and the toxic masculinity associated with it in the face of rapidly transforming gender dynamics. The chapter discusses several male TV drama characters who suffer from the condition who have been singled out as targets for feminist fury in recent years. In presenting the views of a variety of informants from the focus group discussions, it also explores the varying reception of and reactions to the characters' misogynist postures.

Chapter 5 focuses on depictions of foreigners and foreignness on the Chinese TV screen. Foreigners were rarely seen on TV during the Mao and early post-Mao eras, with the notable exception of Japanese soldiers played by Chinese actors, but they are ubiquitous today. In addition to Japanese actors hired to play Japanese officers and soldiers in anti-Japanese TV dramas (actors who are mockingly referred to as "professional devils" by the Chinese media), increasing numbers of Caucasian actors are starring in a range of TV dramas. Catering to both nationalist and cosmopolitan fantasies, images of foreigners have, to a certain extent, become an indispensable element of televisual displays of national pride and are playing an important role in forming a cosmopolitan and modern image of China. Offering close readings of three TV dramas, the chapter explores the changing visions of national selfhood and otherness in contemporary China and how they are expressed through the prism of gender and sexuality. The non-Chinese characters in these dramas are also examined to see how masculinity and femininity are represented as reflecting the confidence and anxiety that are paradoxically associated with China's rise, as well as how the national Other is being both demonized and idolized in stereotyped fashion, particularly through inscriptions of the female body.

From the combined perspective of masculinity, queerness, and nationalism, Chapter 6 explores the proliferation of effeminate male images known as "little fresh meat" in Chinese TV in recent years. The "little fresh meat" images reflect both a reversal of the male gaze on women and a continuation of the colonial gaze on Asian men. In line with the creation of "desiring subjects," the young celebrities who are labeled "little fresh meat" are primarily created and driven by consumerism. They embody shifting masculinity in a consumer society that responds to female desires. The media analysis in this chapter also reveals the internalization of Asian men as the weak Other to White men and anxiety over what an effeminate younger generation will mean for China. By analyzing TV programs and web dramas that feature this type of embodied masculinity, as well as media criticism of the "sissy" aesthetic trend, the chapter illustrates how effeminate male images originated from and are interacting with the transnational consumption of male beauty, particularly in female-oriented BL culture, and how transgressive gender expressions are denounced, censored, and contained by both the hegemonic gender discourse and nationalist politics.

The heterogeneity of female images and discourse of femininity in the televisual space reveal the many faces of Chineseness in the global age. Chapter 7 provides critical readings of a wide range of female characters on the small screen and traces the transformation of ideal womanhood over a span of three decades. The images under scrutiny include "virtuous wives and good mothers" in the domestic space, successful white-collar women who break free of tradition, and back-stabbing imperial concubines in the popular subgenre of "palace intrigue dramas." Censorship and criticism of female characters on TV are indicative of growing concerns about presenting "proper" Chinese womanhood to the world as part of China's soft power endeavor. At the same time, however, women are also being constructed as autonomous agents with an entrepreneurial self who can determine and change their fate in a rapidly changing society through constant self-improvement. The success of these women symbolizes the success of China. Taken together, the female images on TV illustrate the negotiations of various identities, discourses, and political investments surrounding the notion of Chineseness.

Finally, the book concludes with an epilogue summing up the major findings presented herein in arguing for the gendered nature of nationalism and neoliberalism. It also points out potential new directions for future studies.

CHAPTER 2

(Post-)Television in China: Entertainment and Censorship

IN CHINA, "the television generation" was not long ago used to describe the generation of people who grew up enjoying the enviable fruits of modern technology and culture. Of late, however, the term has been replaced by "the Internet generation." Television has been refashioned and even absorbed by the rise and rapid growth of the multiplatform digital entertainment industry. Although its boundaries have been blurred, television culture has by no means disappeared, but has been expanded and even reinforced. Drawing on its massive popularity, it is now exerting unprecedented influence on subjecthood in China's fast transforming society.

CHINESE TELEVISION: EVOLUTION AND TRANSFORMATIONS

Television came to China as an icon and product of modernity. When the country's first TV network, Beijing Television (renamed China Central Television, a.k.a. CCTV, in 1978),[1] began broadcasting in 1958, its symbolic function as an embodiment of the mastery and ownership of the most advanced technology and culture by the new regime outweighed its practical function.[2] During most of the Maoist period, except for the privileged families of high-ranking officials, television remained accessible only in communal viewing spaces, such as government institutions, factories, schools, and neighborhood committees (H. Wu 2008, 65). It was not until the implementation of Deng Xiaoping's economic reforms and "open door" policy in the late 1970s that television sets entered the private lives of ordinary Chinese families. During the 1980s, TV technology was quickly embraced and fetishized as part and parcel of the cult of materialist consumer culture that followed the collapse of Maoist ideology. In such propagandist media as newspapers, magazines, and posters, the black and white TV set (which already seemed old-fashioned in the United States and Europe), along with other modern household appliances such as the refrigerator and washing machine, was depicted as evidence of the improved living standard in urban and rural China and a symbol of a modern lifestyle that attested to the success of Deng's reforms and his ideological stance that "to get rich is glorious" (see Wen 2015). As TV programs constituted an important source of knowledge about the outside world during the early years of the post-Mao, pre-Internet period, TV viewing was also regarded as providing cultural capital to an engaged audience in addition to constituting a symbol of the citizenry's economic capital.

The ruling Chinese Communist Party soon recognized this new media technology's potential for political education and mass entertainment and made concerted efforts to capitalize on that potential. Television's development galloped ahead in the 1980s, and a four-layer network of TV stations at the central, provincial, municipal, and county levels—mirroring the administrative structure of the country—was established. By the early 1990s, with more than five hundred TV stations and nearly one billion viewers scattered across the country, television had overtaken newspapers and radio as the most influential medium in China. In addition to serving as an important propaganda outlet for the party-state apparatus, it also began to function as "a touchstone and trigger for public opinion and social emotions" (S. Kong 2014, 4).

Throughout the 1980s and 1990s, TV programs developed a deep-rooted relationship with politics and ideology in China, emerging as an affective infrastructure to mobilize imaginations of the nation.[3] China's television craze witnessed a host of media events that were of great significance for the metamorphosis of ideology in the post-Mao era, including the first wave of state-sanctioned nationalist sentiments sparked by the live broadcasting of the Chinese women's national volleyball team's "five consecutive championships,"[4] the debates surrounding the polemic TV documentary *River Elegy* (*Heshang*, 1988) and its condemnation of Chinese feudalism on the eve of the 1989 political movement,[5] and the shift to a sentimental economy marked by the overwhelming popularity of the country's first commercially successful TV drama series, *Yearnings* (*Kewang*, 1990), following the Tiananmen crackdown and failure of "elite culture" (see Barmé 1999; Rofel 2007). As

Jingsi Wu (2017, 3) points out, television "facilitates the creation of a public sphere that is so far underdeveloped in [China]." Through contested narratives of nation building and modernity, television, for the first time in Chinese history, powerfully combined entertainment with political pedagogy, knowledge production, and negotiation of the self in the context of pleasurable viewing.

In the process, TV drama series (*dianshi lianxuju*) have emerged as the most watched TV genre and "principal form of storytelling in contemporary China" (S. Kong 2014, 4). In the 1980s, imported TV dramas from Japan, Hong Kong, Singapore, the United States, and Latin America (Mexico and Brazil in particular) dominated the Chinese TV screen and opened the first window onto the outside world for ordinary Chinese families. The enormous popularity of the Japanese drama *The Blood Enigma* (*Akai giwaku*, Chinese title: *Xueyi*) in the mid-1980s, for instance, engendered the first generation of TV fandom in China, with Japanese actress Momoe Yamaguchi and her boyfriend (and later husband) Tomokazu Miura admired and imitated by millions of young people in Chinese cities. Owing to Chinese government efforts to combat the country's cultural deficit and the accelerating development of China's TV production market, however, the 1990s witnessed an explosion of domestically produced TV dramas, with the total number of episodes broadcast skyrocketing from 2,000 in 1989 to 14,498 in 2008 (Mingpin Yang 2011, 10). Several hit dramas, including the aforementioned *Yearnings* and *Beijingers in New York* (*Beijingren zai Niuyue*, 1994) and such "imperial court dramas" as *Yongzheng Dynasty* (*Yongzheng wangchao*, 1999), achieved extremely high ratings, with the images and imaginaries presented therein engraved upon the collective memory of the entire Chinese generation that came of age during the reform era.

Owing to its huge market potential, television was among the first media to undergo commercialization and privatization in China's state-led marketization project. Thanks to the significant reduction in state subsidies for TV production since the early 1990s, TV stations have become increasingly reliant on advertising as their major source of fiscal revenue, with nonstate investors and private TV production companies entering the industry as energetic players. Statistics show that 80 percent of the 9,000-plus TV drama episodes produced in China in 2003 were funded by nonstate TV production companies and independent investors (Mingpin Yang 2011, 13). As discussed later in this chapter, the decentralization of TV production has meant that CCTV has to vie with provincial TV stations for audience share.

In this increasingly competitive field, market demand and audience taste have naturally become the decisive factors in investment decisions and have thus sparked seismic changes in the style and format of Chinese television in the twenty-first century (see Keane 2015; Bai and Song 2015). This transformation of the political economy also explains the shift in Chinese television's (and Chinese media's more broadly) major function of knowledge production from "party politics" to "identity politics," as Haiqing Yu (2009) has observed.

The new millennium has witnessed the dramatic transformation of television and its cultural significance in China, a transformation wrought by two major technological advances: the development of satellite TV and cable TV followed by digitalization and the ensuing seismic convergence of media. The fast-paced development and widespread adoption of satellite TV and cable TV since the late 1990s have greatly increased the number of channels available to ordinary households. Tellingly, whereas in the 1980s, a typical Beijing family could watch only two central channels (CCTV 2 and 8) and one local one (Beijing TV) on a traditional TV set, by the mid-2000s it had access to more than a dozen CCTV channels (including news, sports, movies, finance, TV drama, Chinese operas, and children's channels), thirty-one provincial satellite channels, and a limited number of overseas TV channels deemed politically safe, such as Hong Kong-based Phoenix TV. Consequently, provincial TV stations such as Hunan TV and Jiangsu TV, which stood at the secondary level in the old hierarchical structure, are now able to compete nationally with CCTV via their more innovative and highly acclaimed entertainment programs, primarily talent and game shows and lifestyle programs modeled on foreign programs. In addition, the adoption of satellite technologies has, according to Sun and Gorfinkel (2015, 23), "played a particularly crucial role in China's nation-building, particularly in terms of bringing audiences in remote and mountainous areas into the 'simultaneous' yet individuated act of 'imagining the nation.'" In the process, they aver, provincial TV stations are also challenging CCTV's monopoly on production of the notion of Chineseness because they are "more interested in promoting and maintaining provincial cultural identities" (Sun and Gorfinkel 2015, 29). As a result, marketization and decentralization have given rise to multiple meanings of Chineseness on the Chinese TV screen.

Although Sun and Gorfinkel (2015) are absolutely right about the multiplicity of choices that commercial competition and satellite technology have afforded Chinese audiences, they are in my view too optimistic about the space for decentralization and diversification that the central/provincial tension has engendered, particularly in terms of the articulation of Chineseness. For one thing, although provincial stations have produced a number of experimental or even transgressive programs in recent years, some of which have been wildly successful, they remain shackled by severe ideological restrictions, as evidenced by the recurrent decrees from the central authorities concerning the "correct guidance of public opinion" expected of their programming. In the words of a former employee of Jiangsu TV, all provincial TV stations constantly struggle with their dual identity as both profit-making enterprises (*qiye danwei*) and state-run institutions (*shiye danwei*), with the two roles more often than not conflicting with each other.[6] Hence they lack any real freedom to articulate an alternative version of China and Chineseness that differs from the official discourse. In other words, despite commercial developments, the choices of TV viewers in China in terms of political voices have not expanded since the 1980s. More importantly, profit outweighs any interest in constructing or promulgating local identities as a major driver for provincial competitors. In fact, most big-budget TV dramas are produced on a cross-regional basis and aired simultaneously on the satellite TV channels of several provinces. For example, although *White Deer Plain* (*Bailu yuan*, 2017), which is based on Chen Zhongshi's prize-winning homonymous novel, features the distinct local culture and dialect of Shaanxi, it was produced by New Classics Media, a media conglomerate based in Beijing, and premiered on the satellite channels of Jiangsu and Anhui, provinces with no geographical or cultural proximity to Shaanxi. It is thus clear that the politics of place and capital in Chinese television today invites more nuanced analysis than the simplistic central/provincial dichotomy.

The same holds true for reality shows. In line with global trends, an increasing number of Western and Korean talent, reality, and game shows are being imported and copycatted by provincial TV in China, with many gaining widespread popularity. Such programs have in fact become provincial TV's trump card in its competition with CCTV.[7] These programs obviously share a number of common components, including overheated competition, scathing assessments by a panel of judges, votes from viewers, the elimination of losers, and, more importantly, an opportunity for ordinary people to realize their dreams of celebrity overnight. Such aspirational dream seeking, in particular, contributes to neoliberal subject making and resonates with the official rhetoric on the Chinese Dream. These programs, however, seldom demonstrate local distinctions. For instance, Jiangsu TV's popular dating show *If You Are the One* (*Feicheng wurao*) recruits participants from cities nationwide and even from select overseas locales, with less than 5 percent coming from Jiangsu province despite the show's being produced by and airing on Jiangsu TV. The ratings success of Anhui Satellite TV's outdoor game show *Race Forward, Boys and Girls* (*Nansheng nüsheng xiang qian chong*), based on the American game show *Wipeout*, spawned a series of interprovincial versions in collaboration with Hainan TV and Qinghai TV that were shot at obstacle courses built in Hainan and Qinghai provinces. It is obvious that the desire to transcend their own localities and reach out to the national market prevails over provincial TV channels' concern with maintaining distinct local identities. Therefore, although there have been more TV programs with a notable regional flavor in recent years, and there is increasing use of local dialects, it is fair to argue that the nativist trend has yielded to a desire to create a sense of national cohesion and homogeneity, a primordial Chinese culture premised on which the official vision of Chinese soft power is built.

In sum, satellite channels targeting a viewership that spans China and even stretches beyond the country's borders are a key profit driver for most provincial TV stations and thus an arena of cutthroat competition. That said, provincial TV stations do operate more locally oriented channels, known as "ground channels" (*dimian pindao*), that are not transmitted via satellite. These channels are positioned to reflect the day-to-day activities of local life, and some provinces and regions even boast channels in local dialects.[8] According to *China TV Ratings Year Book 2017*, CCTV channels, provincial satellite channels, and locally oriented ground channels each occupy roughly one-third of the overall audience market share (L. Xu 2017, 29).[9] However, that was the case before the entry of multiplatform media companies as new industry players in the past couple of years, a phenomenon that will be discussed in detail in the next section.

"ANYWHERE BUT ON TELEVISION": A NEW ERA OF TV ENTERTAINMENT

Digitalization and the Internet have, in unprecedented fashion, transformed the production and consumption modes of television and ushered in a "matrix era" of convergent media, which, according to Michael Curtin

(2009), are "characterized by interactive exchanges, multiple sites of productivity, and diverse modes of interpretation and use" (13). In brief, the traditional one-to-many mode of broadcasting is being replaced by a user-generated mode, with the rapid development of new transmitting technologies and devices such as Internet TV (the digital distribution of TV content via the Internet), Smart TV (technological convergence between computers and flat-screen television sets and set-top boxes), and P2PTV (peer-to-peer software that allows users to watch TV programs from any country in real time on the Internet) in recent years (Keane 2015, 2016). Such technological innovations have also ushered in new ways of watching television that have significantly altered viewing patterns. Most of the young people (aged eighteen to twenty-eight) interviewed during my fieldwork reported that they watch TV programs on PCs, tablets, and smartphones rather than on conventional network TV channels. They download TV dramas for future viewing on buses and airplanes and, with the aid of a virtual private network (VPN), sometimes watch foreign TV programs that are unavailable on the mainland TV screen. These viewing habits attest to the accuracy of the widely circulated quip that "television content is accessed these days anywhere but on television" (Sun and Gorfinkel 2015, 33).

As a consequence of these changes, the online video-on-demand (VOD) services of such streaming sites as v.qq, Youku, iQiyi, LeTV, and Tudou are booming, and, together with video sharing on social media sites such as WeChat and TikTok, are posing a significant challenge to TV stations' position as the central players in the production and distribution of television entertainment content.[10] The new media ecology has given rise to drama serials and reality shows that are made exclusively for online delivery. Driven by the huge potential profits, production companies backed by such digital media giants as Tencent, Alibaba, and Baidu have also entered the industry, which has been described as a "game changer for Chinese television" (Bai 2020, 369). These companies outshine traditional TV stations by producing big-budget entertainment programs that appeal to members of the younger generation, who have not conventionally been fans of Chinese TV programs, and, by dint of these programs, are aggressively competing with TV stations for media attention and social impact.

As far as TV drama is concerned, video streaming sites are no longer simply platforms for watching existing TV programs, but have become a hub for the premiere of made-for-the-web hit dramas. For example, a common practice in China is for two episodes of a TV drama series to be aired on several provincial satellite channels during the "golden slot" (7:30–9:30 pm), with those episodes subsequently made available after midnight for free viewing on such major video portals as iQiyi, LeTV, Youku, and Tudou. However, since the runaway success of *The Story of Yanxi Palace*, which premiered on iQiyi in July 2018, the order has been reversed. Increasing numbers of dramas are being shown on the web first, and then later purchased by TV stations for rebroadcasting on satellite channels. The censorship regime for web dramas is also relatively more lenient than that for TV dramas, which grants the genre more room for creative output that caters to the tastes of young audiences. Most web dramas fall into the category known as "IP (intellectual property) dramas," which refers to serial adaptations of original online novels, games, and animations, thereby capitalizing on the existing popularity and fan base of those works. Given their financial and technological privileges, the producers of web dramas are good at augmenting the dramas' social impacts through successful public relations and digital marketing strategies. For instance, after the airing of the hit drama *The Journey of Flowers* (*Hua qiangu*, 2015), comments on and discussions of the program in the blogosphere (encompassing blogs, bulletin boards, instant messaging sites, etc.) increased by a phenomenal 711 percent in just two months.[11] Indeed, recent ratings successes have been, without exception, multimedia events, with major social media platforms and portals flooded with commentaries, interviews, behind-the-scenes stories, discussions, memes, and video remixes for weeks following a drama's premiere, making people feel that it is compulsory to watch it if they do not want to be "left out" (Bai 2020, 366).

Keane (2015, 40) has remarked that marketization led to a fundamental reimagining of the masses who constitute the Chinese audience—from a singular corpus defined by political criteria to a polymorphic presence defined by market share—or, in other words, from "audience-as-public" to "audience-as-market." Identifying the most frequent viewers of television in China, however, is no easy task. Commercial audience surveys conducted by TV stations and media research companies such as CSM and AGB Nielsen are also flawed in that the analytical methods and sample sizes of different surveys are inconsistent, and transparency is generally lacking, with ratings regarded as a business secret by some media companies (Schneider 2012, 135).[12] Based on available information and his own fieldwork data, however, Schneider (2012, 139) maintains that housewives, laid-off workers, and retired people constitute the core fan base of domestic TV dramas, with the educated young urban elite showing relatively little interest. Schneider's contention is contradicted by the development of postbroadcast televisual texts targeting a youthful audience with consuming power. As one TV industry practitioner remarked during an interview, the typical consumer of drama serials has shifted from an "auntie" (*dama*) in the broadcast era to a "young sister-in-law" (*xiao saozi*) in the web era, with the latter referring to a woman in her late twenties or early thirties who is employed and most likely childless, and thus has the time to watch dramas online and the money to pay for subscriptions to video portals.[13] Young women of this type also constitute a strong fan base for the star-making campaigns triggered by the most popular of these dramas. For example, tickets to a concert given by the male stars made famous by *The Untamed* (*Chenqing ling*, 2019), a web drama with ambivalent BL elements favored by many young female viewers (see chapter 6), were bid up to more than 150,000 yuan per ticket, attesting to the remarkable buying power of this female fan base.[14]

Online social media and video-sharing sites have thus made TV viewing both an individualized and socially interactive activity. For example, most video portals in China have adopted a commentary sharing system called a "bullet curtain" (*danmu*). Originating in Japanese ACG (Anime, Comics, and Games) culture (*danmaku* in Japanese), the bullet curtain enables viewers to post comments directly onscreen while watching a video online. Those watching the same program can also entertain one another and form small online communities through their viewing. Indeed, many drama serials today need to be examined in the interactive web of online youth culture characterized by memes, fan re-creations, and games.

It is beyond the scope of this book to delineate all the technological innovations related to television or the impact of those innovations. Suffice it to say that increasing media convergence and the multiplicity of platforms have rendered the awkward question of "What is television?" difficult indeed to answer. Scholars and media commentators in the West have been discussing the distinction between "television" and "TV" for some time, claiming that we have entered "the post-television TV era."[15] Hence China is unexceptional in this regard. According to a comparative study of several countries conducted in 2012, China is the largest consumer of online TV content (Keane 2015, 13). But as Turner and Tay (2009, 4) argue:

On the one hand, the notions of mass communication which underpinned the earlier model and, on the other hand, the expectations of a homogenizing process of globalization both need to be revisited if we are to develop an accurate map of the contemporary television landscape.

Study of China has contributed to the mapping of television and its cultural politics in today's globalized and digitalized era. The resilience of state control over and the social engineering function of Chinese television, as well as the interaction between power and capital, attest to the "possibility that current instantiations of media formats, audience behaviors and technological apparatuses might reinscribe—rather than challenge—existent power relations" (Kackman et al. 2011, 3).

Although some scholars talk about the "disappearance of television" in the digital era, I am more inclined to regard web dramas and other post-broadcast televisual texts as an expansion and renewal of television culture. For one thing, despite the institutional transformation of the industry and changes in transmitting media, the core elements or defining features of Chinese television remain unchanged. Those elements and features include the mechanisms of production and censorship, the distinctive format and aesthetic style of drama serials, and the social functions of TV entertainment programs. Given their appeal to a younger, better capitalized audience cohort, web dramas are continuing and further developing the apparatus of subject making through complicity with and negotiations between capital and state intervention. Therefore, rather than being a stand-alone medium, "television" in this book refers to a multiplatform culture that effectively mediates interactions between the state, capital, and the individual.

(SELF-)CENSORSHIP AND PATRIARCHAL POWER

Privatization has not led to the liberalization and loosening of censorship that many scholars in the West expected.[16] On the contrary, even more stringent ideological controls and surveillance have been enforced in recent years, giving rise to a distinct complicity or, as some scholars put it, "happy marriage" between political constraints and commercial incentives in China's changing media landscape (Sun 2002a, 126). TV production has never been a wholly commercial operation in China, as all TV channels are state-owned, and television has long been and still is regarded as an important tool for propaganda and education by the government. The approval and censorship of TV programs come under the jurisdiction of the National

Radio and Television Administration, which is directly controlled by the CCP's Publicity Department.[17] Under the TV production licensing system, for instance, only licensed companies are allowed to engage in program production. In addition, TV dramas have to pass a heavy-handed two-round censorship procedure before being allowed to air. The first round is called *lixiang* (project application or preproduction approval), and involves the drama's script (or a synopsis of each episode) and other materials being examined by the authorities before a permit to begin shooting is issued. The second round takes place after the principal shooting is finished, when a complete sample of the drama (*yangpian*) must be sent to a committee of censors for a second review, this time to apply for a distribution license.

According to its official positioning, television's primary goal is education rather than entertainment. Therefore, television has never been labeled a "mediocre and trivial popular culture" in China as it often is in the West (Lodziak 1986, 2). Instead, it has been saddled with the social functions of cultivating patriotic sentiments, advocating "uplifting" modes of life, and promoting social harmony and stability. In fact, the government has launched several waves of its "Cleaning Up the Screen" campaign since the 2000s to guard against vulgar forms of entertainment and "excessive entertainment," that is, pure entertainment without any positive ideological message (Bai 2014).

One major consequence of the country's distinctive management and censorship system is a correspondingly distinctive television format. Chinese TV dramas are more akin to extended films with a continuing plot and predetermined number of episodes because prior to their broadcast, producers must complete the entire series and submit it for government review (Schneider 2012, 145). As for reality shows, although onsite control and monitoring are technically more difficult to exert, the mechanisms of censorship and self-censorship are highly effective in ensuring that no messages or styles deemed "harmful" or "disharmonious" by the government appear on air. Two widely discussed instances of party-state intervention in recent years were the suspension of Hunan TV's *Super Girl* (*Chaoji nüsheng*)—a singing contest reality show modeled on *American Idol*—and government regulation of Jiangsu TV's popular dating show *If You Are the One*.

Super Girl, a singing talent show with female contestants, was launched by Hunan Satellite TV in 2004 and soon achieved record high ratings nationwide. Millions of young people across the country voted for their favorite contestants via text message, an exercise described by one foreign journalist as the largest "democratic" voting exercise in mainland China.[18] In 2006, however, the program was suspended for three years after SARFT issued a series of directives warning against the "vulgar and gross style" of such programs. It is widely believed that a major reason for the state's intervention was *Super Girl*'s demonstrated power to mobilize viewers, which disturbed officials (Bai and Song 2015, 5; see also J. Wu 2017). The gender-neutral look of Li Yuchun, the winner of the competition, was also frowned upon by expert critics and officials. The program was relaunched in 2009 with the new title *Happy Girls* (*Kuaile nüsheng*), albeit without its public voting component. *If You Are the One* is a dating show loosely based on the *Taken Out* format, whereby twenty-four women standing in a row on a platform meet five men one by one in each episode. After several rounds of questions and viewing short videos about the men, the women make their choices by switching off the lights in front of them (and those who keep their lights on have the chance to be selected by the men). The program is successful not only in China, but is also broadcast in Australia and Malaysia and is gaining international popularity. But it was criticized by SARFT in 2011 for giving voice to materialistic values and promoting "money fetishism" (Bai 2015). To curb these "incorrect" values, the program format was subsequently substantially revised to allow more postshooting editing and to prohibit any direct mentions of wealth and salary. An additional host, who is a teacher in the CCP Party School and a self-proclaimed expert in marital psychology, was also added to provide guidance on the "correct" attitude toward relationships and marriage.

Contrary to common speculation, most recent cases of government intervention in Chinese TV programs have focused on moralistic, rather than political, censorship. In fact, political control is exercised primarily through self-censorship by TV stations and production companies, with sensitive topics and words avoided or removed before shooting begins.[19] This is the case because the political red lines are relatively clear-cut and crossing them can place the entire drama in peril. Thus, no investor will risk his or her money by violating political taboos. Moralistic restrictions, however, are more obscure, with blurred boundaries, and hence there is always room for negotiation. Even if certain scenes in a drama are banned, there is still a chance of the censored version being permitted to air. The potential profits of dramas with some "bold" content, such as depictions of nonconforming genders and sexuality, lure producers into testing the limits of government tolerance. At the same time, official censorship and media criticisms of a drama will more often than not generate unpredicted public interest in the program, consequently boosting its marketability. This phenomenon has been summarized by How Wee Ng as a "productive" aspect of Chinese TV censorship (Ng 2015).

The increasing frequency of moralistic censorship of adulterous content and actors, explicit LGBTQ depictions, and "immoral" female images (see chapter 7), however, indicates a tendency toward a more conservative gender ideology, one centered on a patriarchy endorsed and promoted by the state. For example, in February 2016, the fifteen-episode web drama *Addiction* (*Shangyin*), which garnered more than a hundred million views following its release, was abruptly taken offline by the authorities. The drama features a predominantly gay cast and tells the story of a romance between two high school boys.[20] Other notable cases of sexuality policing include the suspension of a popular web drama titled *Go Princess Go!* (*Taizifei shengzhiji*) because of its discernible homoerotic overtones (see Lavin, Yang, and Zhao 2017, 1). More recently, the twenty-nine-year-old actress Zheng Shuang was blacklisted by state media and had her past awards rescinded after the press dredged up news that her two children had been born via surrogacy in the United States. Her ex-boyfriend also accused her of attempting to abandon the children after their relationship turned sour. CCTV soon issued a statement condemning surrogacy, which is illegal in China. The National Radio and Television Administration also said in a statement that it would never "give a chance to those who have committed ugly scandals and misdeeds to show their face [on TV again]."[21]

CHINESE TELEVISION AS A FIELD OF STUDY

The study of Chinese television is an emergent field, with a growing body of scholarly work exploring it from a variety of perspectives (Lull 1991; Hong 1998; Donald, Keane and Yin 2002; Moran and Keane 2004; Keane 2007, 2015; Keane, Fung, and Moran 2007; Zhu 2008, 2012; Zhu, Keane, and Bai 2008; Zhu and Berry 2009; Zhong 2010; Schneider 2012; Bai 2014; Kong 2014; Bai and Song 2015; Cai 2016; Lewis, Martin, and Sun 2016; J. Wu 2017; Gorfinkel 2018; Gong 2021). Such studies, whether they discuss Chinese television exclusively or devote a significant portion of their discussion to it, cover a wide range of areas, including the institutional restructuring, technological evolution, ideological control, and cultural transformation of Chinese television. Among them, the following books are of particular relevance to the current one. Shuyu Kong's *Popular Media, Social Emotion and Public Discourse in Contemporary China* (2014) focuses on the "affective articulation" of Chinese popular media texts, borrowing Lawrence Grossberg's conceptualization of affect, and rightfully argues that instead of the end products, more attention needs to be paid to "the agency of audiences in consuming these media products and the affective communications taking place in this process" (12). Kong's book brings to the fore the emotional function of popular culture in understanding the powerful appeal of television, and popular culture in general, for the Chinese. Focusing on readings of six filmic and televisual texts, however, she touches upon the interrelationship between public sentiments and national identity only in passing (S. Kong 2014, 29–33). In *Telemodernities: Television and Transforming Lives in Asia*, Tania Lewis, Fran Martin, and Wanning Sun (2016) examine the rise of popular advice and infotainment TV programs in China, Taiwan, and India in relation to subject positioning and the question of how to cope with the pressures of late-modern existence. According to these authors, lifestyle advice television, which is premised on the discourse of middle-class modernity, "constitutes an important reflection of and agent for subjectification, mediating between emergent and residual social norms and, in particular, playing a crucial role in inciting capacities for self-government through discourses and practices of self-improvement" (Lewis, Martin, and Sun 2016, 255). Their book provides inspiration for the current study, which, from a China studies perspective, identifies television as a site of negotiation between the postsocialist state and the individual. Also addressing the relationship between popular media and politics, Jingsi Wu (2017), in her book *Entertainment and Politics in Contemporary China*, resorts to the notions of cultural citizenship and "the aesthetic public sphere," the latter based on the Habermasian public sphere, tailored for the Chinese context. She argues that television, along with the Internet and social media, constitutes an "aesthetic public sphere" that is becoming increasingly important to the formation of public opinion in China. As the study reported in the current book will illustrate, gender identities and discourses constitute an important yet understudied dimension of the aesthetic public sphere. In *Chinese Television and National Identity Construction: The Cultural Politics of Music-Entertainment Programmes*, Lauren Gorfinkel (2018) discusses the construction of a mainland-centered Chinese identity and the imaginary of a China-centric world in CCTV's music entertainment programs. She examines the images of and performances by ethnic minorities, the Chinese of Greater China (i.e., Hong Kong, Taiwan, and overseas Chinese), and foreigners in these programs. Her work functions as a good reference for this book, which focuses on the dynamics between national and gender selfhood and chooses TV drama, the most powerful and influential form of storytelling in China, as its main subject.

Engaging in dialogue with the approaches and theories outlined above, modernity, nationhood, and affective articulation in particular, this book places Chinese television, narrative entertainment programs in particular, and its connection to the wider processes of identity, subject, and subjectivity formation, in the context of the dynamic interplay between globalization and Chineseness. The mammoth body of TV programs produced in China every year and the fascination with them of billions of Chinese viewers provide a bonanza of topics for researchers of Chinese nationalism and subject making, particularly those concerned with one of the most important aspects of postsocialist subject making in China: the construction of a Chinese identity through the dichotomous imagination of national selfhood/otherness. Indeed, the dynamic link between television and subjectivation in reform-era China is attracting growing scholarly attention in China studies and media studies alike (see Sun 2002a, 2002b; Lewis, Martin, and Sun 2016). Yet what remains a potentially fruitful area of exploration is gender identity and gender politics as effective and important dimensions of the technology of the self and indispensable components of the nation-building narrative. Regarding Chineseness as an affective impact achieved through imaginations of gender, this book delves into a host of issues—some of them hotly debated within and outside China—that lie at the intersection of gender, nation, and modernity.

CONCLUSION

Television constitutes an important apparatus of cultural governance in postsocialist China. It is rapidly evolving and, owing to technological convergence with other media platforms, gaining a new level of cultural importance in the twenty-first century. The unique mechanism of production and censorship in China makes this form of popular culture an effective mediator between popular desires and the state's agenda. The growth of the digital entertainment industry, "IP dramas" in particular, has effected significant changes to the demographics of the domestic TV audience, which is traditionally believed to primarily comprise the middle-aged and elderly. Empowered by the liberal market, young middle-class women living in urban areas have emerged as the primary target audience of drama serials. Their desires and fantasies are pivotal in molding the gender ideals these programs convey, which renders the gender dynamics of narrative programs a particularly interesting site of examination from the perspectives of affect, modernity, and nation. The following chapters will approach this central theme by scrutinizing a variety of subgenres, images, discourses, and ideologies in Chinese television, with a synthesized interest in text, context, and audience.

CHAPTER 3

Anti-Japanese Dramas and Patriotic Patriarchy

As DEMONSTRATED BY the success of patriotic action films such as *Wolf Warrior II* (2017),[1] gender images and imaginaries catering to popular stereotypes and imaginations of the national Self and Other have been part and parcel of a "commercialized nationalism" that is delivering the ideological pedagogy of the state through spectacular film and television entertainment. In this regard, anti-Japanese drama, a subgenre of TV drama depicting the atrocities committed and resistance faced by the Japanese army during the Anti-Japanese War (1931–1945) in China,[2] has become a unique phenomenon on the Chinese small screen. Despite increasing criticism and concern from the media and even the government about its quality,[3] anti-Japanese drama has continued to flourish, and it reached new heights in 2015 with the high-profile celebration of the seventieth anniversary of the war's end. Although the subgenre of "mythological" anti-Japanese drama (*Kang-Ri shenju*), as it is sarcastically termed by netizens, has exhibited a tendency toward decline in the past couple of years, TV dramas set during the Anti-Japanese War are still plentiful. The phenomenon has attracted extensive discussion and mass media attention both within and outside China, and is attributed primarily to the political tensions between China and Japan in recent years and the patriotic education campaign promoted by the Chinese government since the early 1990s.[4] But the continued obsession with a war that ended more than seventy years ago requires a more complex explanation than the sheer manipulation of public sentiment from the top, and it may be more fruitfully explored from the perspective of television's role in reconfiguring gender and national imaginaries.

This subgenre exemplifies the inextricable relationship between patriarchy and nationalism. The masculinist, phallocentric discourse of patriotism justifies and bolsters the reproduction of patriarchy, which conspicuously denigrates the feminine and the queer in cultural representations. The gender stereotypes and dynamics in the dramas under discussion are thus part and parcel of a larger project of epistemological gender regulation endorsed by the state. This chapter embeds anti-Japanese dramas and their gender constructions in the broader context of the economy of consumerist nationalism in contemporary China and investigates the dynamic relationship among government manipulation, market demand, and popular imagination that underlies this peculiar phenomenon. It also seeks to explain the proliferation and popularity of this subgenre by examining TV viewers' meaning-making practices, which often differ from or even oppose the officially endorsed ideology. Thus, to identify the factors that give rise to the flourishing of anti-Japanese drama and its gendered stereotypes, the chapter combines and synthesizes multidimensional methods, including institutional studies of TV drama production and circulation, textual readings of the images of Japanese men and women on the small screen, and empirical studies on the reception, resistance, and manipulation of select examples of this popular TV genre by Chinese audiences.

THE NARRATIVE ECONOMY OF ANTI-JAPANESE DRAMAS

As discussed in the previous chapter, owing to their mammoth potential audience, TV drama series have become one of the most profitable media undertakings in China. As the most-watched genre, TV drama tops all other program types in generating advertising revenue for TV stations. Currently, there are three types of institutions engaged in TV drama production in China: the more than three hundred TV stations at various levels across the nation, large-scale media production companies, and independent investors. The seven fastest growing listed companies in the industry are gradually taking a market lead, indicating a tendency toward intensive, large-scale production.[5] Depending on the expected audience rating, a producer's profit from selling one episode of a drama to TV stations ranges from a few thousand to more than seventy thousand yuan, and that's without other potential income such as corporate sponsorship or copyright sales to audio-visual companies after the initial broadcast.[6] TV drama production is a booming industry in China, recruiting a large body of personnel ranging from script writers, directors, actors, and professional circulation teams to the tens of thousands of "professional crowd members" in major shooting bases such as Hengdian in Zhejiang Province.

At the same time, however, TV drama production is an industry that is severely constrained by heavy-handed political and moral censorship. As noted in the previous chapter, TV drama series have to pass two rounds of examination and censorship—namely, preproduction approval of the entire project and postproduction censorship of sample episodes—before being allowed to air. For most dramas, both procedures are conducted at the provincial level, and the review is generally completed within two months. But if the drama features any "special themes" such as sensitive historical topics or involves international collaboration (such as the presence of foreign capital, shooting crews, actors, and so on), then special approval must be obtained from the central government, and the review period is generally significantly prolonged (Laws and Regulations Department 2013, 402–16).

Needless to say, if a drama fails to obtain the necessary distribution license, then all the money invested in it goes down the drain. Investors also cannot afford a lengthy censorship period, which significantly delays the cycle of capital return. As a result, investors and producers are careful to avoid sensitive topics in their choice of drama scripts (see Niedenführ 2013). Such self-censorship constitutes the first and most effective "fire wall" of the political control and engineering of TV programs in China.[7] It is noteworthy that a wide range of topics is regarded as "sensitive" or even taboo in this system, and the list grows ever longer. According to Article 11 of the current "Rules for the Administration of the Content of Television Dramas," applicants for a permit need to provide

> [a] written opinion provided by the competent authorities of the people's government at or above the provincial, autonomous regional or directly administered municipal level or by the relevant authorities if the dramas involve significant themes or sensitive content such as politics, military affairs, diplomatic affairs, national security, cooperation with non-party members, ethnicity, religion, the judicial system and public security.
> (Laws and Regulations Department 2013, 407)

TV producers are thus left with few safe topic choices. Particular minefields include anything touching on contemporary political and social issues such as graft and corruption among government officials and awkward chapters in the country's history such as the Great Leap Forward and Cultural Revolution.[8] Out of international relations concerns, representations of more recent wars such as the Korean War (1950–1953), Sino-Vietnamese War of 1979, and even the Chinese Civil War (1946–1949) are also discouraged.[9]

During my fieldwork for this book, several industry practitioners also mentioned a government funding project (known as the "Excellence Project") whose aim is to promote the quality production of domestic TV dramas and which allows producers to make ends meet even when no TV stations purchase their dramas. Anti-Japanese dramas stand an exceptionally good chance of winning such funding, as the theme is favored by the government.[10] As a result, the Anti-Japanese War has been singled out as a safe historical period for government-favored profit-making cultural production.

For the Chinese state, memories of the Anti-Japanese War feed the imagination of a much-needed enemy Other against whom a national identity and essentialist "Chinese spirit" can be constructed. William Callahan (2006) maintains that a nation is not simply a question of people or territory, but also of time. The Anti-Japanese War has become just such a temporal event in constructing contemporary Chinese identity. Through the nationalist reconstruction of history, Chineseness is defined, imagined, and negotiated.

This government-sponsored, market-oriented consumerist nationalism, "a hybrid between the commercial and the national" (F. Yang 2016, 66), forms an important part of "a symbolic economy that generates identity" (Callahan 2006, 179). Televisual narratives of the Anti-Japanese War have become both a politically safe form of entertainment and a profit-making industry, in which various popular tastes and desires are cloaked in the overcoat of nationalism. TV drama has also given impetus to the flourishing of a variety of business sectors that capitalize on popular interest in the anti-Japanese theme, such as tourism involving historical sites related to the CCP's role in the war. For example, in 2011, an Eighth Route Army theme park opened in Wuxiang, Shanxi Province, at the wartime headquarters of the CCP-led Eighth Route Army. In addition to viewing a museum-style exhibition and watching live shows, visitors can also join war games reenacting episodes in the battles between the Eighth Route Army and the Japanese to "personally experience" the war (Yau 2013, 69). Such "red tourism" has become a pillar industry for many local economies. As one web essay sarcastically asks, "Has killing Japs turned into a business?" (*Da guizi zenme biancheng shengyi le?*).[11]

Nevertheless, the profound spectacularization of a war that ended seventy years ago invites more nuanced analysis than simple attribution to directives and encouragement from the top. Instead of being a passive reflection of the perceived "authoritarian resilience" of the CCP, for example, Schneider (2012) regards television as a dynamic mode of political communication that forms an important part of "cultural governance" in China. In two-way communication, the role played by the audience cannot be ignored. Therefore, in addition to political agendas and commercial motivations, the tastes and mentalities of TV audiences are also indispensable factors that give rise to the proliferation and popularity of these dramas. For one thing, the wartime violence in the dramas presents a familiar aesthetic for audience members above the age of fifty, who grew up watching propaganda films about revolutionary wars, and thus caters to their collective nostalgia.

The preferred taste of the audience is reflected in the aesthetic features of "mythological" anti-Japanese drama. The government has become increasingly concerned about the quality of this genre, issuing alerts about a trend toward "low taste" and excessive entertainment. The elements that have come in for particular criticism include the dramas' "unfaithful" representation of history, such as their portrayal of overwhelmingly stupid Japanese officers and soldiers, absurdly exaggerated plots (such as those involving the destruction of enemy planes through hand grenades tossed into the sky), and vulgarity and obscenity presented under the cloak of patriotism. The most notorious examples discussed in the Chinese media include a brutal scene in which a character is able to slice an enemy soldier in half from top to bottom using just his hands in *Anti-Japanese Knights-Errant* (*Kang-Ri qixia*, 2011) and one in which a young woman is able to kill dozens of armed Japanese soldiers with arrows after being raped in *An Arrow on the Bowstring* (*Jianzai xianshang*, 2012). In another TV series that caused controversy, *Together Let's Kill the Devils* (*Yiqi da guizi*, 2015), a woman visits her lover who has been locked up by the Japanese army. When he fondles her, he finds a hand grenade hidden in her crotch, which he then uses in a suicidal act of resistance against his Japanese captors (episode 29).[12] Frowned upon by the authorities and elite critics, such lurid plotlines and scenes may cater to the desires, fantasies, and tastes of audiences with a lower educational background.[13] Although these sensationalistic dramas have drawn considerable criticism in recent years, it is surprising that few domestic critics have targeted their excess of violence. Indeed, many a foreign viewer would find the bloody wartime scenes quite upsetting, particularly given that most of the dramas in question air during the golden slot (7:30–9:30 p.m.), which is meant for family viewing. Patriotism has legitimized their gratuitous brutality and bloodiness. As Chinese web writer Murong Xuecun (2014, par. 2) points out, the violent scenes send a clear message that killing is acceptable as long as the targets are "Japanese devils."

THE DOG-BEATING STAFF: PATRIOTIC PATRIARCHY AND PHALLIC POWER

Masculinity and nationalism are jointly articulated in many cultures (Nagel 1998, 249). As Todd Reeser (2010) points out, the analogies and connections made between masculinity and nation demonstrate an underlying anxiety about both:

> [M]asculinity might be linked to the nation precisely because the nation needs to be buttressed by another incarnation of power or because masculinity needs to be helped by the representational power of the nation. A nation that has suffered, or fears suffering, military defeat may use images of masculinity to revitalize or revirilize itself. . . . A man who fears castration or emasculation may turn to patriotism or to more extreme nationalisms [. . .] to assuage his own anxiety about being a man. (189)

Existing research on the interplay between masculinity and nationalism generally focuses on how standards of masculinity have rendered nationalism a masculine identity or on metaphorical analogies between powerful masculinity and the nation from the political studies perspective (Enloe 1990; Nagel 1998), whereas this chapter, which adopts a cultural studies perspective, is concerned with how nationalist ideology and education have influenced the discourse on masculinity in the process of knowledge production. In anti-Japanese dramas, the male characters' self-sacrifice and devotion to their motherland render them paramount examples of the masculine *yang* identity in terms of the Confucian *yin/yang* matrix. It is against this patriotic backdrop that other masculine qualities, such as courage, wisdom, brotherhood, and faithfulness in love, are represented and praised. In other words, national loyalty has become the primary criterion for judging masculinity.

The performance of masculinity in the context of Chinese nationalism can be traced back to at least the late Qing dynasty, but has been reinvigorated by the conspicuous rise of nationalism in popular culture since the early 1990s.[14] The following pages illustrate the interplay between masculinity and nationalism through a close reading of *The Dog-Beating Staff* (*Dagou gun*, 2013), which, to a large extent, epitomizes the male heroism celebrated by the subgenre of anti-Japanese drama.

The Dog-Beating Staff is a seventy-episode drama series jointly produced by CCTV and several TV production companies under the auspices of the Propaganda Department of the Hebei Provincial Committee of the CCP. Its director and screenwriter, Guo Jingyu, is known for his popularity among middle-aged and older audiences and the less-educated members of the populace. The drama tells the life story of Dai Tianli (played by Weizi; *Tianli* literally means "heavenly principles"), a fictional national hero in Rehe Province (which is also known as Jehol, a now defunct province that existed during the Republican period), during the half century from the Boxer Rebellion in 1900 to the communists' victory in 1949, with a special focus on the Japanese Occupation (1932–1945). Like many other TV dramas with a similar theme, the series reiterates the clichéd discourse of a century of national humiliation and drives home the didactic message that none but the Communist Party could have saved China. At the center of the series lies the enmity between the Dai and Na families, neighbors in the Rehe capital of Chengde. The Dai family comprises good characters embodying the spirit of patriotism, with Tianli's father and daughter both dying heroic deaths fighting the Japanese, whereas their rivals, the Nas, who are of Manchu ancestry, make a fortune trafficking opium. Na Tulu (Heizi), the drama's no. 1 villain, ends the series in disgrace, labeled a *hanjian* (traitor to the Chinese nation). In line with nativist nationalist performance, the dog-beating staff, a weapon used to beat "mad, vicious dogs, traitor dogs, and invader dogs," is a symbol of patriotism and the supposed Chinese spirit throughout the series.

In the Chinese language, dogs generally conjure up derogatory images and associations, as evidenced by the many dog-related idioms and proverbs, most of which are highly insulting and carry the connotation of shameless servility. In Chinese cyberspace, "dog" is a common label used by ultranationalist *fenqing* (angry youth) to attack their opponents (Song and Hird 2014, 115).[15] In terms of gender, the image of the dog denotes spinelessness and a lack of principle and thus connotes a lack of masculinity in the Chinese symbolic order, a point we will revisit later in the chapter. The dog-beating staff in this series is a symbol of power for the chieftain of a beggar sect known as the *ganzi bang*. As guard dogs and stray dogs constitute a major nuisance for beggars, the staff, which is also a martial arts weapon, is meant to protect and unite the beggars.[16] When Dai Tianli is bestowed with the dog-beating staff by his predecessor, who died fighting the Eight Power Alliance invaders, and becomes chief of the beggar sect, he discovers an inscription carrying the motto "Protect the family, guard the nation, and enrich the country" (*Baojia, weiguo xingbang*), which attaches a nationalist meaning to

Figure 1. Dai Tianli wielding the dog-beating staff. *The Dog-Beating Staff* (2013).

the weapon (episode 11). In addition to "mad and vicious dogs," Dai later adds "invader dogs and traitor dogs" to the targets of punishment to be meted out by the dog-beating staff. With this mighty weapon, he valiantly kills numerous Japanese officers and soldiers, as well as Chinese villains and betrayers. The staff, as a signifier of the phallus, thus symbolizes the masculine power bestowed by patriotic politics and is associated with the chivalrous deeds that the drama extols (figure 1).

Masculinity is primarily defined in the drama by three Chinese keywords that defy easy translation, *xuexing* (hot-bloodedness), *xinyi* (keeping faith), and *qingyi* (loyalty and emotional attachments), which are linked by the central theme of nationalist loyalty. They echo the trend in public discourse toward restoring "traditional" types of masculinity in pursuit of a Chinese national identity. In *The Dog-Beating Staff*, the three keywords appear repeatedly as touchstones of genuine masculinity, being used to describe those embodying true manhood in contrast to unworthy men who lack the characteristics of *xuexing*, *xinyi*, and *qingyi*. From the outset, that dichotomy is represented by the patriarchs of the two households, the upright Dai Hanting, a loyal guard of the former Qing court, and the unprincipled Na Pingshan (known as "Pockmarked Na"), owner of an herbal medicine shop and underground opium den. Their sons, Dai Tianli and Na Tulu, were childhood friends who studied martial arts together with a mysterious Kung Fu master. When the two are confronted with a national crisis, however, it becomes clear that they are morally poles apart. Dai Tianli and his gang, including his sworn brother "God of Fortune," as well as his rival in love and later ally the effeminate but brave "Old Second Aunt" (Yu Yi) and Dai's son Ma Jiujin (Yang Zhigang), embody real Chinese manhood because they stand up to the Japanese at the risk of their own lives. They are contrasted with less worthy men such as Na Tulu who are physically manly but are cowards on the inside. Like Na, the hypocrite Fang Mengqiao (Niu Baojun) and Dai's son-in-law Bai Jingui (Liu Zhiyang) both descend to *hanjian* status owing to their moral weakness and are eventually punished as "dogs." It is noteworthy that masculinity thus defined is not the exclusive reserve of men in this drama. Various admirable masculine traits are also found in several female characters, such as Dai Tianli's adopted daughter Dai Ruobing, his childhood love Na Suzhi (Yue Lina), and Na's niece, a mute girl named Gege ("Princess"). The female masculinity they display is in line with Mencius's definition of masculinity as political adherence and moral power.

Xuexing, or hot-bloodedness, is often used to refer to a man's courage, uprightness, and determination, the virtues that blood symbolizes in Chinese culture. A man with *xuexing* is not only a man with guts, but also one of morality who is instilled with a strong sense of justice. One of the drama's central themes is resistance to the opium trade. In the official discourse of victimhood that prevails in China, opium was a central part of the foreign powers' scheme to ravage the Chinese people and enslave the country. During the Boxer Rebellion, Dai Tianli kills two foreign opium traders and then goes on the run for thirteen years. He returns to his hometown when the Manchu Qing government is overturned by the Republicans, only to discover that his neighbors, the Nas, are secretly trafficking the drug. An honest and upright man, he then uncovers collusion between the Nas and Rehe governor Fang Mengqiao, who also happens to be the biological father of Dai's adopted daughter, and publicly destroys all of their opium. Accordingly, Na Tulu now holds a grudge against him. As a foil to true masculinity, the malevolent Na Tulu is a macho man in appearance, with a strong build and good martial arts skills, but he is weak inside. He becomes addicted to opium, which leads to the suicide of his first wife (episode 20). When the Japanese invaders arrive, he initially fights as a Guomindang officer, but eventually submits to the Japanese when they threaten the lives of his wife and son and take advantage of his eagerness to pursue revenge against Dai. Na Tulu subsequently becomes the police commissioner of Rehe under the Japanese Occupation and reopens his opium den by order of the Japanese. As previously noted, *xuexing* is not represented as exclusive to the male body, thus rendering masculinity a constructed space outside the biological binary of the two sexes. The quality is lacking in Na Tulu, but it is incarnated in the heroic deeds of some of the women in the series. For example, Dai Tianli's adopted daughter Dai Ruobing is a communist who, although weak in appearance, is instilled with a kind of toughness and resistance to yielding to the enemy. She refuses to surrender when caught by the Japanese and is executed together with her husband, a communist leader, after a sentimental wedding on the execution grounds (episode 67). Another example is Na Tulu's daughter, the mute Gege, who stitches up the heads of three heroes beheaded by the Japanese and then buries them using only her hands (episode 66). Through these women, the drama reiterates the hackneyed discourse that men such as Na Tulu who lack *xuexing* should feel shame when faced with women who display masculine courage and morality.

Xinyi refers to the virtue of keeping faith. Na Tulu's sister Na Suzhi is Dai Tianli's childhood sweetheart, and the two become engaged before Dai flees town. When he returns thirteen years later, however, he brings with him a little girl who calls him Daddy, which causes a misunderstanding between the two families and the eventual revocation of the marriage contract. The truth is that Dai remained faithful to his fiancée throughout his long exile. The girl in question had been entrusted to his care by his friend Fang Mengqiao, a fanatical revolutionary who sets out to assassinate a Manchu high official. Dai hides himself deep in the forest for thirteen years and endures numerous hardships in bringing up the girl alone because of his promise to his friend. Because he had also promised Fang that he would keep his secret, Dai makes no attempt to explain the situation to his fiancée when she misunderstands. The girl's real father, in contrast, is a hypocrite and coward who dare not recognize his own daughter when he returns to Rehe as a Republican official, having been tamed by the arbitrary whims of his wife, the daughter of a powerful official (episode 14). Exemplary masculinity is also demonstrated through various attitudes toward the homosocial code of brotherhood depicted in the series. As "brothers" who learned martial arts from the same teacher (and were in fact the teacher's sole disciples), Dai and Na were taught a special whistle, the "brother whistle" (*xiongdi shao*), to use as a signal for help. Whenever one party was in danger, he was to whistle loudly to summon the other's help. When Na Tulu is surrounded by Japanese troops and, on the verge of death, desperately sounds the "brother whistle," Dai, who is now the head of the anti-Japanese guerrillas, happens to be nearby and rushes to rescue his erstwhile brother regardless of the danger (episode 53). It is not long, however, before the ungrateful Na Tulu betrays Dai in the face of Japanese threats and temptations. When Dai is trapped in an old temple because of a plot hatched by Na and the Japanese, unaware of the former's betrayal, he whistles for help. In stark contrast to Dai's earlier courage and loyalty, Na pretends not to have heard the signal and turns his back on his brother (episode 55). As noted above, through this good/evil dichotomy the drama resorts to imagined "traditional" values and rhetoric, which lie at the core of the nationalist discourse, to construct the idealized Chinese man.

The third keyword, *qingyi*, emphasizes male loyalty, but *qing* (feelings, emotions) also connotes compassion and sentimental attachment. When Dai Tianli leaves his fiancée, he promises that he will come back to marry her and says, "One cannot fail in *qingyi*, even at the cost of one's life. Whoever has *qingyi* is complete in humanity; one lacking in it is just a beast" (*you qing you yi de shi ren, wu qing wu yi de shi chusheng*). This saying becomes one of the drama's recurring themes and is closely linked to masculinity. *Qingyi* morality is best illustrated by the love between Dai Tianli and Na Suzhi. They grew up together and became engaged at a young age. But Na's father, a greedy and fiendish man, breaks his promise to Dai and marries his daughter to the adopted son of a eunuch in exchange for two hundred taels of gold, with which he then opens an opium den. After Dai Tianli exposes him, the government cracks down on the Nas' opium business, and Na Suzhi's father is executed (episodes 13–14). The former couple thus become implacable foes, and they each marry others (with Dai's wife dying after giving birth to his son). Later in the series, however, Dai's newborn son is stolen by a thief at the instigation of Na Tulu, who, as noted, is out for revenge.

The thief, who is reluctant to kill a baby, sends the boy to Na Suzhi and her husband, who has become a bandit chieftain on Cockscomb Mountain since the confiscation of his family's property (episode 20). Na Suzhi adopts the boy and brings him up as her own son, teaching him the principle of *qingyi* using the very saying uttered earlier in the series by Dai. At series end, Ma Jiujin, as Dai's son becomes known, is told the truth about his father, and the three are reunited as a family following the death of Na's husband on the battlefield. *Qingyi* can be characterized by loyalty to women, brothers, and family, but the paramount form of *qingyi* is loyalty to one's homeland, as discussed in detail below.

The three patrilineal generations of men in the Dai family (protagonist Dai Tianli, Dai's father Dai Hanting, who is killed by the Japanese after chopping off the head of the very first Japanese soldier to enter Chengde, and Dai's son Ma Jiujin, who eventually becomes a communist fighter) epitomize the moral accomplishments of *wu* masculinity. *Wu* refers not only to physical strength and military prowess, but also to the wisdom and morality of knowing when and when not to resort to violence (Louie 2002, 14).[17] Patriotism is constructed as the primary criterion of *wu* masculinity in *The Dog-Beating Staff*. As Dai Tianli says at one point, "in the face of the formidable enemy, kill the devils and defend our country; that's what a disciple of *wu* should do" (episode 42). This quasi-religious principle determines his actions and distinguishes humans from "dogs." For instance, when Na Tulu is encircled by the Japanese and seeks his help, Dai rescues his sworn brother regardless of the opposition between them. For him, personal enmity must be forgotten at a time of national crisis. When he meets Na Tulu on the battlefield, he shouts, "You are a real Chinese man now!" (*ni shi yige zhenzheng de Zhongguo ye'mer le*) (episode 53). Patriotic politics are considered a major avenue for establishing one's masculinity, and they have been internalized as the unyielding obligation of a real man. As Dai's given name indicates, a man who betrays his nation is "*tianli nanrong*" (not to be forgiven by Providence).[18]

As mentioned above, the love-hate relationship between Dai Tianli and Na Suzhi constitutes a central theme of the drama. When investigating the Na family's secret opium trade, Dai makes use of Na Suzhi's confidence in him to obtain evidence of her father Na Pingshan's crimes. He promises to intercede with the authorities to save her father's life, but the governor, Dai's former friend Fang Mengqiao, who is also—unbeknown to Dai—involved in opium trafficking, decides to make Na Pingshan a scapegoat and has him executed in front of his family. Na Suzhi, feeling guilty about her betrayal of her father, thus comes to regard her erstwhile fiancé as her principal foe and vows to obtain revenge. Although Dai does his best to keep his promise to her, when faced with a conflict between personal love and the national interest, he unhesitatingly chooses to sacrifice the woman he loves for the sake of the nation's welfare (*minzu dayi*). He says, "As a Chinese, I cannot sit by while foreigners dump opium in China and harm my countrymen" (episode 13). By the drama's end, Na Suzhi comes to understand Dai's patriotic deeds and forgives him for killing her father, and the two are reconciled and reunited.

The patriotic message had a mixed reception among the audience members in my focus group discussions. Most of the informants in the migrant worker and retiree groups praised the drama for its correct "three outlooks" (*san guan*), a term frequently used by the Chinese media to refer to one's outlook on the world, life, and values. The most negative feedback came from the group of female university students. For them, the drama was "old-fashioned" with a predictable plot and ridiculous stereotypes. They pointed in particular to the drama's obsession with male heirs and reduction of women to tools of reproduction. These informants are right in that having a son is depicted as a boon for the positive characters in *The Dog-Beating Staff*, which is in keeping with the narrative tradition in Chinese folklore. Although Dai is forcibly separated from his son, who is dutifully brought up by Na Suzhi and her husband, for many years, father and son are ultimately reunited. Conversely, the characters who are insufficiently masculine apparently do not deserve a son. Na Tulu only has a daughter, who ultimately betrays him, and, as discussed in the following section, Na Suzhi's husband can only steal a son from Dai, as he is both impotent and a "sissy."

The most severe criticism of the young female audience members, however, focused on a subplot in which Dai's wife Xiu'er dies while giving birth to her second child. Xiu'er, a matchmaker's daughter who admires Dai's heroic deeds, is a virtuous wife to Dai who treats his adoptive daughter as if she were her own. Her first child with Dai is a son, the soon-to-be Ma Jiujin, who is stolen soon after birth. After that terrible loss, Xiu'er is desperate to give birth to another son to carry on the Dai family line, and so disregards doctors' warnings about the danger to her health. She finally becomes pregnant, but the labor turns difficult, and the doctor says that he can save only the mother or the child. Xiu'er insists on sacrificing herself, shouting, "Please cut open my belly! I know it is a son!" Upon learning from Dai that the newborn baby is a boy, a white lie because it is actually a girl, she dies content. After her death, her father-in-law bows deeply toward her room to show his gratitude for her contributions to the Dais. The baby girl is named Ruonan (meaning "like a boy") (episode 22). Several of the informants laughed at these scenes for being "hyperbolic," and criticized them for conveying the message that "a woman's worth lies in her ability to give birth to a son." The drama's preoccupation with fertility and male heirs who can carry on the family line is in fact a recurrent theme in Guo Jingyu's work, as will be discussed in chapter 6.

QUEERNESS AND THE NONMASCULINE OTHER: SUBVERSION AND CONTAINMENT

In *The Dog-Beating Staff*, in direct contrast to the heroic patriots of the Dai family are the shameful "dogs" who deserve to be beaten. The nonmasculine Other is embodied not only in the Japanese invaders but also in the unworthy Chinese men who betray their nation. While the forceful yet feeble Na Tulu serves as foil to our primary hero, Dai Tianli, Dai's son-in-law Bai Jingui, who embodies the "small man" image in Confucian discourse, can be regarded as the opposite of the drama's younger hero, Ma Jiujin. Bai was originally an apprentice in Dai's grain shop. An orphan who was adopted by Dai at an early age, he is treated as a family member by the Dais and is particularly well-liked by the grandmother, Dai Tianli's mother-in-law. He grows up with Dai's second daughter Ruonan and later passionately pursues her. When Ruonan is carried off by a local tyrant who wants her beauty for himself, Ma Jiujin, who also desires Ruonan without realizing that she is his sister, ventures into the tyrant's house alone and rescues her. He then leaves the unconscious girl with Bai Jingui after Bai promises that he will make her happy for the rest of her life. When Ruonan comes to, Bai mendaciously claims credit for saving her life and thus becomes her husband, lying his way into the Dai family's confidence (episode 35). Subsequently, as a husband and father of three, he prioritizes the interests of his "small family" over the interests of the nation and becomes a *hanjian* when the Japanese arrive. He leads the Japanese troops into Rehe City and then cooperates with the invaders.[19] Although he behaved like a humble servant to the Dais before his marriage, he reveals his cloven hooves as soon as his status changes. He betrays his father-in-law to the Japanese and with his own hands kills the grandmother who once loved him, before ultimately suffering a shameful death himself (episode 69). Online commentary on the series construes Bai as a "family man" who has no thoughts of patriotism and thus degenerates into a betrayer of the nation:

> Of humble origins, Bai Jingui sells himself at an early age in order to bury his father. His lower status means that he learns how to hold himself in different situations, and the wealth of the Dai family is what he pines for. Given a choice, he will never choose to return to poverty. So he works for the Japanese in order to protect his family and preserve his current life. . . . But he sincerely loves Ruonan. In order to save her, he leads the Japanese in and betrays his own people. . . . Bai Jingui represents a lot of us, who would rather betray the nation for the sake of the small family. He is a good family man but a harmful element for the nation.[20]

This denunciation of the family man is reminiscent of the condemnation of selfish, family-centered men found in traditional Chinese literature.[21] It is considered shameful and lacking in masculinity to be concerned about one's immediate family when the nation is endangered. In sharp contrast to Bai's selfishness are the sacrifices made by the aforementioned communist couple, Dai Tianli's adopted daughter Ruobing and her husband Gao Jinghu. Gao presents a weak scholarly image on the surface, but he inducts Ruobing into the Communist Party and the two become fearless anti-Japanese fighters. When they are eventually captured by the Japanese, they choose to die for the nation. Dai Tianli initially looks down upon his frail-looking son-in-law but is later deeply moved by his patriotic spirit and praises his manhood. Once again, the national interest serves as a touchstone for true masculinity.

Another male character in the drama who merits particular attention is Na Suzhi's husband, the bandit chieftain nicknamed "Old Second Aunt" (*Lao er shen*).[22] This type of heroic man (and form of masculinity) is uncommon in anti-Japanese TV dramas. As the adopted son of a eunuch who wins Na Suzhi with his father's wealth, this man presents a negative image when he first appears on screen. Compared with Dai Tianli, he is effeminate, talking and moving about in a womanish manner; that is, he has a typical *weiniang* image.[23] Online commentary compares him to a fox, thus eliciting the transgender "Fox Man" image popular in cyberspace (see Song and Hird 2014, 100–101):

> The four main characters in the drama represent four types of man, which resemble a donkey (Dai Tianli), wolf (Na Tulu), leopard (Ma Jiujin) and fox (Ma Yi, a.k.a. "Second Daughter" or "Old Second Aunt"), respectively. . . . The audience is so amazed when the "Second Daughter" played by Yu Yi first appears in the drama. His skin is as white as a woman's, he speaks in a girlie manner and walks with a sway of his hips. His powdered face, the green earring on one ear and the gesture of "orchid fingers" when he is talking . . . all leave the audience dumbfounded—"What a womanish man!"[24]

Some readily associate this image with homosexuality.[25] But the nonnormative gender expression is soon contained and countered by the depiction of Old Second Aunt as a loyal (heterosexual) lover and even a model husband. Na Suzhi does not like him at first and guards herself against him with scissors on their wedding night. But this effeminate man turns out to be a subservient husband and treats Na very well after their marriage. To please his wife, who is a fan of Peking Opera, he even arranges for an opera troupe to visit Cockscomb Mountain, and he becomes a cross-dresser when he plays the concubine in the play *Farewell My Concubine* (*Bawang bieji*) (figure 2).

Old Second Aunt becomes incredibly determined and valiant when facing the Japanese, and he dies a heroic death on the battlefield. He turns his bandit gang into an anti-Japanese guerrilla force and proclaims himself their commander-in-chief. These men fight side by side with Old Second Aunt's rival in love, Dai Tianli, in striking against the Japanese troops. Because of a Japanese agent in their camp, however, they are soon defeated and surrounded by the Japanese. Old Second Aunt fights until his last breath, pulling out a grenade to die together with his enemies. Lying in his wife's arms, his last words are "I have been playing the concubine all my life, and in the end I played the king (Xiang Yu) once" (figure 3). Here, the concubine (feminine)/king (masculine) dichotomy symbolically represents the distinction between appearance/fantasy and reality, and it unmistakably normalizes this character's gender transgression and cross-dressing through political validation.

As his wife says, Old Second Aunt is a "real man with a woman's look." This displacement between real life and fantasy and between outer appearance and the inner heart significantly reveals the meaning of true masculinity, which is fundamentally defined in the drama as inner moral power rather than physical appearance or strength. Men such as Na Tulu who appear strong and macho on the surface ultimately turn out to be cowards,

Figure 2. "Old Second Aunt" cross-dressed as the concubine in the Peking Opera *Farewell My Concubine. The Dog-Beating Staff* (2013).

Figure 3. "Old Second Aunt" dying a heroic death on the battlefield. His left hand displays the feminine hand gesture known as "orchid fingers." *The Dog-Beating Staff* (2013).

and therefore nonmasculine, whereas it is possible for effeminate men like Old Second Aunt to represent the true spirit of Chinese masculinity, that is, the valor to fight and die for the nation. In other words, his masculinity is validated by the heroic deeds he performs, which are prescribed by nationalist politics, thereby demonstrating a thought-provoking split between mind and body. As studies on masculinities in traditional China (Song 2004) reveal, true masculinity can be accommodated in feminine or even female bodies. Interestingly, the depiction of Old Second Aunt in the drama intertextually refers to the story of Xiang Yu, the hero par excellence, and his concubine, who is normally played by a male *dan* actor in traditional operas.[26] The play is now known for its cross-dressing and homoerotic overtones thanks to Chen Kaige's prize-winning film *Farewell My Concubine*. In terms of the *yin/yang* matrix, however, it goes without saying that Xiang Yu represents the *yang* and the concubine the *yin* in both heterosexual and homosexual contexts. Yet in *The Dog-Beating Staff*, this dichotomy is significantly subverted by Old Second Aunt, who looks *yin* on the outside but bears a *yang* spirit on the inside. Patriotism is therefore the power that engenders the ultimate *yang* identity.

This displacement of the body and mind, however, is unusual in anti-

Japanese dramas, wherein the construction of heroic masculinity is usually conspicuously premised on repudiation of the feminine, with womanish villains appearing in these dramas as contrasts to the manly heroes. The fascination with excessive femininity can be traced back to the time-honored tradition of amusing the audience through mimicry of women by male actors in the traditional Chinese comedic performing arts, such as *xiangsheng*. In the words of Tiantian Zheng (2015b, 352), effeminate men have become a "comic spectacle" in the Chinese media. At the same time, however, apart from its amusement purposes, male femininity in dramas with an anti-Japanese theme also serves to depict the abnormality and pathology of the Japanese "devils" and the moral weakness of their Chinese collaborators. Womanish Japanese men are weird, sinister predators, particularly when juxtaposed with "normal" upright Chinese masculinity. A recent example is Kaede Sendo in *Rookie Agent Rouge* (*Yanzhi*, 2016) (figure 4). The name Kaede Sendo demonstrates the discernible influence of Japanese ACG culture. It is a combination of Akira Sendoh and Kaede Rukawa, two teenage basketball players in the bestselling manga series *Slam Dunk* and the main characters in the self-published homoerotic *yaoi* manga *Deep Purple*. The name of this character in *Rookie Agent Rouge* thus carries a strong queer implication. Sendo (Su Xiaoding) is the head of the Special Higher Police in Shanghai. His father is a Japanese general, and his mother is Chinese. As an epitome of "feminine monstrosity" (T. Edwards 2006, 126), the character's effeminate appearance and behavior have been described as "witchy" (*yaoqi*) by online commentators. In fact, the actor gained such unexpected popularity following his performance that he felt forced to clarify during an interview that he is a "100 percent straight man" (*chun yemen'er*) in reality.[27] Sendo is depicted as a highly intelligent, and thus very dangerous, predator hunting the communist agents hidden within the Special Higher Police. He has exceptional skills and pathological zeal for detecting spies and then torturing them. Toward the end of the series, Sendo takes a fancy to his subordinate, Feng Manna (Tao Xinran), a beautiful but paranoid female officer working for the Japanese. Feng, however, despises his unmanly manners and is instead infatuated with the good-looking—and masculine—communist agent Zhou Yuhao (Lu Yi), the drama's primary hero. The contrast between these two men highlights the dominant and privileged position of heteronormativity and denigration of queer elements in the construction of nationalist heroism by Chinese television. As Tiantian Zheng (2015b) points out, in media portrayals effeminate men are "considered a peril to the security of the

Figure 4. The "witchy" appearance of Kaede Sendo. *Rookie Agent Rouge* (2016).

nation" because they reflect "powerlessness, inferiority, feminized passivity, and social deterioration, reminiscent of the colonial past when China was defeated by the colonizing West and plagued by its image as the 'sick man' of East Asia" (par. 5).

Male effeminacy and queerness are deployed to depict the detestable nature of evil characters or, at best, the flaws of good characters. Despite carrying strong implications of gayness, the effeminate characters without exception prove to be heterosexual in the dramas under study. In this sense, the queer elements in Chinese TV dramas are reminiscent of Stephen Greenblatt's theory of "subversion and containment": the dominant order sometimes generates subversive elements in order to make use of them and contain them within its parameters (Greenblatt 1988). The nonmasculine Other, be they Japanese or Chinese men, is created in this manner to suppress any possibility of deviant sexuality and accentuate the images of the heteronormative patriotic heroes.

A WAR OF WOMEN: EVIL JAPANESE AND GOOD JAPANESE

Homi Bhabha (1983) contends that stereotype, as a discursive strategy, is a form of knowledge and identification that vacillates between what is always "in place," already known, and "something that must be anxiously repeated" (18). Constituting the source of knowledge about Japanese people and culture for most Chinese, television and film contribute significantly to a well-defined imaginative space of the Japanese as the Other. Compared with images of the Japanese in Chinese films (see Yau 2013), however, the subject of the overwhelming number of "Japanese devils" on the small screen remains largely understudied. The issue of how the Japanese are imagined and represented as an Other to be feared and hated in this form of popular entertainment is thus ripe for investigation.

In the huge array of TV drama series under discussion, the Japaneseness of characters is portrayed in different ways. In the first type of portrayal, Japanese characters are played by Chinese actors speaking ordinary Chinese, leaving the audience to identify their nationality solely from their costumes and makeup such as the famous Jintan mustache, a marker of "Japanese devils" in film and TV alike. In the second type, which has become more common in the past decade or so, Japanese actors are hired to play Japanese roles. The Japanese characters speak fluent Japanese, subtitled in Chinese, among themselves, and they generally speak Chinese with a Japanese accent when talking to Chinese characters, thereby creating a sense of authenticity while satisfying the audience's curiosity about the Other. The result is that a group of amateur actors from Japan have become household names—and earned a considerable amount of money—in China by working as "professional devils" in anti-Japanese dramas.

A third type of portrayal, however, has appeared more recently. The most recent of these dramas tend to replace Japanese actors with Chinese actors who imitate a Japanese style of speaking Chinese. Even when speaking among themselves, the characters use this make-believe language, which is essentially Chinese mixed with a few token Japanese words such as *hai* (yes) and *baka* (idiot). This linguistic strategy is in line with an ideology of cultural superiority, which places the Japanese in an inadequate "learner" position relative to the Chinese. The ugly, even silly, Japanese-style pronunciation of Chinese in these dramas has become a new marker of Japanese national identity that, according to some audience members, feels "more like the Japanese than the real Japanese" (Mr. Li, thirty-year-old technician).

In discussing the censorship of TV dramas in China, Michel Keane (2015) notes that although images and language that are overtly sexual or violent or that incite ethnic hatred or discrimination are banned, "laws are intended to protect the Chinese people from vilification by outsiders, [and] a great deal more latitude is extended to Chinese narratives of anti-Japanese resistance. In many of these dramas Japanese people are stereotyped as evil and subhuman" (23). Indeed, most of the dramas under discussion are prone to the use of violent language. Japanese soldiers are almost always called "devils" (*guizi*), a pejorative term that can be used to refer to any foreigner but is generally reserved specifically for the Japanese in these dramas, or other such derogatory terms as "bastards" (*gouride*). A recurrent scene is that of the enraged hero, following the death of his loved ones, rising abruptly with machine gun in hand and shouting something like, "Jap suckers, I fuck your ancestors!" (*Xiao Riben'er, wo cao ni zuzong*). Many of the lines spoken in these dramas subscribe to a type of essentialist racial ideology that delineates the Japanese as the subhuman or even nonhuman Other. For example, in *Women of Luolong Town* (*Luolongzhen nüren*, 2014), when a middle-aged peasant woman kills a Japanese soldier for the first time, she at first trembles and says, "I killed someone!" After a moment, she then murmurs to herself, "No, no, it's a devil, it's not a human!" (episode 41).

The characterization of Japanese officers and soldiers relies on stereotypes that have become deeply rooted in the Chinese collective memory and imagination over generations, albeit gained from watching films and TV rather than from actual experience. For instance, the cold-blooded Japanese commander predictably commits *hara-kiri* when ultimately faced with defeat. The Japanese officer regularly slaps his subordinates in a fit of anger, with *baka* always on his lips. He also treats women like slaves, yet his submissive wife bows deeply to welcome him home every evening. It is common to portray the Japanese invaders as casting a covetous eye on China's cultural heritage, echoing a time-honored imagination of the Japanese as "thieves" of Chinese culture.[28] In many recent dramas, including *The Jade Phoenix* (*Feicui fenghuang*, 2009), *Sons and Daughters of the River* (*Dahe ernü*, 2014), *The Masters of Business* (*Da zhangmen*, 2013), and *Women of Luolong Town*, the plot centers on the insidious Japanese attempting to lay their hands on a Chinese cultural treasure, be it a priceless artifact, a secret recipe, or a special technique, with the Chinese characters, usually the members of two feuding families, burying the hatchet to defend that treasure together. In the aforementioned *The Dog-Beating Staff*, for example, in order to discover the whereabouts of the dog-beating staff, which, as noted, is regarded as an embodiment of the "Chinese spirit," the Japanese commander asks his own son, Ochiai Jiro, who is also an officer leading the invading troops, to disguise himself as a mute (so that his true identity will not be revealed by speaking) and mingle with the Chinese. He insinuates himself into Dai's confidence and becomes one of his two martial arts disciples. As the most dangerous enemy in Dai's midst, Ochiai not only steals his martial arts techniques, but also spies on him and gains information on the guerrillas, thereby causing the death of Old Second Aunt. Ochiai embodies one of the most entrenched stereotypes of the Japanese, which is that they learned everything they know from Chinese culture and yet still have the nerve to bite the hand that fed them.

This cultural pride (and anxiety) sometimes verges on chauvinism. In *When the Student Meets the Soldier* (*Xiucai yudao bing*, 2015), for instance, when the hero Long Qianyan is offered *sashimi* and Japanese tea by a heinous Imperial Army officer named Kitahara Hiroyuki, he sneers and says:

> The *sashimi* tastes good, but you made a common mistake by calling it Japanese cuisine. It is actually not Japanese. It originated from China, [where it is] known as *yukuai* [fish slice], which can be traced back to the Zhou Dynasty [ca. 1100–256 B.C.E]. And *Sado* (tea ceremony) is also from China! Thousands of years back, you should all call Chinese people your ancestors! (episode 3)

This kind of sentiment is common in these dramas and finds resonance in online discussions. The self-aggrandizement of "Chinese culture" reflects and reinforces the cultural essentialism that "draws an imaginary boundary between China and the rest of the world" (Chow 2000, 5).

One phenomenon in the televisual depiction of the Japanese in recent years warrants special attention. That is the increasing appearance of female "devils," even though, according to historians, there were no female soldiers or officers in the Japanese Imperial Army. As Iwata Takanori rightly observes, female Japanese "devils" on the TV screen are usually beautiful young women clad in close-fitting uniforms.[29] As an embodiment of both national and gender otherness, these characters are normally cold-blooded army officers or, more remarkably, spies who use their bodies to achieve their ends. The representation of such Japanese "sex spies" shows the conspicuous influence of the widely circulated legend about the female Japanese spy Kawashima Yoshiko during World War II.[30] According to Louise Edwards (2016, 8), in war narratives, sex spies are central to establishing the contrast between the high moral standards of the desexualized space of "our side" and the hypersexual, corrupted space of the "enemy side."

In addition to being objectified to cater to the male gaze, these women also illustrate the symbolic power relations of gender in war. Normally, women who go to war destabilize the gendered principle that "war enhances the masculine power of men by granting them, by dint of their sex, the role of protector of women and their virtue" (L. Edwards 2016, 8). In these dramas, however, Japanese women, regardless of whether they are good or evil, are usually passive victims of war and militarism. In most cases, they join the army and become fanatics because of their husbands or other men they love. Their presence in the drama therefore reinforces, rather than challenges, the notion of war as a masculine struggle between nations.

A notable example is Sakko in *A War of Women* (*Nüren de kangzhan*, 2014). The play, a "main melody" drama produced by the Television Arts Center under the auspices of the Political Department of the People's Liberation Army (PLA) Shenyang Military Region, centers on the heroic deeds of a group of Chinese women, including guerrilla soldiers and underground workers, during the war. Presumably inspired by the textbook story of eight female guerrilla fighters who martyred themselves by jumping into a river when besieged by the enemy,[31] the drama also ends with the women fighters, led by the protagonist Du Xueyan (Wen Zhengrong), committing suicide in front of the Japanese soldiers. Du is a communist agent whose husband is a police officer working for the pro-Japanese government. Her nemesis, a female Japanese officer named Sakko (Zeng Li), is the fiancée of the captain of the Japanese Military Police Corps, a man named Sato. As shrewd an officer and agent as she is, Sakko is extremely submissive toward and obedient to Sato and is always sexually available for him. In one scene, after discussing a plan to eliminate the anti-Japanese guerrillas, Sato carries her behind a folding screen. The sexual innuendo of a man holding a woman horizontally is commonly used in film and TV to convey women's passivity and sexuality (figure 5).

To help her fiancé to complete his mission of wiping out the anti-Japanese forces, Sakko risks her life by impersonating a Korean woman who lost her family during the Japanese invasion to infiltrate the guerrilla base. She successfully uses her sex appeal to elicit information from the deputy commander and a cipher officer in the guerrilla forces. Her sexuality therefore becomes a grave danger to the anti-Japanese troops. Later on, when Sakko's cover is blown, she is shot in the chest and falls down into a snow-covered valley while being chased by the guerrillas. Although she is rescued by the Japanese army, she suffers frostbite, and her wounds leave her permanently infertile. Interestingly, her primary opponent, Du Xueqing, gives birth to a

Figure 5. Sato holding Sakko horizontally in an intimate scene. *A War of Women* (2014).

healthy son at the same time that Sakko is hospitalized and learns of her infertility. As punishment for the atrocities she has committed, Sakko loses her reproductive capacity and thus her worth as a woman. From this point onward, she becomes pathologically cruel and takes pleasure in torturing people. She harbors a particular hatred for Du owing to jealousy over the latter's fertility. Different from Maoist narratives on female revolutionaries, the female fighters and soldiers in *A War of Women* never cross the boundaries of domestic and reproductive concerns. As a result, the images of both the Japanese and Chinese female combatants never pose a challenge to the patriarchal ideology that underlies this genre of TV drama.[32]

Japanese women can also be good characters, reflecting the long-standing link between femininity and victimhood in war narratives. Although positive images of the Japanese have existed in films and literature on the Anti-Japanese War since the Maoist and early post-Maoist eras, their ideological implications have changed over time. In Maoist ideology, the war was launched by the militarist ruling class in Japan, and thus both ordinary Chinese and Japanese people were victims. Hence, the good Japanese characters in Mao-era films and dramas are meant to illustrate the innocence and compassion of the Japanese oppressed classes. But with the ideology of class and class struggle replaced by an essentialist cultural nationalism in more recent TV programs, the symbolism and function of the good Japanese characters have changed. Although they are significantly reduced in number compared to the early and mid-1980s, when Sino-Japanese relations enjoyed something of a honeymoon period, good Japanese characters can still be found in some anti-Japanese dramas. Their existence, however, serves primarily to evidence the moral power of the Chinese people and Chinese culture. For example, in *The War-Time Duo* (*Fenghuo shuangxiong*, 2014), a Japanese soldier named Akiyama Taro, after being saved many times by Chinese characters at the cost of their own lives, is so moved by the heroism and selflessness of the Chinese people that he joins the Eighth Route Army and becomes a Pythagorean friend to Chinese communist fighter Chen Tiequan. Generally speaking, women significantly outnumber men among "good Japanese" portrayals on the small screen, which reflects the stereotypical image of Japanese women as less aggressive than their male counterparts.

During my interviews with TV audiences, many of the informants, men in particular, unexpectedly singled out one character as being among the most impressive Japanese characters on the TV screen in their recollections of the anti-Japanese dramas they had watched: Rieko (Liu Zhihan) in *The Patriots* (*Aiguo zhe*, 2018). Rieko is a fairly minor character in the series, the wife of a Japanese secret agent named Kishitani (Lu Fangsheng). An innocent and naïve woman, she accompanies her husband to Manchuria, where she obediently waits upon him, only to find that he does not love her at all. In her isolation and loneliness, Rieko befriends the young Chinese woman living next door to them, Shu Jie (Tong Liya), who is a communist agent, and inadvertently helps her to complete her missions. When she later discovers her husband's infatuation with Shu, Rieko falls apart. In an attempt to retaliate, she ties Kishitani up after incapacitating him with a drug, but is easily deceived by his sweet words when he wakes up. She imprudently releases him, only to be strangled to death. In online forums and personal discussions, many male viewers described Rieko as the ideal wife and expressed a desire to find a woman just like her. They commented that Rieko embodied Japanese womanhood, characterized not only by obedience and submissiveness to her husband but also by virtue of enduring her husband's abuses without complaint (*ni lai shun shou*). Her tragic end makes one "achingly sad" (*rang ren xinteng*) because she remains "pure and kindhearted" (*chunzhen shanliang*) even when facing her demonic husband (Mr. Zhang, thirty-two-year-old manager). In an interview published by an online magazine, the actress who played Reiko, Liu Zhihan, said that "in order to demonstrate the features of Japanese women of that era in both appearance and tempera-ment," she had watched *Oshin*, an NHK TV drama that was sweepingly popu-lar in China in the 1980s, repeatedly and painstakingly imitating the man-ner of speaking and moving about of the eponymous character.[33] In the popular imagination, Oshin is widely regarded as an exemplar of Japanese womanhood—and the "good wife, wise mother" ideology—and is still beloved by many Chinese today.

Female Japanese characters on the Chinese TV screen, be they good or evil, reflect not only (mis)readings of the national Other but also the blatant projection of male desires onto women. They are mostly imagined as sexu-ally available and intellectually controllable subjects. Anti-Japanese ideol-ogy has legitimized sexual explicitness in portrayals of these women as the subhuman "enemy," thus catering to the phallic imagination of male audi-ences. Their submission to patriarchal power is more often than not exagger-ated with exaltation. In *The Patriots*, after murdering his wife, Kishitani com-placently boasts about his male power to Shu Jie:

> Do you know why Rieko loved me so much? Why she followed me from Japan
> to Manchuria and never left me? She trusted me until her death even when I
> treated her like this. Because . . . you will know later, I am capable of making
> you surrender your whole heart and whole body. (episode 34)

RED: AUDIENCE NEGOTIATIONS OF MEANING

Although anti-Japanese dramas are an essential pedagogic tool of patriotic education, an important yet largely neglected factor that has given rise to their proliferation is the space they provide for irony and mockery of the official discourse. As defined by Ien Ang (2007) in her study of TV dramas in the West, irony is

> a form of cultural capital that empowers those who possess it to construct a
> relativist relationship to television; it is appreciative of its pleasures but [has]
> not fully succumbed to it; "in the know" about its textual tricks and therefore
> able to good humouredly play with them. (22)

During my fieldwork, I found that although many informants admitted watching this type of TV drama, none identified him- or herself as a big fan.

Everyone, including retired people and people with lower incomes, burst into laughter when the term "mythological anti-Japanese drama" was mentioned, and all were highly critical of the quality of such programs. Common complaints included that the topic has been done to death, that people are tired of being spoon-fed hackneyed messages about the abhorrent acts of Japanese soldiers and the suffering and patriotic spirit of the Chinese people, and that the plots have become very formulaic and scripted along official lines. Some also bemoaned the incredible amount of bloodshed. For many, anti-Japanese dramas are nothing but travesties of official propaganda on patriotic and revolutionary themes and exemplars of the "low-taste" culture that dominates the Chinese media today. In fact, the term *Kang-Ri shenju* itself reflects audiences' sarcastic reception of the subgenre, with the character *shen* connoting meanings more along the lines of crazy, unbelievable, absurd, lurid, preposterous, or ridiculous.

Apparently, many of the dramas under discussion address their lofty patriotic theme with a touch of ironic playfulness. Compared with the propaganda films on the Anti-Japanese War produced in the 1950s and 1960s, their contemporary TV counterparts treat their historical narrative with a pointed self-parody, paradoxically fulfilling the functions of both patriotic education and postmodern entertainment. Scenes such as the aforementioned "crotch grenade" scene unmistakably convey a ludic irony toward the official discourse. As far as the audience is concerned, it is questionable how seriously the anti-Japanese message in these dramas is taken. Indeed, viewers' online comments paint a diverse and sometimes unexpected picture of the way in which the dramas' intended political message is understood and its meaning negotiated.[34]

When discussing the audience reception of this subgenre of TV drama, a more nuanced analysis that takes into consideration the diversity of viewers in terms of gender, age, class, and education level is clearly in order. As many scholars have pointed out, TV audiences must always be understood in the plural and with sensitivity toward their diversity in terms of background and needs. In addition, instead of passively receiving the intended meanings of TV programs, diverse audiences are involved, often unconsciously, in making sense of these "texts" from their own personal and social perspectives. Ethnographic research on the active audience has therefore emerged as a new and promising path in television studies (see Ang 1991, 1996; Morley 1992, 1993). The last section of this chapter explores various reasons for the popularity of this subgenre by discussing focus group work with a sample of television audiences in Beijing. The size of the sample is admittedly very small in view of the large diversity of the Chinese TV audience for anti-Japanese dramas. The focus group results, however, help to illustrate the stark age differences in those who watch these dramas, and they also reveal that different viewers consume TV drama programs (and the gender discourses associated with them) for different reasons.

War dramas are traditionally believed to be the favorite genre of male audiences. Individual and focus group interviews with TV viewers during my fieldwork, however, indicated no particular gender distinctions among those who frequently watch anti-Japanese dramas. Many women said they enjoyed watching them for a variety of reasons. To unravel the complex entanglement between such factors as gender and age in interpreting the dramas under discussion, I interviewed twelve female audience members in Beijing in February 2015 about their responses to a recent popular TV drama series called *Red* (*Hongse*). The series was actually brought to my attention by a female respondent. According to online information, *Red*, a hit TV drama in 2014, appeals to a wide range of audiences and is particularly popular among the younger generation and women. The drama achieved a high rating of 9.2 on Douban.com, a Chinese equivalent to IMDb. Instead of a typically shoddy "mythological" anti-Japanese drama, it features sensitive emotions, delicate performances, and a suspenseful plot. The informants, who were initially recruited with the help of my local collaborator at the Communication University of China and then expanded through snowball sampling, all claimed to have followed the drama when it aired on several major TV channels. They were divided into two focus groups. The first group (group 1) comprised five middle-aged women, most of them retired (average age: sixty-two), and the second group (group 2) consisted of seven undergraduate and postgraduate students (average age: twenty-two). The focus groups began with a brief overview of the plot, followed by the screening of the last episode of the series. The informants then engaged in an unstructured discussion centering on the drama's characters and storyline.[35]

The male protagonist in *Red*, Xu Tian (Zhang Luyi), is a homebody who hides his exceptional abilities to seek a humble and ordinary life in Japanese-occupied Shanghai in the 1940s, only to be forced into becoming a lone hero. At the outset, he works as a low-level accountant in a fresh food market. A shy and reserved man in his thirties who still lives with his mother (his father died during the communist rebellion), Xu remains single and has never dated. He is a filial son who brings food home from the market every day and has dinner with his mother. None of those around him has the slightest inclination of his extraordinary gifts, which include unusually keen observation skills and reasoning power, or of his ten years of military training in Japan (it is not explained in the drama who sent him to Japan or why). Xu chooses to lead this prosaic life until he meets the love of his life, the female protagonist Tian Dan (Tao Hong).

Xu first meets Tian on the street on the day that Japanese troops occupy Shanghai as she is rushing to the airport to join her fiancé in fleeing the city. The fiancé soon abandons her, however, choosing to save himself when one person has to step off the overloaded aircraft. Her parents are then killed by the Japanese for secretly helping the communists, and she becomes homeless after her house burns down. Xu, who falls in love with her at first sight, persuades her to rent the upstairs room of the house in which he and his mother live. He soon discovers that Tian, a pharmacist, is making use of her medical and chemistry knowledge to kill the Japanese to avenge her dead parents. Out of love for her, Xu secretly helps Tian using his superior intelligence and physical power, although Tian remains unaware of his help or that he has rescued her from Japanese clutches many times at the risk of his own life. In her eyes, he is just a considerate, thoughtful but humble boyman. The bulk of the drama thus depicts the breathtaking adventures of Xu repeatedly covering for the object of his affection using his wisdom and courage. After enduring horrific torture at Japanese hands, Xu finally succeeds in escaping to reunite with his mother and now lover Tian, who has finally recognized his true worth, in a communist stronghold.

One online comment on *Red* describes it as a hotchpotch of *Sherlock Holmes*, *In the Mood for Love*, *Mr. & Mrs. Smith*, and *Love Hina*.[36] It is clear that a variety of popular motifs, such as the whodunit, clichéd romance between a landlord and tenant, and nostalgia for old Shanghai, are strategically combined and packaged into a politically favorable anti-Japanese setting to engender maximum market appeal. It thus exemplifies contemporary Chinese TV's market-driven enticement of a diverse audience.

The two focus groups in this study had remarkably different readings of the program. The first group, comprising middle-aged women, demonstrated emotional engagement with the heroic deeds of the protagonists and brutality of the Japanese during the viewing session. They all appeared happy and relieved when, at the end of the program, the primary antagonist, a Japanese officer named Kasega (Xu's former tutor in Japan), and his aide Hase are killed, commenting that they "well deserved" (*zizuo zishou*) their shameful ending. They also described Kasega as a pathological pervert (*biantai*) who is obsessed with spying on his prey in addition to torturing them physically, psychologically, and sexually. They noted that he could have killed Xu when he first suspected him but instead chose to torture him by taking advantage of Xu's love for Tian. One informant particularly disliked Kasega's hyperbolic fake laughter, linking it with her unfavorable impression of Japanese men in general. The other informants agreed with her. Most of them also found the electric torture imposed on Xu by the Japanese to be particularly cruel and inhumane (*canwu rendao*). Two women said they watched the torture scene in tears. The informants attributed Kasega's behavior to the "national character" of the Japanese people.

With regard to their impression of the drama's male protagonist, one informant mentioned that she was moved by the loving relationship between Xu and his mother and said that the use of the Shanghainese dialect made the drama "true to life" (*bizhen*)[37]:

> The play is about Xu and two women in his life, instead of one, that is, his mother and his girlfriend. I was so moved and happy when I saw that Xu escapes Japanese-occupied Shanghai and reunites with his mother and Tian in a liberated area in the end. This ending makes the drama special. If it were another drama, most likely the guerrilla would only rescue his girlfriend, and the two would be allowed to live happily together. . . . I like the dialogue between Xu and his mum, all of it in Shanghainese or Mandarin with a strong Shanghai accent. So mundane and authentic. This is also unusual in TV dramas. Xu Tian's filial piety (*xiao*) is in harmony with his loyalty to the nation (*zhong*).
>
> (Ms. Deng, fifty-eight-year-old retiree)

When the two focus groups were asked to use key phrases to describe their feelings about the male protagonist, four of those in group 1 used "patriotic" (*aiguo*), a term that none of their group 2 counterparts mentioned. Almost all the informants in the second group, made up of students, identified with the female protagonist, Tian Dan. The romance between the two main protagonists was central to their enjoyment of the drama, and their discussion focused on the desirability of the male protagonist from the perspective of young women. The anti-Japanese theme, by contrast, was largely neglected. The key phrases they chose to describe Xu were "homebody" (*zhainan*), "cute and boyish" (*meng*), and "warm man" (*nuan-*

nan). Rather ironically, the first two of these phrases originate from Japanese popular culture, unmistakably attesting to the influence of Japanese pop culture on young audiences in China.[38]

As Song and Hird (2014, 79–92) discuss in some detail, the trendy word *zhainan* originates from the Japanese term *otaku* and has taken on the connotation of a desirable form of masculinity in the Chinese context, echoing the discourse on the obsession and purity of the good man in premodern Chinese culture. Several of the group 2 informants referred to Xu as a *zhainan* who had had no contact with women before meeting his true love. They indicated that this "purity" made him particularly attractive: "He is a big, timid boy who goes home to have dinner with his mum on time every day and would faint at the sight of blood. He is a reliable *zhainan*!" (Ms. Tan, nineteen-year-old undergraduate student). In fact, the drama's title, *Red*, was taken by this group of informants to refer to the color of blood, and specifically to Xu's likelihood of fainting at the sight of blood, rather than to the color of revolution, which would be the traditional symbolic interpretation.

The word *meng* bears an even more direct link to Japanese pop culture, being the Chinese pronunciation of the Japanese character *moe*. *Moe*, which originally meant "budding" or "burning," now refers to a particular kind of "adorable" or "cute" preadolescent girl in the fantasy world of ACG culture. The word carries hints of lust and denotes feelings of desire by ACG fans for imaginary figures who do not exist in reality. Like *otaku*, the word has undergone transformations in meaning and usage during its migration to China. In the Chinese context, *meng*, which can be used as a noun, an adjective, or even a verb, has become a trendy word among young people, particularly in cyberspace. It can be used to describe a wide range of things: from children's expressions to President Xi Jinping's new hairstyle. Notably, it is increasingly used to describe loveliness in men, and when a man is referred to as *meng*, there is a (positive) implication of femininity. The popularity of *zhainan* and *meng* in China, on the whole, represents a growing cultural convergence among East Asian countries, a kind of "Asianisation" of Asia (Ang 2004, 305–6). At the same time, the transnational circulation and interaction of images and discourses are coterminous with nationalistic expressions of national pride and anxiety on Chinese TV.

Coinciding with the views expressed in many online comments on *Red*, the young female viewers in focus group 2 unanimously expressed a euphoric response to the *meng* expression in Xu's eyes (see figure 6). One informant

Figure 6. Xu Tian. *Red* (2014).

said, "Although he is a hero, he looks so innocent and boyish. I am bewitched by Zhang Luyi's *meng* appearance in the drama!" (Ms. Liang, twenty-year-old undergraduate student). In her usage, *meng* represents a kind of feminine beauty in men, or an androgynous glamor that is reminiscent of the feminine scholar in premodern Chinese culture (see Song 2004). It is no wonder that an online article praises Xu as "the most graceful anti-Japanese hero."[39]

Another trendy word associated with this male image is *nuannan* (warm man). It refers to sensitive men who harbor warm emotions for women, men who bear some similarities to the herbivore men (*Soshoku danshi*) of Japanese society. They are slender and clean in appearance and often display an understanding of women and their feelings. According to the informants in focus group 2, Xu Tian exemplifies the attractive features of a *nuannan*. His masculinity is exhibited through his delicate and thoughtful care for his girlfriend. One informant said he possesses the typical attributes of a Shanghainese man, such as cooking skills and being considerate to women (Ms. Xue, twenty-three-year-old postgraduate student). Another said that this image of a homely "little man" (*xiao nanren*) is juxtaposed in the drama with the heroism of a "great man" who shows no fear in the face of torture by the Japanese and refuses to betray his woman (Ms. Chen, twenty-year-old undergraduate student). Many of the young women in this group said that Xu is the type of boyfriend they dream of:

I like this TV series very much for a reason that may be different from, say, my mother's. My mother likes it because she hates the Japanese and feels satisfied when they are punished. But for me, I find the male protagonist played by Zhang Luyi to be the type of ideal boyfriend that every girl would fancy. Whenever his girlfriend gets herself into trouble, he solves the problem for her even without her knowledge. This unselfish love is the highest level of romance.

(Ms. Hu, twenty-three-year-old postgraduate student)

Domestic TV dramas in China, which traditionally cater to middle-aged and older audiences, as noted, are now trying to reach out to young viewers through a more creative style and more nuanced stories (W. Xu 2015). *Red*, with its refined cinematography, engaging plot, and charming actors, appears to constitute a successful such attempt. Although the stereotyped images of the Japanese as cold-blooded, perverted killers and the patriotic education agenda familiar from other anti-Japanese dramas persist, young audiences are attracted to *Red* by its romantic elements and, surprisingly, by gender ideals that show the conspicuous influence of Japanese pop culture. The responses of audiences of different age groups reveal the tension-fraught, paradox-permeated conditions of today's Chinese television (Bai and Song 2015).

The "unorthodox" audience reception of anti-Japanese dramas is by no means exclusive to *Red*. Dramas such as *Drawing Sword* (*Liang jian*, 2005), *My Chief and My Regiment* (*Wo de tuanzhang wo de tuan*, 2009), and *The Disguiser*, which all received scores above 8.5 on Douban, are wildly popular across generations and are known for their deviation from the official historical narrative on the Anti-Japanese War. Some of these dramas are regarded by young viewers as classic queer dramas for their representations of ambiguous homosocial or homoerotic relationships (see Song 2010). This all attests to the increasing diversity of this subgenre in content and theme and the grow-ing space for alternative interpretations and recreations by TV fans.

CONCLUSION

The proliferation of TV dramas set during the Anti-Japanese War cannot be sufficiently explained simply as the government's strategy of stirring up nationalist sentiments. Adopting the combined methods of institutional analysis, textual reading, and audience reception study, this chapter approaches this subgenre of TV drama from various perspectives. Anti-

Japanese drama reflects the authority of the state in entertainment production, which can be said to be a distinct feature of Chinese TV relative to that of other countries. In terms of gender construction, the anti-Japanese subgenre is a typical vehicle for patriotic patriarchy, which derides and diminishes femininity and queerness. At the same time, however, the comedic effects, intended or unintended, generated by some of these dramas render them a form of carnivalesque entertainment cloaked in a nationalist overcoat. To cater to the tastes and desires of the diverse "active audience" in the Chinese market, anti-Japanese dramas are increasingly becoming a hotchpotch of different discourses, motifs, and themes. Nowhere else in the mediascape can we find such a congenial coexistence of revolutionary heroism, cultural nationalism, neoliberal consumerism, and postmodern black humor.

The outcomes of the audience reception study in this chapter reflect the general trend of Chinese television's transformation from blatant political pedagogy to commodified entertainment. In the process, young women have emerged as the primary target audience for many TV drama producers. Anti-Japanese dramas are not just about struggle and conflict but can also indicate cultural proximity and convergence. Through textual analysis of *Red* and a focus group study of its audience, the final section of this chapter demonstrates how nationalistic heroism is able to negotiate and achieve synthesis with new trends and new identities of masculinity that result from the convergence of East Asian popular cultures while maintaining an anti-Japanese theme.

In sum, the production and circulation of anti-Japanese dramas illustrate a new mode of cultural governance that is built on the intertwined forces of commercial incentives and political constraints. At the same time, however, the irony, mockery, and space for alternative subjectivity engendered by the reception of this subgenre raise questions about the effectiveness of the stale mode of nationalist education and expose the cracks in the formation of this new mode of cultural governance.

CHAPTER 4

"Straight-Man Cancer" and "Bossy CEO"

Sexism with Chinese Characteristics

RECENT YEARS HAVE witnessed growing public debate over gender issues in China, influenced in part by such global trends as the #MeToo movement and fueled by the expanding space for speech enabled by social media platforms. One prominent characteristic of these debates is the entanglement of gender and nation. Although the discursive interconnectedness of gender and nation (and race) is not limited to China amid a global rise in nationalism and populism (e.g., the male chauvinism, American exceptionalism, and white supremacy simultaneously espoused by the Proud Boys in the United States), the Chinese obsession with a masculine nation has given rise to both anxiety about Chinese men and misogynist and sexist postures. In China, social concerns over gender issues are usually intertwined with handwringing over the nation. For example, in the aforementioned debate on the standard of masculinity triggered by *niangpao* images, both critics and defenders of the aesthetic exhibit deep-seated concern about representing Chinese men, as a symbol of the Chinese nation, in the correct manner on the international stage (see chapter 6).

A more recent example is the controversial remarks made by education billionaire Yu Minhong. Yu suggested that Chinese women, who allegedly choose men based solely on their ability to make money, should be held responsible for the decline of the nation, although he apologized after being accused of sexism.[1] These debates, which bespeak the tension between a patriarchal/sexist ideology and the grassroots awakening of female subjectivity and burgeoning influence of feminist thinking, are in many ways echoing and reinforcing the entrenched affective link between gender and nation. In the process, a number of television programs, TV dramas in particular, have been singled out as a target of feminist fury. Television programs and their reception also allow us to discern an ever-widening generation gap in today's China over issues of gender and sexuality.

Men such as Yu who display chauvinist thinking are often described in cyberspace as sufferers of "terminal 'straight-man cancer' (*zhinan'ai*)." The jokingly coined neologism "straight-man cancer" is pronounced similarly to "rectal cancer" (*zhichang'ai*) in Chinese, and thus carries the connotation of a hopeless condition. According to several online articles, a man who suffers from "straight-man cancer" shows traits of toxic masculinity. He is cynical, chauvinist, and prone to sexist behavior and language. He is prejudiced against women and, out of deep-seated male anxiety, typically confirms his own worth by belittling women, especially women who are superior to him in education, family background, or professional achievement.[2] Moreover, these men are extremely possessive of women and are more often than not single-minded in love. They have a strong desire to control and manipulate the women with whom they form relationships. From a female perspective, the term emphasizes the "straightness" of these men and thus questions heteronormativity and its ideological link with patriarchy in the context of growing awareness of the diversity and pluralism of gender and sexuality.

This chapter delves into recent TV dramas featuring male characters who have been labeled as sufferers of "straight-man cancer" by audiences and online critics, and it uses them as examples to examine the coupling of patriarchy and nationalism, as well as resistance to the prevailing patriarchal ideology. It also discusses a particular type of male chauvinist fantasy, the "bossy CEO" motif in online romantic stories and TV (and web) drama series adapted from them. These stories follow a certain stereotyped formula, depicting the love between a wealthy and domineering young man, a member of the business elite or a success in another social arena, and a girl of humble background with modest accomplishments. Although there are variations of the story pattern in terms of setting and characterization, the essential constituents never change: a Cinderella-type fantasy that normalizes the male protagonists who patronize and the female protagonists who organize their behaviors to ultimately deserve that patronage.

CHINESE-STYLE RELATIONSHIP: CRISIS OF MASCULINITY
AND IMAGINED CHINESENESS

One of the examples of a TV character suffering from "straight-man cancer" singled out by audience members during interviews is Ma Guoliang, a middle-aged entrepreneur in *Chinese-Style Relationship* (*Zhongguo shi guanxi*, 2016). The TV drama's title echoes that of the earlier hit drama *A Chinese-Style Divorce* (*Zhongguo shi lihun*, 2004), which itself alludes to that of the celebrated film *Divorce Italian Style*.[3] The passion for identifying things as "Chinese style" reflects an ingrained obsession with the uniqueness of Chinese culture in the global era. This thirty-six-episode series highlights the contrast between the "Chinese style" of socializing and conducting business and the perceived *haigui* (returnees from overseas) style. National pride and confidence are entangled with the "crisis of masculinity" faced by the drama's middle-aged entrepreneurial protagonist. At the beginning of the series, Ma Guoliang (Chen Jianbin), a man in his mid-forties, is deputy head of the City Planning Institute, a government department charged with approving and monitoring property development projects. In the course of his work, he meets a U.S.-educated female architect named Jiang Yinan (Ma Yili) whose design of a proposed apartment complex for the elderly is submitted for his approval. The two experience a number of conflicts and misunderstandings due to differences in their cultural assumptions and mindsets. Shortly after their first encounter, Ma experiences an unprecedented crisis in both his personal and professional life: his wife of twenty years leaves him to marry his subordinate and longtime friend Shen Yun (Zhao Lixin). Shen is also his rival for promotion to head of the institute, a position that Ma longs for. Because of Shen's betrayal, however, Ma loses out on the promotion. Aggravated by the turn of events, Ma quits his job and, with the help of Jiang and a young man named Guan Qiang, sets up his own construction company. The trio undergoes various trials before finally achieving success. During the process, our hero wins Jiang's heart through his honesty, warmheartedness, wisdom, and spirit of self-sacrifice, and the pair finally embarks on a "Chinese-style" relationship.

At the story's heart lies the deep-seated fear of midlife crisis and cuckoldry-related anxiety common to middle-aged men. Cuckoldry, "as a form of competition between men in a patriarchal culture" (Cohen 2004, 6), evinces emasculation and, according to studies on literary representations of this theme, leads to "psychological castration":

[T]o be betrayed by a woman [. . .] is to be humiliated or dishonored, and thus placed in a position of vulnerability that makes [the cuckold] psychologically like a castrated man, and thus womanish. To defend against the fear of such castration, men anticipate it in fantasy, and turn it against women by calling them whores. To be betrayed by a woman thus threatens a man's very masculinity—his identity as a man. (Kahn 1981, 132)

In Ma's case, losing his wife to his best friend not only threatens his masculinity but also directly results in career failure. The humiliation is particularly acute because Ma actually witnesses a secret tryst between his wife and Shen upon returning home from the office (episode 2), and it is exacerbated by his snobbish mother-in-law's enmity and support for the divorce. What happens to Ma is evidence that "[m]en with economic and political power become sexually potent, whereas men who have lost such power feel emasculated by the market reforms" in today's China (T. Zheng 2015b, 350). Predictably, it is entrepreneurial success that eventually revalidates Ma's masculinity. As an added boon, he obtains a woman far superior to his previous one and even overcomes his ex-mother-in-law's hostility.

Guanxi, a keyword in the series title, refers to both the networks of influence that are needed for business success in China and the romantic relationship that develops between the two protagonists. A word that has become widely known in the West and even absorbed into the English language, guanxi is often negatively associated with the corrupt business culture of mainland China. In Chinese-Style Relationship, however, rather than an indicator of corruption or nepotism, guanxi is positively presented and justified as a unique characteristic of Chinese culture. In cultural relativist terms, guanxi is interpreted in the drama as the necessary interpersonal ties that nourish trust and respect between individuals and is thus linked with the power of masculinity. Ma's success is attributed to his skillful mastery of the art of guanxi and his familiarity with the rules of doing business in China. For instance, in episode 12, Ma and Jiang eagerly solicit an investment from an uncouth tycoon called Brother Hao, who insists that the decision must be approved by his company's board of directors. It turns out that the board consists exclusively of Hao's immediate family members and relatives, and the board meeting is held in a foot massage parlor, a locale known for its popularity among the Chinese nouveau riche. Jiang feels deeply insulted by having to give her presentation to a group of inattentive boors enjoying a foot massage, whereas Ma patiently socializes with them, allowing him to notice subtle tensions among the family members at the mahjong table, tensions that he then makes skillful use of to attain his goal.

The usefulness of *guanxi* is compared with the perceived "Western" style of doing business in dichotomous fashion. In episode 1, for example, Jiang is invited to a banquet to introduce her project, but instead finds herself repeatedly urged to drink by Ma and the other men at the table. Disappointed, Ma takes her refusal to drink as a lack of sincerity:

> JIANG: I've said only sixty words since I entered this room two hours ago.
> MA: You've been in this room for two hours but only drank one sip of wine. I have failed to do my job.
> JIANG: I'm sorry, but I'm here to present my proposal, not to eat and drink.
> MA: In fact, eating and drinking show your sincerity [about cooperating] . . . it's all about etiquette.

Upon hearing that, the other male guests pass a wine glass to Jiang and urge her to toast to Ma, but she refuses to do so. Not only that, she even inadvertently spills wine on his shirt, thereby spoiling the dinner. This imagined cultural conflict between the Chinese and American ways of thinking actually begins when the two meet for the first time on a flight from the United States. Ma answers his cell phone before the plane has come to a complete stop, and Jiang, who happens to be sitting next to him, becomes so angry that she grabs the phone and switches it off. A quarrel ensues. Ma insists that disobeying the rule is not such a big deal as the plane had already landed and criticizes Jiang for being an inflexible fussbudget. Leaving the airport in Beijing, both are soon caught in a major traffic jam. Jiang demands that her taxi driver adhere strictly to the traffic rules and, as a result, is late for an important meal organized by the property developer (she has no idea that Ma is the man she is going to meet at the meal). After a series of similar setbacks, Jiang gradually realizes the importance of *guanxi* and begins to change her "Westernized" mindset, as shown by her remarks near the series end:

> I was very frustrated when I returned to China and met with failure in whatever I did. You said it was because I knew nothing about Chinese-style *guanxi*. Then I began to ponder what *guanxi* is. . . . Now I understand that *guanxi* not only exists in business and official circles; it also permeates humanity. It is

linked to the moral principles and emotions that have lasted for thousands of years in Chinese culture. Only by understanding this can you become invincible in China. (episode 36)

This justification of *guanxi* in a cultural relativist manner echoes the advocacy of the "four confidences" ("confidence in our chosen path, confidence in our political system, confidence in our guiding theories, and confidence in our culture") by Xi Jinping in recent speeches. Of the four, Xi highlights cultural confidence in particular as "a more fundamental, a broader, a more profound type of confidence" (Feng 2016). Accordingly, enhancing China's soft power and "the power of speech" (*huayu quan*) in the world has become a priority concern in the government's recent cultural policies, with television the predominant site for constructing and promoting confidence in China's national culture and identity. *Chinese-Style Relationship* serves as a good example in this regard. Ma's masculinity is regained and consolidated not only through "self-entrepreneurization" in the context of neoliberal market reforms but also through his possession of "Chinese" wisdom as a form of cultural capital, which includes his shrewdness in debt collection (episodes 11–12) and resourcefulness in thwarting Shen Yun's scheme to frame Jiang and undermine her elderly housing project (episodes 34–36).

Perhaps the most controversial aspects of *Chinese-Style Relationship* are Ma's attitude toward women and his wife's infidelity. When discussing Ma's divorce, the male and female members of the focus group divided themselves into two camps, with his lack of manners and respect for women garnering him harsh criticism from the latter, while the former were largely sympathetic. Informants of both sexes, however, likened his divorce to the sensational Wang Baoqiang incident:[4]

> Ma Guoliang is the TV incarnation of Wang Baoqiang. He is an ill-tempered man, and during his twenty-year marriage to his ex-wife, he seldom cared about her emotional needs. That led directly to his ex-wife's infidelity. When she complains that he returns home drunk [because of the socializing requirements of his work] every day and does not even have time to talk with her and their daughter, Ma replies, "I provide you with food and shelter and give all my salary to you every month; what else do you want?" What a typical mindset of Chinese husbands! Ma is a middle-aged greasy man [i.e., a man who does not care about his appearance]. . . . But, just like in reality [in the case of Wang Baoqiang], most people sympathize with [the man], and few care about

his estranged wife's feelings. In the drama, Ma is presented as a good man who [is supposed to] deserve audience sympathy. (Ms. Xu, forty-one-year-old marketing executive)

Another female focus group member added that Ma comes across as an arrogant man who always speaks in an annoyingly condescending, lecturing tone when talking to women. Jiang does not like him initially because he is always astringent and is sometimes downright rude to her (Ms. Zhang, thirty-two-year-old office clerk). The same woman also pointed out that Ma is an inattentive husband and father. For example, when he and his wife fight for custody of their daughter during the divorce case, Ma cannot even remember which grade his daughter is in. Most male audience members, however, were defensive of Ma and thought that his ex-wife should be blamed for her betrayal. One male informant expressed his indignation toward Liu Lili—Ma's ex-wife—and her mother as follows.

It is evident that Liu Lili has had an affair, and yet she always suggests that she has been treated poorly—saying "Is there a need for this attitude, can we not speak in a civil manner?" Does she expect her husband to speak to her in a calm and peaceful manner with a massive smile on his face when it was she who had an affair behind his back? Also, when they are already divorced and Liu has gotten together with Shen Yun, she is still unhappy over the fact that Ma is living with a young lady—what does [she] have to do with this? Ma is being courteous by allowing his ex-wife to temporarily live in his house. In return, Liu calls for her lover to move into the house. She turns her ex-husband's house into her newlywed house and has sex with another man on her ex-husband's bed. If she is all right with this, on what basis should she be making a fuss about Ma and the young lady? This is a typical example of how someone is being a bitch while still wanting to [maintain] a decent reputation. Another funnier character is Liu's mother, as she asks Ma to provide evidence of her daughter's affair. Isn't this the formula of the one who is at fault demanding evidence and then accusing the victim despite the fact that they are at fault to begin with, like that in Wang Baoqiang's case? Seriously, if it wasn't for the fact that [the series] was filmed beforehand, I really would think that it was based on Wang's case. (Mr. Huang, twenty-eight-year-old clerk)

The conflicting debate about this character is most interesting inasmuch as it reflects the dynamics of gender relations and contested expectations of marriage in contemporary China. Yet in the drama, Ma's "symptoms," such as arrogance and male chauvinism, are justified through approval of his true "Chinese-style" masculinity, which is demonstrated by Jiang's gradual realization and acceptance of his merits. In the final episode (episode 36), Jiang professes:

> When we first met, I didn't like him at all. He was arrogant, slothful, chauvinist, and arbitrary. My first response was that I could never in my life become his friend. But suddenly I realized that, even at the lowest ebb of his life, he still treated old people kindly, such as his ex-mother-in-law and Granny Gu, whom he met by chance, and his neighbors. . . . Whether one is able to adhere to kindness and filial piety in times of difficulty is a benchmark of his humanity.

Ma's parents had passed away long ago. As a filial son, however, he cherishes elderly people like his own parents and dreams of building comfortable and affordable apartments for them to live in, which is why Jiang's proposed apartments for the elderly hold a particular attraction for him. The project also serves as a common pursuit that binds the two emotionally. While working on it, they encounter Granny Gu, an eccentric old lady who lives alone in a courtyard house in Beijing. Ma treats her as if she were a member of his own family, thereby winning her trust and regard. When she passes away, she leaves her house to Ma and Jiang as a gift. Another incident that causes Jiang to view Ma in a new light is his courageous self-sacrifice when their company faces a threat in the form of Shen Yun. The elderly housing project has to be approved and endorsed by Shen, who is now head of the City Planning Institute. Worrying that Shen might use his position to retaliate against Ma and impede the project, Ma decides to resign from the company that he had established. Compared with these masculine qualities and merits, namely, filial piety, comradeship and brotherhood, a spirit of self-sacrifice, and a sense of responsibility, Ma's sexist remarks and behaviors and lack of manners are presented as innocuous trifles or even humorous stunts. In other words, sexism is excused as part and parcel of the patriarchal "Chinese style."

Another testament to Ma's masculinity is his sexual power, although it is again exhibited in a "Chinese" way, that is, through his ability to restrain his sexual desire.[5] In depicting the protagonist's virtues as those of a true man, the drama resorts to two recurring, and clichéd, motifs in Chinese TV dramas, namely, that of the man who is loved and admired by more than one woman and that of the man who controls himself and refrains from sex even with women living under the same roof. *Chinese-Style Relationship*, as summarized by some of the audience members interviewed, focuses on the story of Ma and the three women in his life: his faithless ex-wife, his business partner and later paramour Jiang, and a young admirer named Huo Yaoyao (Ye Yiyun). Huo is a good-looking model in her early twenties with a university degree in accounting. She comes from a poor rural family and is heavily burdened economically by the need to support her father and brother at home. At one point in the drama, Huo is working as a waitress in a bar, and Ma protects her from harassment by Brother Hao's son and his gang. Falling in love with Ma, she declares that she has no home to return to and asks Ma to take her in. The young woman then moves into Ma's apartment and refuses to leave. The love and comfort of two women—Jiang and Huo—assuage and compensate for the catastrophic harm to Ma's masculinity caused by his wife's infidelity. When Ma receives his ex-wife's wedding invitation, he initially hesitates about whether to go. Jiang, who is sympathetic toward him and understands him, persuades him to go and even helps him choose what to wear. At the wedding banquet, to the surprise of the other guests, Jiang and Ma suddenly appear on stage singing karaoke, soon joined by Huo. The trio steals the show before Ma triumphally leaves the banquet with his arms around the shoulders of the two beautiful women (episode 8; see figure 7).

At the same time, however, Ma is an honest and upright man who would never take advantage of Huo's emotional reliance upon him. Although he admits to finding Huo attractive and secretly harbors sexual desire for her, he refrains from having sex with her throughout the series despite several attempts on her part to arouse him sexually. In the end, Huo joins Ma's company as an accountant and loyally treats him as a big brother. This plotline has been jokingly described by one online commentator as the story of "a lolita [a term borrowed from Japanese ACG culture in which it means a lovely young girl] chasing after an uncle" (*luoli zhui dashu*) and criticized for being too prudish. But it reflects a long-standing tendency in Chinese popular culture toward constructing masculinity through the refusal and repudiation of female sexuality.

In this regard, the foil to Ma's true manhood is Jiang's ex-husband He Junxian (Ding Zijun). His background is not clearly explained in the drama, but his name, appearance, and manners are all suggestive of overseas Chinese men or Hong Kong or Taiwanese men. Also an architect, he is a partner

Figure 7. Ma Guoliang triumphantly leaving his ex-wife's wedding banquet with his arms around the shoulders of Jiang Yinan (left) and Huo Yaoyao (right). *Chinese-Style Relationship* (2016).

in Jiang's business in the United States. He looks like a gentleman and behaves in a refined and civilized manner, sending flowers to Jiang and kissing her in public, but in fact he is selfish, cruel, and hypocritical. He abuses Jiang's trust and has an affair with her assistant, a young mainland Chinese woman, under her nose. When the affair is discovered, He shows his true colors and threatens to sue Jiang for ownership of her designs. This highly educated *haigui* man, however, ultimately turns out to be a coward and is outwitted by Ma. By juxtaposing this diasporic, "unorthodox" version of Chinese masculinity with the genuine "Chinese-style" manhood embodied by Ma, the drama highlights a China-centered vision of Chineseness. Through the gendered rhetoric of cultural nationalism, this imagined Chineseness is represented as a source of cultural and social capital that assuages and overcomes the crisis of masculinity and anxiety over cuckoldry.

BOSS AND ME: "POSITIVE ENERGY" AND CINDERELLA FANTASY

In keeping with the desire to enhance China's soft power and regain cultural confidence, the country's deficit in the balance of trade in cultural content is a deeply troubling concern for the Chinese authorities and Chinese intellectuals alike, with numerous efforts made to counter such foreign influences as the Korean Wave. Yet, perhaps contrary to government expectations, Chinese web fiction, stories written by ordinary Chinese netizens and posted in installments on the Internet, has emerged as a new form of soft power in recent years. There have been media reports about foreign fans who have learned Chinese in order to read web novels without having to wait for translations, and even about an American man who unexpectedly overcame drug addiction by indulging himself in reading these enchanting stories.[6] In an online article, Zhang Yiwu, a Peking University professor and renowned cultural critic, predicts that the popularity of a subgenre of online romantic stories known as "bossy CEO stories" (*badao zongcai wen*), in which the core content is a love story between a domineering wealthy and powerful young man and a young woman of modest means, will give rise to a "Chinese Wave" of popular culture to succeed the Korean Wave. He applauds such stories for "creating an alternative path for the spread of Chinese literature, aiding the spread of Chinese culture."[7]

In "bossy CEO" stories, the male protagonist is generally good-looking, with an egoistic personality and a brusque and cold manner, albeit consistent in love. The female protagonist, in contrast, is often of a humble background. She is generally rather plain, with modest accomplishments. Sometimes she is timid or shy, conveying an image of purity and weakness for the male protagonist. As the story progresses, the hero suddenly falls madly in love with the heroine and expresses his admiration and affection forcefully and in a brusque manner, to the extent that he could be suspected of trying to force himself upon her. Without exception, however, the stories have a happy ending: the two marry, with the heroine thus gaining entry to upper-class society and obtaining both a wonderful love life and a luxurious lifestyle.

The Chinese version of the popular Cinderella fantasy of hypergamy can be traced back to the novels of Taiwanese writer Qiong Yao, which achieved widespread popularity on the mainland in the 1980s, whereas the storyline of the "bossy CEO" subgenre has its roots in the work of another Taiwanese romance novelist, Xi Juan, who was popular in the 1990s. For example, her 1995 novel *The Poppy Lover* (*Yingsu de qingren*) concerns the headstrong son of the owner of a large company in Taiwan who forces an impoverished young woman to become his mistress, although true love wins out and the two marry at the novel's end (Liang 2015). "Bossy CEO" stories are increasing in popularity with the rise of online literature, especially among young female readers. The settings of such stories vary—from modern corporations to ancient times and fairyland—and the young male lead can be an entrepreneur, a lawyer, a military commander, a high-ranking official, or even a king or emperor. What remains unchanged, however, is his power to control his environment and issue commands.

Of course, the image and story pattern of the "bossy CEO" are by no means unique to Chinese culture. Instead, they show the influence of the circulation of global pop cultural products featuring a revamped Cinderella fantasy. As will be discussed in chapter 6, the Japanese manga *Boys Over Flowers* (*Hana yori dango*) and its film and TV adaptations in South Korea, Taiwan, and mainland China are typical examples of this romantic pattern. American bestsellers such as *Fifty Shades of Grey* and the Twilight Saga, which have also been adapted into popular film series, feature male characters similar to the "bossy CEO" (being cool, aloof, and sometimes rude to women) and demonstrate the global appeal of such a gendered image, a charming victor in the neoliberal economy.

Labeled as "fast food reading," this type of romantic fiction has come in for severe criticism in recent years. One online commentator, for instance, describes it as a "cultural freak" that combines "the remnants of feudal thinking in modern Chinese society, the extreme individualism of commercial society and the low-quality creation of small intellectuals."[8] The values of such stories have also been condemned for showing "a strong sense of worship of the strong and also despotism." The commentator uses a novel set in a fictional police state as an example: the male protagonist is a high-ranking official in the secret police who rapes and imprisons a young Chinese woman and murders her friend. But the two eventually still fall in love. The commentator also questions how plausible this subgenre of literature is, given that the male protagonist can invariably bypass the law and do anything he likes in industry. Despite such criticisms, however, "bossy CEO" narratives continue to flourish and have even reached the small screen, giving birth to a popular new genre of TV consumption.

As noted in chapter 2, since the early 2010s "IP dramas" adapted from web fiction have become a burgeoning arena of TV drama production, particularly since the policy known as "one drama, two satellite [channels]" came into force in 2015, rendering big-budget drama series much costlier for small TV stations.[9] Many "bossy CEO" online novels have since been adapted for television, with some achieving high ratings. Among the most influential are *Boss and Me* (*Shanshan laile*, 2014), *My Sunshine* (*Heyi shengxiaomo*, 2015), and *Summer Desire* (*Paomo zhi xia*, 2017). The following analysis focuses on the first of these.

Boss and Me, adapted from Gu Man's web novella *Shanshan lai chi* (literally, "Shanshan comes to eat") and directed by Taiwanese director Liu Chunchieh, was produced by GCoo Entertainment in Shanghai and premiered in 2014. The series, a typical Cinderella story, portrays the romance between Xue Shanshan (Zhao Liying), a naïve young woman from a small town, and her boss Feng Teng (Zhang Han, a.k.a. Hans Zhang). Shanshan graduated from a second-class university in China and regards herself as an average girl. She is overjoyed when she is offered a highly competitive job as a financial assistant by the illustrious Feng Teng Group (of which Feng Teng is the CEO), but she soon discovers that she was given the job because of her rare blood type: AB negative. It so happens that Feng Teng's sister Feng Yue shares this blood type, and the company thus gives priority to fellow carriers when recruiting new members to reserve potential blood donors. This "bloodsucking" ploy is reminiscent of the vampires in the Twilight series and helps to create an atmosphere of mystique surrounding the wealthy Feng family.

After donating blood to Feng Yue while she is giving birth, Shanshan is summoned to the boss's office at the top of the building for lunch. The kindhearted Feng Yue has prepared pork liver, a blood tonic in traditional Chinese medicine, for Shanshan as a token of thanks. Feng Teng, who is attracted by Shanshan's cute manner of eating, then asks her to have lunch with him every day, giving the excuse that he needs someone to remove vegetables he dislikes from his lunchbox. The two soon embark on a relationship in which Feng plays the role of overbearing protector and benefactor. Fully aware of the huge social gap between them, Shanshan makes a concerted effort to improve herself. Through hard work, she not only passes the challenging CPA examination, but also becomes a successful businessperson herself.

The relationship is decidedly unequal from the outset. Feng Teng, in his early thirties, epitomizes the "tall, rich, and handsome" stereotype of masculinity. As the only male heir of the Feng family, he inherited the giant company from his grandfather at a young age (his parents both passed away in a traffic accident when he and his sister were still children). He possesses not only a distinguished family background but also impressive overseas educational credentials. Young, rich, and single, he owns numerous properties, including an old house in an elite neighborhood and an upscale apartment in Lujiazui, the new financial center of Shanghai, between which he alternates. Everyone in the company calls Feng "Big Boss" and treats him with fear and reverence, whereas he always exhibits a grim countenance and appears aloof. By contrast, Xue Shanshan, the daughter of a small-town tailor, shares a small rented apartment in Shanghai with her cousin and constantly worries about the security of her job before she begins dating Feng. Owing to the unequal power relations between them, Feng continues to play the role of boss throughout their relationship, especially in its initial stages, speaking to Shanshan in a commanding tone and jokingly or half-jokingly threatening her with dismissal or a pay cut. Shanshan never attempts to challenge his authority or complain about his domineering manner. Although the drama highlights her spirit of self-reliance, as discussed in detail below, such gestures as having her hide the relationship from colleagues and rejecting Feng's favors and gifts failed to convince the audience, with some respondents describing them as "cosmetic" in nature. When Shanshan's grandfather falls seriously ill, for example, the Xue family sends him to Shanghai, but he is turned away by hospital after hospital because of a lack of vacant beds. The helpless Shanshan can only turn to Feng for help, and he soon makes arrangements to send her grandfather to the best hospital and receive the best treatments. Referring to this plotline, one female informant lamented, "I would gladly sacrifice my independence and freedom for such an overbearing boyfriend who can easily provide the best for me" (Ms. Li, twenty-one-year-old university student).

The pork liver lunchbox is a plot device that warrants special attention. It is initially Feng Yue who asks her brother to bring the lunchbox to Shanshan to thank her for her donation of blood. Subsequently, however, Feng Teng continues to bring the same lunch, greasy pork liver, which Shanshan loathes the sight of, and forces her to have lunch with him. Not daring to refuse, Shanshan implores Feng's secretary to stop bringing her pork liver to eat, only to be told that she should talk to the boss herself. She ultimately ends up eating this loathsome food every day for a whole month! This mischievous behavior is meant to demonstrate Feng's interest in Shanshan. As his sister Feng Yue says, the only way her brother can express his love for the woman he desires is to bully her. Several online commentators, however, have speculated that the real reason for the daily pork liver lunch is that Feng "enjoys seeing how Shanshan has to swallow her anger out of fear."[10] His behavior is reminiscent of the well-known scene in Cao Yu's (1910–1996) 1934 masterpiece *Thunderstorm* (*Leiyu*), in which the tyrannical patriarch

Zhou Puyuan, the owner of a coal mine, forces his wife to drink liquid medicine despite her strong reluctance to do so.[11] In both cases, forcing women to eat or drink is a way to demonstrate male authority and becomes a morbid source of male pleasure. Unlike the case in *Thunderstorm*, however, Feng's behavior in *Boss and Me* is approvingly depicted as a sign of "bossy" love rather than male despotism.

The scene in which Feng is first attracted to Shanshan also signifies the hierarchical relationship between them. Feng occupies a spacious, book-lined office at the top of the building. Through his huge plate glass window, he can see the roof area outside his office, but no one can see inside. To extricate herself from colleagues who are gossiping about the lunchboxes provided by the boss's secretary, Shanshan one day takes her lunchbox to the rooftop area to eat alone. From behind the blinds, Feng observes with interest every move of Shanshan, who, without knowing that she is visible from the other side, shouts to her reflection in the window, "Shanshan is a ball of sunshine that is always filled with positive energy!" His one-way gaze not only exemplifies the much-discussed "to-be-looked-at-ness" of the female body (Mulvey 2009), but also symbolically reflects the unequal class positions of the two. To be precise, Feng's condescending gaze is enabled by his privileged viewing position (figure 8).

Compared with the other women who court Feng, including a wealthy movie star, a woman he grew up with, and the daughters of business tycoons, Xue Shanshan's attraction lies in her simplicity and naïveté, which have been extolled as desirable feminine traits. Many online commentaries use the word "adorkable" (*dai meng*) to describe her image. Originating in Japanese ACG culture, "adorkable" is normally used to refer to girls who are cute and pure and react slowly while appearing a bit silly. In this drama, Shanshan is regularly shown eating snacks. She presents an innocent look whenever wronged in the workplace. She likes talking to herself and smiles in a doll-like manner, reflecting Japanese *kawaii* culture in many ways (figure 9). Feminist studies have unraveled the sexist overtone of childishness in the portrayal of women, and, according to recent research on the "infantilized images of femininity" in *feizhuliu* (nonmainstream) youth culture in China, female cuteness not only implies the dependence and vulnerability of women but also conveys a cosmopolitan quality that lies at the center of postsocialist modernity (Qiu 2013). As a type of gender performance (Butler 1990), highly stylized images influenced by the Japanese *kawaii* culture of cuteness flourish in Chinese cyberspace:

Figure 8. Feng Teng peering at Xue Shanshan from his office. *Boss and Me* (2014).

The majority of *feizhuliu* girls appearing online are photographed wearing contact lenses that enlarge or change the colour of their irises. Girls often stare at the camera lens directly, with an exaggeratedly innocent look that is accentuated by pursed lips. In the sea of online images of *feizhuliu* from *feizhuliu* websites one can easily observe conventions with semiotic associations that conjure up popular images of the feminine youth who is child-like and playful: lollipops, cheeky faces, hot-pink hair clips, colourful nail polish and bracelets, Hello Kitty necklaces, tongues stuck out and cartoon-style decorations abound. Both cute and coy, they overwhelmingly convey an innocent yet precocious doll-like image. (Qiu 2013, 234)

Although the drama itself does not fall into the category of *feizhuliu* youth culture, the way Shanshan is portrayed exhibits the obvious influence of the trend of celebrating the cuteness and childishness of young women, a portrayal to which, according to online comments, the popularity of the series can be largely attributed. That influence becomes particularly clear when one compares Shanshan's portrayal with that of her love rivals, all of whom are presented as scheming, snobbish, or pompous, personality characteristics that are labeled as unfavorable feminine traits in a male-dominant society.

Given the tyrannical character of the male protagonist and the somewhat clichéd plotline, it is surprising that *Boss and Me* has been so well-received by audiences of various ages and genders. It has achieved consis-

Figure 9. The ador-
able image of Xue
Shanshan. *Boss and
Me* (2014).

tently high ratings in its numerous reruns since its premiere in 2014. In fact,
when the controversial *The Story of the Yanxi Palace* was taken off the air in
January 2019, the drama that replaced it on Jiangsu Television was *Boss and
Me*, a move that reveals the contestation between different visions of Chineseness and feminist subjectivity, a point that will be revisited in the final
chapter of this book. One comment made repeatedly by my informants, as
well as in online commentaries, is that Xue Shanshan embodies the "positive energy" (*zheng nengliang*) that young women need and thus that the
drama is uplifting and advocates a neoliberal womanhood characterized by
the discourse of self-improvement. As one online article contends, Shanshan carries "the genes of a good girl" that we should all learn from.[12]

    As noted, instead of feeling self-abased, Shanshan does everything she
can to narrow the gap between herself and the boss by improving herself.
She says to Feng Teng, "Although I may not be the best match for you, I will
try to become the best version of myself to match you" (episode 22). Whenever she faces difficulties, she goes to the roof and shouts to her reflection in
the window. In elaborating on "the genes of a good girl," the aforementioned
online article spells out Shanshan's attitudes toward life, love, and career:

> The story stages Shanshan into a foodie—not the kind of foodie who is overly
> picky about what she eats; rather the kind of foodie that would be satisfied
> with a full belly. This is just another way of saying that Shanshan is really easy

to please, she does not have any big ambitions, she is kind and simple, treats others with passion and sincerity, is considerate for others—she is just a well-mannered girl who does not cause issues nor is melodramatic. There is indeed a huge gap between Shanshan and Feng Teng. She does not know how to dance, how to fish and nor does she have a passport. However, she never runs away from the details of the difference between the two of them, instead she deals with them directly.[13]

Tellingly, when Shanshan finally becomes a successful entrepreneur through her hard work and inherent wisdom, she decides to close her business and return to her role as "Mrs. Feng." She declares that she is actually not ambitious at all nor interested in earning money. Her sole purpose in embarking on a business career was to prove her value so that she could stand on an equal footing with Feng (episode 33). In other words, female power obtained through career success serves only as capital to win and retain an ideal husband. Shanshan's temporary transgression of the male-dominated field is reminiscent of the woman warrior Hua Mulan in Chinese folklore, who disguises herself as a man to fight on behalf of her father and then immediately returns to the conventional role of daughter at the war's end.

The commendation of Shanshan's inspirational spirit was echoed by my informants. Regardless of their gender or educational background, most of these informants were favorably impressed by Shanshan's positivity. Among them, the young women particularly identified with Shanshan, admiring her ability to improve herself and become stronger both mentally and financially. One of them commented that Shanshan, "an ordinary girl," wins Feng's heart with nothing other than her "positive energy," which is the only thing able to "bring some sense of ease to the ice-cold face of the big boss" (Ms. Liang, thirty-four, sales). Another commended Shanshan's bravery in facing up to the class gap between the two and the maturity she achieves in making efforts to narrow it:

I think the most important thing in love is not whether there is a gap between the couple; it is more about how they deal with the gap between them. Shanshan eventually stops using her eyes to signal admiration when she is with Feng Teng as she starts to grow; instead she becomes more and more natural when she is around him, and she eventually obtains the ability to protect herself. This is in fact a process through which her mentality becomes stronger. (Ms. Zhang, thirty-year-old yoga teacher)

The male informants further linked Shanshan's positivity with desirable femininity and Chinese womanhood, paying special attention to her success and subsequent retreat. More than one of them mentioned that Shanshan, with her self-esteem and self-confidence (*zizun zixin*), is a "representative of new women in the new era," a subject position known for positioning womanly virtue as "the secret engine of China's march to the neoliberal world order" (H. Lee 2014, 263). One male informant, for instance, pointed out that Shanshan differs significantly from other "silly, white and sweet" girl (*sha bai tian*) images commonly seen on the small screen:

> Regardless of it being in the workplace or the field of love, regardless of it being actual hardship or the gossip of other people, Shanshan has her moments of confusion and stops, and yet she only becomes braver and braver. She got into the company with her special blood type, gets questioned about her capabilities, and yet Shanshan never runs away or complains; instead she works harder and harder with a stronger mentality. For example, when she faces confrontation with her colleagues, she takes the initiative to explain and to reconcile with them. Later on, during the startup of her own business, the Shanshan who was previously undetermined cannot be found; instead she seizes all opportunities to promote [her business]. It is enough to touch others even if it is just her spirit of confronting hardships head on and dealing with all problems. Apart from the love story, Shanshan embodies the spirit of Chinese women in the reform era. (Mr. Mo, thirty-one-year-old manager)

In addition, the formation of neoliberal subjectivity echoes an imagined, ahistorical Chineseness that is conspicuously associated with pedigree, wealth, power, and, by extension, the patriarchy. The fabulous wealth of the Feng family was originally generated by a figure who never appears in the drama, Feng Teng's grandfather, who founded the Feng Teng Group and passed it on to his grandson when he died. From the lips of Feng Teng and his sister, we know that the grandfather was a benevolent yet conservative patriarch who established all the rules and traditions of the clan, ranging from the dishes served for Chinese New Year's Eve dinner to rigid wedding rituals. These family traditions, along with the images of loyal servants who have waited upon the family for more than thirty years, articulate a fantasy of a continuous "Chinese" elite culture, as if the revolutions of the twentieth century had never taken place. Contrary to the stereotype of the boorish nouveau riche, the wealthy elite in *Boss and Me* are depicted—in an ahistori-

Figure 10. Feng Teng as a child playing chess with his parents. *Boss and Me* (2014).

cal manner—as an aristocracy with a rich cultural inheritance and refined bourgeois taste. For instance, in episode 12, there is a flashback to Feng Teng's childhood in which he, wearing a shirt and bow tie, witnesses his parents playing chess in a cozy home setting. Chess, also known as "international chess" in China, is associated with high-class taste and bourgeois culture in popular media. The scene also shows the young Feng Teng reading an English novel before his father calls him to watch the game (figure 10).

As indicated by the above example, the English language and an imagined Western lifestyle, paradoxically combined with nationalist cultural obsession (Feng Teng is shown reciting a Tang poem to his girlfriend immediately after the chess scene in episode 12), function as both cultural capital and symbols of class distinction. Feng Teng is regularly depicted reading English-language newspapers (e.g., *China Daily*) in his office, and he travels frequently to the United States and Britain. In fact, some episodes were partially shot in Britain to demonstrate how familiar and at ease Feng and his admirer Yuan Lishu (the daughter of Feng's nanny, who grew up with Feng and is treated as a child of the Feng family), both educated in the United Kingdom, are with high-class "Western" culture. By contrast, Shanshan lacks such markers of class status. She has never been abroad and does not even possess a passport. She can barely communicate in English. Accordingly, when she phones the hotel reception in Britain to speak to Feng, she has to rely on Yuan's translation and is laughed at by Yuan in return (episode 19). In line with Bourdieu's theory (1984), traditions, taste, and knowledge are inextricably tied up with class distinction and, by extension, serve to approve of the boss's "bossy" attitude.

As noted, this class-based "bossy CEO" pattern is commonly found in TV dramas adapted from web fiction. In *Love Me, If You Dare* (*Ta laile, qing biyan,* 2015), for instance, the manners and attitude toward his girlfriend-cum-assistant Jian Yao (Ma Sichun) of the male protagonist, Bo Jinyan (Wallace Huo), earn him a reputation as another sufferer of "straight-man cancer." Rather than an entrepreneur, Bo is a professor and criminal psychologist who has returned from overseas and is invited by the Chinese police to assist in their investigation of a serial killer. The two first meet when Jian, who is in her final year of college studying English, comes to Bo's home to apply for a part-time translation job Bo has advertised. He is looking for someone to translate his English journal articles into Chinese because, as a *haigui* who received a Western education, his Chinese is not good enough. The relationship is patronizing from the outset, with Bo, who is hiding upstairs, casting an examining gaze at the young woman being interviewed and tested by his best friend Fu Ziyu (Yin Zheng). Belying his stony face and icy manner, Bo actually appreciates Jian's reasoning powers, which he discovers in the process of working with her, and he falls in love with her. But when explaining to Jian why he hired her, a college student with no knowledge of criminal psychology, he blatantly objectifies her: "Every time you wear make-up, the pleasant [scene] gives me inspiration and expedites my thinking" (episode 15). He proposes to the local police that Jian be appointed as his personal assistant and even takes the liberty of high-handedly informing the company with which Jian has already signed an employment contract of his decision to hire her. In response, Jian appears more flattered than offended. She is always in the position of follower, with the arrogant Bo exhibiting boundless self-esteem throughout. In addition to knowledge and wisdom, which typically legitimize male dominance in terms of the Cartesian mind/body dichotomy (Hesse-Biber 2006), Bo's power fundamentally derives from his class background. He is from a wealthy family that owns flashy cars and a European-style luxury villa atop a hill and, more importantly, can afford his elite education in the West. In the scene in which he confesses his love (episode 13), after a candlelight dinner in a big hall accompanied by a violin performance, Bo takes Jian to an opulent suite on the top floor of a five-star hotel with a bird's-eye view of the entire city, from where they view the National Day fireworks.

The debates surrounding the "bossy CEO" genre reflect the entangled interrelations between gender and class in public discourse. On the one hand, the images of cute, consumerist, self-motivated young women are supposed to represent a new mode of womanhood in line with China's post-socialist modernity; on the other, the revamped Cinderella-type hypergamic fantasy and misogynist posture of the male protagonists strongly indicate the restoration of a patriarchal ideology. We now turn to an important issue in the context of Chinese culture, namely, the politics of fertility, to lay bare the latter point.

MOTHER'S LIFE: GENERATION GAP AND THE POLITICS OF FERTILITY

TV viewing has long been the site of generational war, particularly where gender ideology is concerned. As noted, TV programs in China often trigger intense social debates, some of which reveal significant generation gaps in perceptions of women, marriage, and reproduction. Such debates also manifest the entrenched discursive link between patriarchal ideology and nationalism. For instance, it is a marked social phenomenon in China for parents to press their adult children, especially daughters, to marry and give birth. Regarding heterosexual marriage and child bearing as the only correct and natural life path, some anxious parents make efforts to look for a marriage partner on behalf of their children, daughters in particular, sometimes even without their knowledge.[14] In a recent episode of the Hunan Satellite TV reality show *My Little One* (*Wojia na xiaozi*), the parents of several female celebrities in their early thirties persuaded their daughters to find boyfriends and even coaxed them into relationships. In commenting on his celebrity daughter's unwed status and childlessness, one father said that it is "a matter of filial piety" and that "[i]n giving birth to a child, [a daughter is] fulfilling [her] responsibility not only to [her] family, but also to [her] country." To this sentiment, many young audience members responded with frustration and acrimony: "These women are obviously leading happy lives, aren't they? [They] have goals and plans and are enjoying their lives—why should they get married?"[15] As such generational antagonism demonstrates, the politics of fertility lie at the center of Chinese womanhood and are closely linked to nationalism, which is evidenced by both online commentaries and focus group discussions with TV audience members across age groups. One recent

TV program that has been dismissed by many netizens as promoting a "feudal" ideology concerning gender roles and reproduction is a drama series titled *Mother's Life* (*Niang dao*, 2018; literally: The Way of Motherhood).

Like *The Dog-Beating Staff*, the script of *Mother's Life* was written by Guo Jingyu, who is also the general director of the series. Produced by Tianjin Jianxin Cultural Communication Group, the series premiered on Beijing and Jiangsu Satellite TV in September 2018. Although it received high ratings, it scored the exceptionally low mark of 2.7 on Douban.com.[16] A common explanation for the discrepancy is that middle-aged or older viewers were responsible for the generally high audience ratings, whereas the more Internet-savvy post-1990 and post-2000 generations were responsible for the ranking on Douban.com.

The drama, set during the Republican era, revolves around the life story of a fictional woman named Yingniang (Yue Lina). When she is a young girl, Yingniang, who is from a poor family, sells herself to the illustrious Long family as a "River Girl" (*he gu*)—a live human sacrifice for the Yellow River—in order to be able to bury her father, who has passed away. She grows up in the ancestral temple of the Long family, and when she reaches the age of eighteen is presented to the river in a sacrificial ceremony. But Yingniang unexpectedly survives being thrown into the river, and she later marries Long Jizong (Yu Yi), the runaway son of the Long family, and gives birth to two daughters. During a third pregnancy, Jizong's mother (Shi Ke) manages to find the couple and sends servants to bring them back to the Long mansion in the hope that Yingniang will give the family a male heir. To the mother's disappointment, however, Yingniang gives birth to another girl. Yingniang is then expelled from the Long family, with her children being regarded as the cause of the family's ill fortune. To protect his wife and daughters, Jizong breaks with his mother and moves out of the Long home, only to be framed by his best friend Shi Shaoqing (Liu Zhiyang), who covets Yingniang, and to die soon thereafter. Yingniang becomes homeless and has to seek shelter with her brother Liu Shuanzi (Wu Liansheng), an opium addict who subsequently trades her youngest daughter for money. To prevent her other daughters from being sold, Yingniang sets fire to Shuanzi's house, an act that lands her in prison. While incarcerated, she finally gives birth to a son, whom she names Laosheng ("being born in prison"). To make Yingniang suffer, the villainous Shi steals her son and takes him to Japan, and she also loses her other children. After being released from prison, Yingniang embarks on a long and difficult journey to find her children. Then, when she has lost all hope of locating them, she attempts suicide, only to be saved by a Guomindang officer nicknamed "Wood-stake Gao" (Heizi). Yingniang subsequently undergoes years of hardship before finally being reunited with her children. Toward the end of the series, her daughters become heroines who fight the Japanese invaders. Long Yanzong (Yu Yi), the twin brother of the late Jizong, becomes the leader of heroic anti-Japanese guerrillas and fights side by side with Wood-stake Gao. The series ends with Yingniang taking a bullet for her son, who is executed in public by Long and Gao after the war's end for collaborating with the Japanese. Her son finally recognizes her and is moved by her motherly love.

The drama continues the discursive tradition of female victimization, which has been an important tool for the allegorical representation of the nation in Chinese cinema since the 1930s. Yingniang, who is supposed to be an embodiment of the average woman in traditional China, endures hardship, and even torture and humiliation, to protect and nurture her children. Her motherly virtues are recurrently associated with an icon popularly referred to in hackneyed fashion as the "mother" of the Chinese nation, i.e., the Yellow River, as seen in the series theme tune:

> My mother walks on the banks of the Yellow River,
> Her blood running inside my body.
> My mother stands on the banks of the Yellow River,
> Her invincible spine is the soul of the River.
>
> . . . .
>
> My roots are planted on the Yellow Earth.
> The invincible spine is the soul of the River.

In the drama's final scene, Yingniang is shown lying on an operating table undergoing surgery to remove the bullet in her abdomen. In hymn-like style, the screen alternates between flashbacks of her motherly deeds and scenes of the roaring torrent of the Yellow River before the words "A tribute to all mothers in the world" appear to conclude the entire series (episode 76). In Chinese political rhetoric, a sacrificing and suffering mother remains a salient symbolic reference to the nation.

Another clichéd articulation of gender stereotypes is the emotional strength of mothers. As many audience members pointed out, the drama's story line seems to have been inspired by and serves to illustrate a widely circulated saying: "women are by nature weak, but they are incredibly strong when they become a mother" (*nüzi ben ruo, wei mu ze gang*). The saying, which actually appears on a promotional poster for the series (figure 11), can be traced back to Liang Qichao's (1873–1929) *Discourse on the New Citizen* (*Xinmin shuo*), a treatise on nation building in modern China that has gained widespread media popularity in recent years.[17] In a social Darwinist manner, Liang sings the praises of the courage and resilience displayed by women in carrying out their motherly duties, which in turn enables the reproduction of the nation. He goes on to quote the foregoing saying, which he attributes to the French writer Victor Hugo, to explain the source of citizens' "martial spirit."[18] By depicting the sacrifices that Yingniang makes to protect her children, her son in particular, *Mother's Life* typifies the long-standing strategy of "turning women's drab plights into visual spectacles" in Chinese film and TV (H. Lee 2014, 264). What is more, through women's self-sacrifice and suffering, female virtue is also exalted in alignment with victimhood nationalism.

Notwithstanding the officially endorsed rhetoric of nation-as-mother and the historical context of the Anti-Japanese War, the drama has been severely criticized by netizens and by some critics for promoting a "feudal" ideology of female virtue and treating women as machines for reproduction. It has aroused heated discussions not only on such social media platforms as WeChat, but also in state media outlets. An article published by the official *China Woman's Daily*, for example, maintains that the way Yingniang is portrayed sends a harmful message about female subjectivity and that the drama lacks basic respect for women:

> When suffering from obstructed labor, [Yingniang] screams, "Save my son, my lowly life is nothing! I must give birth to a son for Jizong!" After the death of her husband, she still insists that "I am Jizhong's woman alive or dead." For many young audience members in front of the TV set, this mentality is really beyond common sense. It is, however, in line with teachings at the "virtue schools" for women nowadays, namely, men are the heaven and women the earth, and giving birth to a son is the primary value of and mission in a woman's life. But the climate of public opinion on the Internet, with the proliferation of new media, will only yield fierce criticism and complaints, rather than sympathy, towards this type of values. No wonder one netizen laments, "My parents are watching *Mother's Life* in the sitting room, while I am watching *A Handmaid's Tale* in my bedroom—between us is the longest distance in the world!" (Q. Wang 2018).[19]

Figure 11. A poster of *Mother's Life* (2018) with the catchline "Women are by nature weak, but they are incredibly strong when they become a mother" in the upper left-hand corner.

To these charges, the director, Guo Jingyu, responded that his intention was to "faithfully reflect" the position of women in history rather than to "promulgate" feudal ideas. Netizens obviously did not buy that explanation, however. An article widely circulated on WeChat highlights the drama's obsession with reproduction, the bearing of a male heir in particular:

> The female protagonist's self-positioning in her marriage is that she is a machine made to give birth: Upon hearing that her husband is having an affair with another woman, her first reaction is that she is not worthy of her husband as she is incapable of producing a male heir—to the extent that she would rather he marry that lady instead of remaining with her! With that said, she urges her husband to divorce her and marry that woman—hoping that the woman will soon give birth to a healthy fat son for him. . . . Her husband names their three daughters "Pandi" (longing for a brother), "Zhaodi" (calling for a brother) and "Niandi" (thinking constantly of a brother). . . . Upon learning that her new-born baby is another daughter, the female lead apologizes to her husband with an expression of disappointment.[20]

Indeed, the nigh-on pathological obsession with a male heir is displayed not only by Yingniang but also by other characters in the drama. In episode 73, for example, the subordinates of Wood-stake Gao draw lots to decide who will carry out the mission of assassinating Long Laosheng, Yingniang's son who is now the leader of a team of pro-Japanese special agents. Pandi is originally chosen, but her sister Zhaodi secretly puts sleeping pills in her wine so that she can undertake the mission instead. Zhaodi eventually loses her life but fails to kill Laosheng. When asked why she has sacrificed herself to save her sister, Zhaodi says without regret, "Pandi is pregnant, and if she bears a son her husband has agreed to adopt the surname Long for the boy!" This spirit of making a sacrifice to ensure a male heir, which is espoused by many of the female characters in the drama, unmistakably sends the message that women's raison d'être is to live and die for the grand objective of carrying on the family line and, by extension, ensuring the continuation of the nation. In the same vein, when Wood-stake Gao is seriously wounded in battle, someone tells him that his daughter-in-law is pregnant. Upon hearing this news, Gao suddenly springs up, fully reenergized, and charges into enemy lines (episode 76). In sum, the obsession with a male heir is central to the politics of fertility and is more often than not intertwined with deep-rooted anxiety over national power and virility.

Most of the young informants in my focus groups echoed the disdain for the drama's sexist tendencies. In fact, no other TV drama discussed generated such a marked generational divide and polarization of opinion during the focus group discussions. An overwhelming majority of those over the age of fifty had watched all or part of the series and thought highly of both its performances and story line. The female informants in this age group were particularly impressed by Yingniang's "true love" for her children, with most of them relating it to their own life stories, recalling the sacrifices they had made for their own children. By contrast, of the forty-eight informants below the age of thirty, only five had watched even part of the drama, and those few confessed that they had watched it as a way of spending time with their parents. As expected, the most severe criticism was expressed by the subgroups of university students and young employees with a tertiary education, the women among them in particular. These informants sneered at the aggrandizement of Yingniang's motherly love and condemned the drama's representation of female virtues as "out of step with the times." One of them, for instance, found its advocacy of female "selflessness" reprehensible: "the [advocacy of a] lack of self for women can only serve male desire—without a self, women are easier to control and enslave. Why should women make sacrifices but not men? This is still the Confucian idea of women playing domestic roles and men public roles (*Nan zhu wai, nü zhu nei*) (Ms. Tan, nineteen-year-old university student). Another commented that Yingniang is "cheap" as a woman:

> Yingniang has been mistreated and tortured by her mother-in-law. But when the Long family faces a crisis and needs her to make a sacrifice, she does so without hesitation. When the bandits besiege the Long family, she voluntarily goes to the bandits' fort to stop them. When the Japanese army are about to arrive, everyone is fleeing but she insists on staying to protect the ancestral hall of the Long family! Isn't this ridiculous? She is a woman who takes pride in giving everything she has to her husband's family. Who benefits from this type of womanly virtue? For today's women, this message is not only funny but also badly harmful. (Ms. Zhao, twenty-three-year-old clerk)

Some of the informants also took issue with the formulaic "Mary Sue" characterization of Yingniang and its hidden ideological implications.[21] In the drama, there are at least four men who fall madly in love with or who desire Yingniang, namely, her husband Jizong, Jizong's twin brother Yanzong,

Jizong's best friend and the primary villain Shi Shaoqing, and the Guomindang officer Wood-stake Gao, and yet Yingniang remains faithful to her late husband throughout her life. For some of the young female informants, this plotline not only highlights the "with one man all the way till the end" (*cong yi er zhong*) prescription on women's chastity, but also drives home the stereotypes that "women can only become successful through men" and that "women survive by showing their weakness to men." These mindsets are reportedly common in Chinese TV programs today (Ms. Hong, twenty-year-old university student).

Relating *Mother's Life* to Guo's earlier productions, such as *The Brave Heart* (*Yonggan de xin*, 2013) and the aforementioned *The Dog-Beating Staff* (see chapter 3), many of the informants contended that these dramas consistently reveal the director's preoccupation, whether consciously or unconsciously, with female fertility, as well as a deep-seated patriarchal mentality packaged with nationalist sentiment. Many were perplexed as to how dramas promoting such a "dated and decadent" ideology could achieve ratings success in today's China. Others, however, were more at ease with the phenomenon, explaining the popularity of Guo's dramas, particularly among middle-aged and older viewers, from the angle of market demand:

> We young people can choose to watch American, Japanese, or Korean TV dramas, but it is harder for our parents to become interested in foreign dramas due to cultural differences. They therefore have fewer choices [for entertainment] and can only kill time by finding pleasure in watching domestic dramas like this one. (Ms. Liu, twenty-one-year-old university student)

CONCLUSION

By focusing on three subgenres of TV drama that enjoy high ratings and have generated heated debate over gender issues, this chapter furthers the exploration on how patriarchy and nationalism intersect in contemporary China. The dramas discussed target different age, gender, and educational background audiences and feature different types of popular gender imaginaries, namely, middle-aged entrepreneurial masculinity, Cinderella-type grassroots girlhood, and patriarchal womanly virtue. What they have in common, however, is the display of a "Chinese-style" sexism, which can be attributed to both the local and global sociopolitical and cultural climates.

At the same time, these dramas and their gender images have sparked alarm among a certain portion of the population, who are highly critical of the fundamental values they promote.

So what exactly are the "Chinese characteristics" of the type of sexism playing out on the Chinese TV screen? To answer this question, let us first have a look at Harrell and Santos's assessment of the "transforming patriarchy" in contemporary China:

> On the one hand, present-day China resembles in many ways the industrial societies in North America and parts of Europe, in which patriarchy in Weber's classic sense no longer exists, while male dominance remains. On the other hand, family relations in today's China display many unique features, many of them linked to specific features of the Chinese patriarchal tradition. . . . [M]aking sense of these specificities requires adopting a model of patriarchy and social change that is sensitive to Chinese realities. (Harrell and Santos 2017, 33)

To be more precise, the distinct nature of those realities lies not only in the resilience of patriarchal ideology in China but also in the recent official stance on the necessity of regaining "cultural confidence" in the global age, a stance that has catalyzed an imagined gender order as part of the country's national essence. In addition, gender hierarchy and ideals are closely associated with the moral value of "positive energy," which emphasizes an optimistic and aspirational attitude in the face of challenges. As a result, in both the media and popular culture, the socialist discourse on gender equality and women's liberation has to coexist and negotiate with the interests, desires, and aspirations of a market that pragmatically promotes neoliberal self-governing subjects. As we have seen, whether we are talking about "straight-man cancer" misogyny, "bossy CEO" arrogance, or the treatment of women as reproduction machines, these gender discourses and imaginaries can be readily traced back to entrenched traditions in Chinese culture and, at the same time, reflect the profound economic and social changes that have taken place in the reform era, as well as the political agenda of perpetuating both national and male chauvinism. In the next chapter, we will have a look at how this chauvinist Chineseness is enhanced through representations of non-Chinese men and women as "the Other."

CHAPTER 5

Foreign Men and Women on the Chinese TV Screen

IN 2018, CCTV's Spring Festival Gala (*chunjie lianhuan wanhui*, or *chunwan* for short), an annual five-hour variety show broadcast on Lunar New Year's Eve that is watched by a one billion-plus audience in China and across the world, delivered the strong message to the world that China desires to be cosmopolitan. An unprecedented number of non-Chinese faces appeared on the program, including Caucasians singing such well-known patriotic songs as "Descendants of the Dragon" (*Long de chuanren*) and "I Love You, China" (*Wo ai ni, Zhongguo*) (figure 12). In one controversial skit, an "African" woman—played by a Chinese actress in blackface—feels so happy when she hears that her daughter will marry a Chinese man and go to China to live that she enthusiastically shouts, "I love China!" As one observant audience member said, "[In the Spring Festival Gala] they let mainlanders say they love China, and then let actors from Hong Kong and Taiwan say they love China. They are not satisfied with that any more. They now take pleasure in hearing foreigners saying they love China."[1]

Indeed, Chinese TV programs have increasingly involved foreigners in production and performance. As both evidence and a result of the rapid globalization undergone by the Chinese media and Chinese society at large, images of foreigners and foreign countries have become ubiquitous on the Chinese TV screen. Foreigners who speak impeccable Mandarin appear in a variety of TV shows, including Chinese-language contests (e.g., *Chinese Bridge*; see Gorfinkel and Chubb 2015), dating shows (e.g., *If You Are the One*), and singing contests (e.g., *Sing! China*), and Chinese-foreigner marriages—how foreign spouses become Sinicized in particular—have become a popular topic on television talk shows (see P. Wang 2015). To a certain extent, foreign-

Figure 12. Caucasian women singing the patriotic song "I Love You, China." *Spring Festival Gala* (2018).

ers have thus become an indispensable element in China's display of national pride, most obviously in their on-screen performance of patriotic Chinese songs (*hongge*) and admiration of Chinese food. The homogenized "foreigner" (which in most cases is a proxy for "American") on Chinese TV thus plays an important role in forming a modern, cosmopolitan image of China and reflects the deeply rooted practice of alluding to the Occident as a contrasting "Other" in defining what one believes to be distinctively "Chinese" (X. Chen 1995, 39). A salient example is the exoticized—and eroticized— bodies of white women seen in some Chinese TV dramas, which has been critically linked to the "libidinal economy" of Chinese men by Sheldon Lu (2000; see also Erwin 1999; Johansson 1999, 2015; DeWoskin 2005).

The foreigners appearing in Chinese TV dramas range from professional actors, who are paid more than fifty thousand yuan for a couple of days' work, to ordinary people in walk-on parts, who earn one hundred yuan per day or even less.[2] Some actors unknown in their home countries have even become household names in China, most notably the group of Japanese actors known as "professional devils" (*guizi zhuanyehu*).[3] Owing to the proliferation of dramas set during the Anti-Japanese War, playing Japanese soldiers and officers has become a lucrative career for such Japanese actors as Koji Yano, Kenichi Miura, and Tenma Shibuya. Their example illustrates how

China's global consumer power is driving changes in acting careers and production processes across the region and even the world. At the same time, a much larger group of foreigners play insignificant roles or merely make an appearance as part of the mise-en-scène to add some "cosmopolitan" atmosphere to the drama. In *Mr. Right* (*Lian'ai xiansheng*, 2017), for example, white people can often be seen wandering in the background of parties or celebrations organized by the male protagonist's dental clinic, thereby demonstrating just how "high-end" the clinic is.

In addition to the aforementioned dramas portraying "Japanese devils," the three following subgroups of TV dramas are particularly prone to featuring foreigners. The first is historical dramas, particularly those with an international espionage theme. Recent examples include *The Last Visa* (*Zuihou yizhang qianzheng*, 2017), a forty-six-episode series based on the true story of a Chinese diplomat in Vienna who saved thousands of Jewish lives by issuing Chinese visas on the eve of the Second World War, and *Peace Hotel* (*Heping fandian*, 2018), which depicts the struggles of a group of international agents in Japanese-occupied Manchuria. These dramas not only express egregiously nationalist sentiments but also reflect China's (imagined) relations with other countries today. The second group of representations, which has become increasingly popular in recent years, concerns the lives of Chinese students, tourists, new immigrants, and merchants in foreign countries. A far-from-exhaustive list of dramas of this category includes *Beijingers in New York* (*Beijingren zai Niuyue*, 1995), *Shanghainese in Tokyo* (*Shanghairen zai Dongjing*, 1996), *So Long, Vancouver* (*Biele, Wengehua*, 2003), *Teenage Overseas Chinese Students* (*Xiao liuxuesheng*, 2005), *Wait for Me in Sydney* (*Zai Xini deng wo*, 2006), *Lost in Los Angeles* (*Mishi Luoshanji*, 2008), *Love Story in Barcelona* (*Qingxian Basailuona*, 2009), *Poor Daddy, Rich Daddy* (*Qiong baba, fu baba*, 2009), *Master Lin in Seoul* (*Lin shifu zai Shouer*, 2012), and *The Way We Were* (*Guiqu lai*, 2018). In addition, it has become trendy for the popular subgenre of "urban love story plays" (*dushi qinggan ju*) to include exterior shots of overseas locales in depictions of the characters' vacations, business trips, study experiences, and so on, as a symbol of their middle-class lifestyles.[4] These programs both satisfy Chinese curiosity about the world beyond and display a fetish exoticism in depicting the Other. Without question, they are also an indicator and product of ordinary Chinese people's increasing contact with the outside world. The third group of representations focuses on the lives of foreigners in China, such as *Foreign Babes in Beijing* (*Yangniu zai Beijing*, 1995), *A Modern Family* (*Modeng jiating*, 2001), and *Chinese Maids in Foreign Families*

(*Shewai baomu*, 2001). As Rachel DeWoskin (2005, 24), an American who had a role in *Foreign Babes in Beijing*, noted, these dramas are "written, directed, produced, and marketed by Chinese to Chinese," and thus represent a "Chinese view of the foreign view" of China.

In all these groups, gender and sexuality constitute an important dimension of identity construction and a productive domain of meaning. Transnational romance and marriage are recurrent motifs in these TV programs, and the affective articulation of masculinity and femininity across national borders tells us a lot about the role played by gender in the imagination and narration of national self/otherness in a globalizing era. This chapter focuses on a number of images on the Chinese TV screen that can be fruitfully explored from the perspective of such articulation, and it diachronically teases out the changes seen in the past two decades in televisual representations of an imagined and imaginary West as the Other and how they relate to the Chinese obsession with national dignity.

A MODERN FAMILY: FANTASIES OF MODERNITY AND COSMOPOLITANISM

A Modern Family is perhaps the most "cosmopolitan" TV drama ever produced in China. Broadcast in 2002, this thirty-three-episode series was a coproduction between CCTV and Korea's Munhwa Broadcasting Corporation (MBC). The codirectors were Zeng Lizhen and Park Yeong-ju. The series inaugurated a new pattern of Sino-foreign cooperation in TV drama production and was also among the earliest TV dramas to be partially shot overseas. Centering on the stories of an old couple in Beijing and their three children, who all go abroad and marry foreigners, the drama series was shot in China, South Korea, Malaysia, and Australia and brought together actors and actresses from South Korea, Italy, Malaysia, Sweden, Morocco, and Russia. Sponsored by airlines, travel companies, and tourism bureaus in Malaysia, South Korea, and Australia, the series showcases beautiful scenery and tourist attractions in these three countries, which were among the most popular destinations when the huge Chinese tourist market began to emerge in the early 2000s. Set in the social milieu of Beijing's bids and preparation for the Olympics, looking at the outside world and becoming a cosmopolitan citizen constitute the central messages of this highly "internationalized" TV drama series.

The title of the series suggests a linear perception of modernity in the context of the largely optimistic sentiments toward globalization in China in the early 2000s. To the amazement of today's TV audiences, the series depicts transnational marriage as a symbol of China's successful opening up and "modernization."[5] The old/modern dichotomy is represented in the drama by two generations of the Xiao family, who live in a traditional court-yard residence (*siheyuan*) in Beijing. The father (Liu Zifeng) is a retired school principal, and the mother (Tong Zhengwei) a funny "neighborhood com-mittee aunt."[6] They are supposed to represent average citizens of the older generation who do not speak English and hold "conservative" views of trans-national marriage. The mother, in particular, dislikes foreigners because of her eldest daughter Yunchu's (Zhao Mingming) unfortunate experience a decade earlier. Despite the strong opposition of her mother, Yunchu had married an Italian "artist," who turned out to be a drunkard and gambler who abused his wife while drunk. At the beginning of the series, Yunchu flees to Beijing with her son to hide from her abusive husband. Her mother, however, cannot forgive her for marrying a foreigner. Worse, the husband follows her to Beijing. Yunchu thus leaves her son with her parents and flies to Malaysia, where she falls in love with her best friend's boyfriend, the son of a rich Malaysian Chinese merchant. After many twists and turns, she finally marries him. At the same time, the son of the family, Yuntian (Liu Yijun), who works as a software engineer in Seoul, wins the heart of his supe-rior, a beautiful and intelligent Korean woman (Lee Tae Ran). They overcome cultural barriers and the biases of both their families and eventually get mar-ried. Meanwhile, the youngest daughter, Yunshu (Bai Yu), travels to Australia in the hope of keeping her boyfriend, an overseas Chinese student who has been "stolen" by an Australian girl. She ends up meeting Le Nei'er, a sunny, warm-hearted young Australian man who lives in a vineyard in South Aus-tralia, and falls in love with him. At the end of the series, the three young couples get together in Beijing to celebrate Chinese New Year. Seeing this big, "modern" family, Mrs. Xiao, who has by now cast aside her prejudice against foreigners, proudly acclaims: "Our family resembles the United Nations!" (figure 13).

The stories in *A Modern Family* reiterate the clichéd theme of how "true love" transcends national borders and overcomes prejudice, which is not uncommon in contemporary Chinese literature and TV drama. A fascinat-ing new message, however, is that a "modern" family is cosmopolitan. As noted above, the obsession with cosmopolitanism may be better understood

Figure 13. The Xiao family. Back row from left: Yunchu, Yuntian, and Yunshu with their partners. Front row: Mr. and Mrs. Xiao with Yunchu's son in the middle. *A Modern Family* (2001).

in the context of Beijing's two bids (in 2000 and 2008) to host the Olympic Games and in the phenomena associated with those bids, such as the nationwide enthusiasm for learning English and the ubiquitous resolution "to connect track with the world."[7] As Liu Kang (2004) points out, "China is perhaps the most enthusiastic of all about globalization, from its leadership to the general public" (4). As illustrated by the slogan of the 2008 Beijing Olympics—"One World, One Dream"—cosmopolitanism is at heart primarily a desire to overcome China's peripheral position in the world. In the popular imagination, that goal can be achieved by the elite of the younger generation, "who are perceived to benefit from [globalization's] commoditized artefacts, able to afford its acquired tastes, travel and consume other cultures" (Theodossopoulos and Kirtsoglou 2010, 6). The names of the three Xiao children—Yunchu, Yuntian, and Yunshu—allude to a famous line in Mao's poem "Swimming" ("To look afar to the open sky of Chu" [*ji mu Chu tian shu*]) leaving the audience with a feeling of openness and wide horizons.[8] The underlying logic of using cosmopolitanism in this way is that the Chinese elite transcend their locality to join the cosmopolitan elite. In doing so, they are worthy representatives of a rising China. In other words, China is strong because it is cosmopolitan.

According to Strathern and Stewart (2010), "peoples who perceive themselves or are perceived by others as belonging to peripheries are likely to develop particular stances towards the issue of cosmopolitanism, because in effect cosmopolitanism is usually seen as belonging to some central metropolis" (23). The image of a cosmopolitan individual implies "an unpleasant posture toward the putative provincial" (Appiah 2006, xiii). In a wide range of popular literature, TV programs, advertisements, magazines, online discussions, and so on in China today, we find dichotomous representations of *yangqi* (Western, modern) vs. *tuqi* (countrified, rustic). This dichotomy, and the disdainful representation of people from the provinces as lacking in cosmopolitan qualities, can be traced at least as far back as colonial Shanghai in the 1920s. In the context of contemporary China, those carrying the *yangqi* connotation are typically returnees from overseas (*haigui*) or white-collar employees (*bailing*) of foreign-backed companies, that is, individuals believed capable of following international trends, whereas *tuqi* stereotypes usually adhere to people from the countryside or small towns and, more recently, to the *baofahu* (nouveau riche), who are low-brow and lacking in taste.

The construction of the cosmopolitan self is part and parcel of the "middle-class" lifestyle. Commodities, even food, are connected to a cosmopolitan subjectivity (see Henningsen 2011). What matters for many consumers is that they can imagine themselves participating in a way of life perceived as foreign. As a footnote to the official discourse of "One World, One Dream," *A Modern Family* represents fantasies about a cosmopolitan lifestyle for ordinary Chinese in the "modern" era. The old couple, for instance, travels freely to Korea, Malaysia, and Australia and they announce toward the end of the series that they will travel around the world to celebrate their fortieth anniversary, as if no visa restrictions for Chinese nationals existed (a particularly unlikely scenario in the early 2000s). The series also hyperbolically depicts the popularity of China and Chinese people around the world. For example, Yunshu's Australian professor at her university in Beijing enthusiastically invites her to study in Australia and offers her a scholarship. Yuntian attracts his eventual Korean wife and wins over her parents with his good looks (in fact he looks rather feminine), hard work, and virtue, filial piety in particular. When Mrs. Xiao gets lost in Australia, she is warmly welcomed and hosted by Roster, an old Australian, when he learns she is from China. At the same time, the drama displays strong nationalist sentiments, manifested, for instance, by an obsession with dignity in the context of transnational marriages and other relationships. The xenophobic mother initially has an aversion to foreigners and foreign countries and tries everything to prevent her children from marrying foreigners instead of eagerly encouraging them to "marry up" and migrate to foreign countries. In episode 10, she initially refuses to attend Yuntian's wedding out of resentment over the family of the bride's domination of the event. She then regains her "face" only when her husband makes a well-received speech at the wedding. All the Chinese characters in the series take pride in their national identity and even display a sense of cultural superiority in their dealings with foreigners. In episode 3, for example, Mr. Xiao and Yunshu laugh up their sleeves when Yunchu's Italian husband wolfs down delicious Chinese noodles and shows a lack of table manners.

As in other Chinese TV dramas of a similar theme, the representation of foreigners in *A Modern Family* is peppered with gendered stereotypes and reflects a gendered imagination of race, as evidenced by the loathsome and violent Italian husband (perhaps revealing the influence of Mafia images in films and TV), the beautiful and submissive Korean wife, the licentious young Australian woman, and the wealthy Malaysian Chinese businessman. Perhaps the most revealing episode is the one in which Mrs. Xiao, out of fear that her son may suffer wrong in a Korean family and from having a wife who is his superior, decides to "evaluate" her Korean daughter-in-law after the wedding. In a bluntly patriarchal and sexist manner, she not only warns her son against excessive sex with Yanji, ostensibly out of concern for his health, but she actually creates a poster listing "ten criteria for a good daughter-in-law" and puts it up on the wall of the new couple's home (episode 12). These criteria include such supposedly "traditional Chinese" standards of womanhood as consent to serve in-laws uncomplainingly (*cihou gongpo, renlao renyuan*), willingness to cook and competent culinary skills (*rude chufang, fancai kekou*), diligence in maintaining a clean and tidy home (*jiating weisheng, shishi yao gao*), and the capacity to get on well with neighbors and her husband's siblings. When her husband and Yuntian worry that Yanji may be vexed at this, Mrs. Xiao says, "she is my son's superior at work, but at home I am her superior!" Contrary to their expectations, however, Yanji is not at all angry when she sees the poster. Instead, clenching her fist in front of her, she determinedly says, "I must try my best to meet mom's standard." Yanji is regularly depicted performing chores such as vacuuming while her husband sits on the sofa. When she finally passes her mother-in-law's trial by proving that she is the perfect wife, she is praised by her in-laws as being "even a better wife than a Chinese girl," which is the highest possible praise for a non-Chinese spouse in media coverage of transnational marriages. The tenth criterion on the poster, however, remains blank, and Mrs. Xiao refuses to reveal it. It is not until she learns of Yanji's pregnancy that she announces that the tenth criterion has also been met: to carry on the family line!

The images and imaginaries of the Other bring another question to the fore. How are China and Chineseness perceived and represented as the Self in a transnational setting? In *A Modern Family*, we can see that the self-congratulating message of national pride and confidence goes hand in hand with a discernible self-Orientalist mentality. One example is the vision of China and Chinese culture as an ahistorical, fixed, and unchanging space, which is expressed through the masculinity of the male characters. For instance, Mr. Xiao is supposed to represent manhood in traditional Chinese culture. His daughter describes him as a man who "would rather eat no meat, cannot live without bamboo," quoting a famous line by Song dynasty literati member Su Shi (1037–1101). His refined masculinity as a scholar is also portrayed through his hobbies of calligraphy and the game *go* (*weiqi*).[9] He befriends his Korean daughter-in-law's father through their common interest in these hobbies, which also serves to demonstrate China's profound cultural influence on neighboring countries. This generalization of Chinese manhood is bereft of historical context, presented as if the upheaval of the Cultural Revolution and other traumatic events of the Mao era had never occurred. At the same time, Yuntian is presented as a hard-working, dutiful, filial son. These flat characters more often than not echo Western stereotypes of Chinese men, and are therefore subject to a "self-Orientalist" reading.

Grace Yan and Carla Santos (2009) define "Self-Orientalism" as "essentially a reconfiguration and, in many ways, an extension of Orientalism" and argue that "Orientalism is not simply the autonomous creation of the West, but rather . . . the Orient itself participates in its construction, reinforcement and circulation" (297). It is manifested not only through the heavy influence of Western conceptions of self-produced images of the Orient (such as the Great Wall), but also through the reinvention of Oriental history to fit into the Western model of social development and modernity. As noted, globalization is seen as a natural and welcome consequence of modernization in the drama's narrative. This optimistic view of globalization is epitomized by

Mr. Xiao's speech at his son's wedding, which is a clichéd paean to globalization.[10] The self-Orientalist construction of the self can also be seen in the attempts to represent China and Chinese people from an imagined "Western perspective." For instance, the Australian Anna is attracted to Yunshu's boyfriend because of the "Oriental scent" of his body.

Foreigners and foreign countries are portrayed in a superficial manner in *A Modern Family* and are sometimes even inadvertently humorous, likely because of the director's limited knowledge. For example, although some episodes are shot in Australia, none of the three "Australian" characters is played by an Australian. Rather, the actors are Chinese, Swedish, and Russian, which reflects a rendition of "the West" as homogeneous from the outside. Some of the characters' names would also sound odd to the Western ear, the Italian husband being called "Allan Poe," for instance, and a young Australian man and his uncle being called "Le Nei'er" and "Roster." Despite its interest in exploring the outside world and seeing China accepted by that world, the drama is peppered with biased and even distorted stereotypes of the Other. For example, Australia is presented as a sexually permissive country. When she tries to stop her daughter from going to Australia to further her studies, Mrs. Xiao yells, "Do you know what kind of place Australia is? It is a 'Cave of Silver Web,' full of demons!"[11] In comparison, the depiction of Korea appears much more "authentic" in terms of plot, scenery, and language, which is unsurprising given the involvement of the MBC director and her production team. With the explosive growth of TV production resources and China's accelerating contacts with the world, however, increasing numbers of TV dramas are today being filmed in foreign locales, with foreign actors playing increasingly important roles, and the representations therein are thus becoming more realistic. As a result, Chinese audiences are gradually losing their curiosity about foreigners. Nevertheless, images of foreigners continue to play a significant role in the televisual construction of national identity and articulation of nationalist ideology.

MY NATASHA: OCCIDENTALISM AND WESTERN WOMEN

Of the various depictions of foreigners in the Chinese media, the image of the Caucasian woman is deserving of particular theoretical attention. Perry Johansson (1999), in discussing the blonde, blue-eyed women who appear in Chinese-produced television dramas and decorate "the covers of magazines, posters, calendars, and advertisements" (377), contends that the white female is constructed as the Occidental other in a clear-cut dichotomy of West and East and that the fetishism of the Caucasian female body reflects a projection of male pleasure and a wish for power over Western women. Perhaps the best illustration is the famous scene in the 1995 TV series *Beijingers in New York* in which the protagonist, a frustrated new Chinese immigrant in the United States, pours dollar bills over the body of a buxom, white, blonde prostitute while demanding that she shout "I love you" repeatedly. According to Geremie Barmé (1995), this "was an extremely popular scene with mainland audiences, in particular with the Chinese intelligentsia" (209). In a tongue-in-cheek manner, he summarizes the drama's sentiments and the reactions of its fans as "to screw foreigners is patriotic" (Barmé 1995, 209). This symbolic position echoes what Xiaomei Chen (1995) terms Occidentalism, namely, "a discursive practice that, by constructing its Western Other, has allowed the Orient to participate actively and with indigenous creativity in the process of self-appropriation" (4–5).

My Natasha (*Wode Natasha*) was the first Chinese TV drama series to give a foreigner a leading role. This forty-one-episode series, produced by Shandong Television Station and Dalian Tiange Intermediary Company and broadcast by the satellite channels of the Shandong, Anhui, Henan, and Jiangxi TV stations in January 2012, tells the half-century-long love story of a Chinese revolutionary soldier and his female Soviet instructor. According to its director, Guo Jingyu, and scriptwriter, Gao Mantang, the drama was based on several real stories of long, tortuous transnational romances between Russian soldiers and Chinese residents of Dalian, a port city in northeastern China that was occupied by the Soviet Army for a short period following World War II.[12] Natasha, played by Ukrainian actress Irina Kaptelova, is a young officer in the Soviet army stationed on the Sino-Soviet border on the eve of the Sino-Japanese War. By accident, she saves a Chinese guerrilla named Pang Tiande, who is being chased and has been injured by Japanese troops. After he recovers, Pang remains in the Soviet camp with three fellow Chinese soldiers to receive training as an undercover agent from the Soviets, and Natasha becomes their instructor. She admires Pang for his bravery and patriotic spirit, and the two gradually fall in love due to their common cause: fighting the Japanese. Disguised as husband and wife, they excel in several tasks in the Japanese-occupied area. But during one mission in which they capture a ship full of Chinese antiquities looted by the Japanese, they disagree about what to do with the antiquities. Pang insists that

Chinese treasure should remain in China, while Natasha, under orders from her superior, attempts to direct the ship toward the Soviet Union. In the end, Pang ties Natasha up and successfully transports the treasure to a Chinese communist area. Natasha is transferred back to the Soviet Union, and Pang is later arrested, tortured, and sent to the Germ Factory by the Japanese.[13] When they eventually meet again, Natasha—now an engineering school graduate—is an "expert" sent to China to assist the newly founded People's Republic of China. She works in the same factory as Pang. They finally decide to get married after obtaining approval from both the Chinese and Soviet authorities, as well as from Pang's father, who initially does not like Natasha because of the cultural barrier. History, however, intervenes, with Natasha ordered to leave China on the eve of their wedding because of the open split between China and the USSR. As a patriot, Pang refuses to leave with her. In the years that follow, the lovers occasionally meet clandestinely in a hut near the Sino-Soviet border. When bilateral relations worsen, however, the couple gives up hope, and they marry others. At the end of the series, the now elderly couple amazingly find each other and, after many setbacks, finally have their long-delayed wedding.

In addition to the love story between Natasha and Pang, another thread running through the drama is the triangle between the pair and a Japanese woman named Noriko Ida. Noriko embodies the merits of "Oriental" womanhood, such as obedience, submissiveness, and perseverance, in contrast to Natasha's tough and aggressive demeanor. Noriko, a nurse, saves Pang from the Germ Factory and carries him all the way back to his hometown. She loves Pang deeply and looks after him and his father single-handedly after Pang's mother dies. Noriko's love is so strong that she even attempts to kill Pang when she realizes that she will never have his heart. As discussed in chapter 3, positive images of the Japanese are rare on the big or small Chinese screen in recent years, and the characterization of Noriko is in keeping with the stereotyped Japanese in Chinese popular media: narrow-minded, paranoid, and fanatical. Even so, Pang marries her when he realizes that he has no hope of finding Natasha, and the two have a daughter together. When Natasha ultimately reappears, however, Noriko gives up and "returns" Pang to his true love, and she and Natasha become "good sisters." In addition to exemplifying male fantasies of concubinage and polygamy, commonly seen on the Chinese TV screen today, some critics have also pointed out that the triangle also metaphorically symbolizes the perceived relationship among the three nations. As a matter of fact, the name "Natasha" itself nostalgically recalls the memory of Soviet influence in China during the 1950s. In the Soviet propaganda film *Lenin in 1918*, Natasha is the wife of Lenin's protégé Vasili, whose line "there will be bread, there will be milk, there will be every-thing" is familiar to an entire generation of Chinese.[14] The eponymous pro-tagonist's name in *My Natasha* is likely derived from this film.

As Rey Chow (1991, 86) argues, the white woman has been made a sym-bol of what China is not or does not have, and has therefore become a fetish. In *My Natasha*, the Western female body is made into a stereotype of strength and power. Natasha, as a Soviet officer, is Pang's superior and com-mander. She is a superb fighter and ace shooter. She fights with Pang and beats him badly when he attempts to escape from the Soviet camp (episode 2). But she is also straightforward and bold in expressing her love for Pang. In their relationship, she always takes the initiative and even attempts to seduce him on the eve of his departure for a battle (episode 8). When Pang is captured by a gang of bandits, Natasha rushes to rescue him. She fights with the bandit chieftain's daughter, who is also attracted to Pang, and finally wins him back (episodes 6–7). To a certain extent, Natasha embodies the discourse of gender reversal and the popular imagination of the West as a powerful, dominant Other.

Paradoxically, however, a more nuanced reading of this character also reveals the objectification of the female body and a desire to tame the Other. The very title of the drama conveys a sense of possession, placing the audi-ence in the position of desiring subject. As a brave soldier, Natasha is pre-sented as an object of (visual and physical) consumption, as far as her body is concerned. Her beauty is used as bait to successfully trap and kill a Russian traitor (episodes 21–22). Sexual temptation lures not only enemies, but also comrades. In one scene, Natasha is taking a bath when Pang Tiande walks in. The close-up shots of her wet, naked body give the audience the pleasure of looking, allowing them to experience a fetishistic scopophilia, to borrow Laura Mulvey's (1975) term. One of the Chinese guerrillas she instructs, a man nicknamed "Moustache Cong," fantasizes about her coveted body with his fellow soldiers: "Look at the big butt and the strong legs. Just think about one pinch of the flesh!" He is later seriously injured in battle and, as a dying wish, asks Natasha if he can hug her because, he confesses, he has never had any physical contact with a woman (despite all of his bragging about how many women he has slept with). A tearful Natasha grants his last request (episode 3). Under the motif of a revolutionary friendship between com-rades, white women are depicted as hypersexual and (at least potentially) as

Figure 14. Pang Tiande and Natasha in their youth. *My Natasha* (2012).

attractive objects awarded to good men (the hug is a reward for Moustache Cong, who has sacrificed his life for his country).

Western women are not only to be consumed, but also to be tamed and conquered. The leitmotif of taming Western women, seen regularly in TV dramas on transnational marriage such as *Foreign Babes in Beijing*, reflects "a desire to have what the Other has, and an aggressive reaction to the fear of Western containment, which reads like the fear of castration" (Johansson 1999, 387). What is interesting about *My Natasha* is that although there are detailed representations of Natasha's sexual attractiveness and the deep love she shares with Pang, the two do not actually have sex until they are middle-aged and meeting secretly in the hut near the border. Up to that point, they deny themselves physical fulfillment, even though they share a bed several times (when disguised as husband and wife). Many reasons are given for their chaste relationship. First, during the war, Pang is not sure whether he will return and therefore does not want to act irresponsibly. Then, after the war, they encounter one barrier after another, not least the presence of Noriko, Pang's father's aversion to Natasha, and the worsening relationship between their two countries, and thus wait for the right time to consummate their relationship. A modern audience might well find it unrealistic, even laughable, that a couple who regularly express their love and longing for each other through letters and diaries would refrain from sexual intimacy despite many obvious opportunities. Granted, their restraint is a plot device to demonstrate the moral power of the Chinese man through his ability to control his sexual desire. At the same time, however, this delayed "consumption" of a white woman can also be interpreted from the Lacanian perspective on male anxiety: the sexuality of Western women is dangerous and should be avoided until they are tamed. In other words, women can be strong, but they have to be contained within the parameters of (Chinese) patriarchy.

Although Natasha is a strong, beautiful woman, she experiences numerous setbacks and frustrations when she lives with Pang and his family disguised as Pang's wife, and she has to overcome many cultural barriers to be accepted as a real Chinese wife. Pang's father, who calls her "a live monkey," disapproves of her energy and spontaneity and prefers Noriko despite his resentment of the Japanese.[15] Although Natasha tries hard to please her father-in-law, she fails time and again. To extend the series so as to generate additional revenue—a common practice in Chinese TV drama productions— many comedic incidents illustrating the imagined confrontation between Eastern and Western cultures occur in episodes 11 through 20. For instance, Natasha crawls to her father-in-law's bed to extend "morning greetings," a practice that greatly annoys him and causes him to feel awkward but that allows the audience to laugh at and feel culturally superior to the funny foreigner. Natasha is also severely punished for her ignorance of the moral requirements of a Chinese wife, most importantly filial piety. When she returns to Pang's hometown with the Soviet occupation army after the Japanese surrender, she is so eager to discover Pang's whereabouts that she arrests Pang's father and Noriko for hiding Pang from her. Pang later complains to Natasha's superior, a Soviet general, about her illegal behavior. When the general criticizes Pang for knowing nothing about love, Pang responds that love should be repressed for the sake of filial piety (episode 30). As a result of this incident, Natasha is sent back to the Soviet Union, and the couple misses the chance to be together. At the end of the series, Natasha finally—after some fifty years—becomes a Chinese wife, an identity she has longed for all her life, through a traditional Chinese wedding ritual.

Both *A Modern Family* and *My Natasha* feature judgment on and the containment of non-Chinese women in a way that verges on sexism. It is noteworthy, however, that the target of the masculinist taming depicted shifts from a Korean woman in the former to a Caucasian woman in the latter, a significant shift in terms of imagining China's rise through gender discourse. There was a span of ten years between the airing of the two dramas, a period in which a series of important events in the Sino-Western relationship occurred, the most notable between China's entry into the World Trade Organization in 2001 and Beijing's hosting of the Olympic Games in 2008. Rapid economic growth and the accumulation of wealth gave rise to explosive growth in national confidence and ambition in the media. In *A Modern Family*, elite members of China's younger generation go abroad in the hope of being absorbed by the outside world and take pride in their cosmopolitan identity, whereas in *My Natasha*, a strong and powerful Russian woman comes to China and is tamed and transformed by the power of Chinese culture. The nationalities of the "Chinese wife," who is subject to Sinicization by a patriarchal China, in the two dramas reflect a growing desire to renegotiate China's place in the world and enhance the country's soft power on a global scale.

The cultural imaginary of China's rise is also expressed through the desirability of Chinese masculinity in both dramas. In *My Natasha*, Pang Tiande is constantly fought over by a Russian woman and Japanese woman, who both love him passionately and lastingly. Natasha is willing to give up everything she has and dumps her Russian boyfriend for Pang's sake. Noriko endures torture in a Japanese prison rather than leak his name, and she risks her own life to save Pang's several times in the series. Pang's masculinity is also praised by his rival, the Soviet lieutenant Vasrov, who is also madly in love with Natasha. Vasrov is subdued by Pang's moral power and manhood and finally gives up Natasha. Pang outshines the burly Soviet in several operations with his wisdom and stratagems, representing the ideal Chinese masculinity, which combines *wen* and *wu* merits (see Louie 2002). In fact, not just Pang, but all of the young men in the anti-Japanese guerrilla force are "real men." Moustache Cong, on the eve of his heroic death, says to Natasha, "Although your Russian men are tall and strong, to be honest, they are not a big deal in my eyes. Tomorrow I will show you what a Chinese man looks like" (episode 3). The issue of heroic Chinese masculinity in a global setting will be discussed more thoroughly in the next section.

THE LAST VISA: RESCUING THE WORLD WITH
CHINESE MASCULINITY

The Last Visa, which was promoted as a Chinese *Schindler's List*, is a forty-six-episode TV drama coproduced by the Omnijoi Media Corporation, Jiangsu TV, and Yijia International Cultural Communication Company in Beijing and Twin Star Film and Film Kolektiv in the Czech Republic. Shooting began in 2015 at the peak of commemorations for the seventieth anniversary of the end of the Second World War, although the drama did not air until January 2017. It is based on the true story of Ho Feng Shan (1901–1997), who, as the Chinese consul general in Vienna on the eve of the Second World War, saved thousands of Jews from the horrors of the Holocaust by issuing them "life visas" to Shanghai. Ho was posthumously recognized as a hero and the savior of many Jewish lives. In *The Last Visa*, however, this historical prototype is split into two characters, Deputy Consul-General Lu Huaishan (Chen Baoguo) and Pu Jizhou (Wang Lei), a visa officer at the Chinese Consulate General in Vienna. In terms of masculinity, they embody middle-aged mature masculinity and young laddish masculinity, respectively, which happen to be the two most popular types of masculinity on the Chinese TV screen. In addition, a large portion of the drama is devoted to a fictional romantic triangle involving Pu Jizhou, his Chinese wife, and a young Jewish woman he saves.

The screenwriter, Gao Mantang, who also wrote *My Natasha*, said during an interview that his aim was "to write a true story of how Chinese people won respect internationally, an emergent task that should have been done much earlier." He also said he regarded *The Last Visa* as a much-needed counteraction to the vulgar anti-Japanese dramas that glut the Chinese TV screen:

> It is ridiculous that the War of Resistance against Japanese Aggression, during which we lost so many lives, has now turned into a subject for entertainment. This kind of "spiritual victory" [that characterizes these dramas] will only confuse our future generations. The drama that I wrote is to correct people's understanding of history.[16]

The drama's antiwar theme constitutes a paean to cosmopolitan humanitarianism, with Chinese in the role of savior. After Austria's annexation by Nazi Germany in 1938, tens of thousands of Austrian Jews desperately sought foreign visas to flee the country. Although many countries refused to issue visas in fear of aggravating the Nazi government, the Chinese Consulate General issued papers to many Jewish people that allowed them to travel to Shanghai, an international port city whose entry did not require a visa. From there, they were then able to travel on to other destinations such as the United States. In the drama, Deputy Consul-General Lu Huaishan disobeys instructions from his superior and insists on issuing visas to save Jewish lives out of humanitarian concerns. This spirit of humanity, which treats foreigners as equal to Chinese people, significantly transcends the conventional Self/Other dichotomy seen in so many Chinese TV dramas. Lu and Pu risk their careers and even their lives to rescue people in danger regardless of their nationality or ethnicity. In justifying their actions in the face of potential tension between moral justice and the national interest, Pu draws an analogy between the Jewish and Chinese people in a vehement tone while dining with Lu at a restaurant on the banks of the Wien River just after Counselor Wang of the Chinese Embassy in Berlin instructs Lu to discontinue visa issuance. Pu tries to persuade Lu to disobey Wang's order:

> Human life is of greater value than everything. There are numerous human lives out there! If your family or friends were among them, would you still say the same thing? . . . Before coming to Vienna, I witnessed how millions of people in Shanghai lost their families, homes, and lives under the gunfire of the Japanese devils, followed by the falls of Nanjing, Hangzhou, and Jinan. Wuhan is also in imminent danger now. What our compatriots are facing is exactly the same as what the Jews are experiencing here. If we give up, one day when all of this is finished, will we have regrets? Will we be able to spend the rest of our lives with a peaceful conscience? (episode 6)

The next scene switches to Shanghai, with close-ups of the Japanese flag waving over a barbed-wire fence. Cosmopolitan humanitarianism is thus strategically incorporated into the narrative of patriotism and official discourse of national humiliation with which Chinese audiences are very familiar. At the same time, however, patriotism transcends the blatant confrontation between the Self and Other depicted in so many anti-Japanese dramas and corresponds to "a new, cosmopolitan Chineseness" (H. Lee 2014, 263).

The pursuit of cosmopolitanism is also reflected in the drama's filming locations and casting. Most of *The Last Visa* was shot in Prague, and an unprecedented number of foreign actors (most of them Czechs or Slovaks), including Jan Révai, Natália Germániová, and Pavel Gaidos, were cast.

Indeed, the performances of the many foreign actors served to lure viewers to the series. Many said through *danmu* that they were eager to see how the foreign actors performed and stated they thought the casting of real foreigners gave the drama a "sense of reality."

The drama, however, was severely criticized by Ho Feng Shan's daughter, Manli Ho, particularly for its lack of historical authenticity. During an interview with *China Daily*, Manli Ho, a retired journalist living in the United States, did not try to hide her disdain for the "laughably unrealistic" drama, describing it as "an embarrassingly bad soap opera with poor production values, an obvious lack of understanding of both the European and Chinese history of that time, and ridiculous cartoonish characters."[17] A particular criticism was the two male leads' conspicuous lack of the "cultural refinement and strict decorum" that defined diplomats of the Nationalist China era. Ho also complained in the interview that

> [b]esides the unbelievable plotline, the details—from the sign in front of the Chinese diplomatic mission, which should have been a bronze plaque in German rather than what looks like a "cultural revolution" (1966–76) poster in Chinese, to the official rank and work of the diplomats, to the ill-fitting costumes, to using Christian crucifixes for Jews—show plain ignorance.

The "unbelievable plotline" she mentioned refers to the fictional Pu risking his life and outwitting the SS time and again to deliver Chinese visas to seven Jewish people on a secret list, a list of scientists and artists who Lu thinks should be afforded priority in their rescue mission. The two men thus become saviors rather than mere helpers, directly fighting with the SS in Vienna, the head of which is an evil character named Hans, who is pathologically fond of playing games with them. It is this plotline that deviates most significantly from the historical record and thus has been singled out for criticism by some audience members. During my interviews, some used such idioms as *duo guan xianshi* (to poke one's nose into something that isn't his or her business) and even *chili pawai* (to do harm to one's own country to help outsiders) to describe the Chinese diplomats' behavior. Others questioned whether a Chinese visa was really so powerful—"as if the Chinese visa were an amulet for the Jews"—given that China was a weak country at the time, having already lost most of its territory to the Japanese.[18]

The discourse of Chinese men as saviors of the world, however, has gained in popularity in film and on TV in recent years. Salient examples include *Wolf Warrior II* and *Operation Red Sea*, which "express[] a cultural imaginary of China's rise through the banal reassertion of masculinity" (C. Wang 2018). But unlike the jingoism in these two films set in the present day, *The Last Visa* is set during the Republican period, and Lu and Pu are both Nationalist officials. To counter the awkwardness of that fact, the drama highlights the contrast between the chivalry and sense of moral justice of individual Chinese men (Pu, Lu, and their colleagues at the Chinese Consulate) and the cowardice and selfishness of the corrupt Guomindang government (embodied by Counselor Wang and other bureaucrats in the Chinese Ministry of Foreign Affairs). Pu and Lu repeatedly defy orders to suspend visa issuance and even openly criticize Chiang Kai-shek's policies. With this sharp contrast between characters, and between the upstanding characters and the government of the day, the drama not only conveys a politically felicitous message, but also successfully aligns the obeisance paid to moral agency and cosmopolitan humanitarianism (the name Pu Jizhou carries the meaning "universal salvation" in Chinese) with the state interest in legitimizing communist rule in China.

As the epitome of true masculinity, Pu is praised by his supervisor Lu as "a man of hot blood, of courageous integrity, [who] dares to tell the truth and dares to take on responsibilities." These masculine merits, particularly the taking on of responsibilities, echo CCP discourse on China being a "responsible great power" (*fuzeren daguo*) in the world and the project to create new images of the country in a personified manner. As the savior of thousands of Jewish lives, Pu is given a hero's welcome when he and his wife visit the Jewish community in Shanghai during a trip back home, which further strengthens his determination to help as many Jews as he can upon his return to Vienna (episode 31). Through such sentimental scenes, masculine honor is woven into the imagination of national esteem and confidence and becomes a cultural signifier of nationalism.

The role played by exotic femininity is also noteworthy. *The Last Visa* features a romantic triangle among Pu, his Chinese wife Yao Jiali (Zhang Jingjing), and a young Jewish woman named Rosa (Natália Germániová). Rosa is pregnant and is eager to leave Austria. She bears a strong resemblance to a famous violinist named Helen Michelle, of whom Pu is a great fan, and Pu mistakes her for Helen. Rosa and her boyfriend David, a Jewish resistance fighter, decide to make use of this case of mistaken identity to obtain a Chinese visa for Rosa, who ends up seeking shelter in Pu's apartment after being pursued by members of the SS. She now has to play the role of Helen full-time, imitating her voice, style of dressing, and living habits, as well as hide her burgeoning baby bump. The situation is agonizing for her, as she struggles between the guilt she feels for fooling Pu and her will to survive. Although there is no indication of Rosa falling in love with Pu, Pu harbors passionate feelings for her, although they take the form of admiration more than desire. Indeed, helping Rosa leave the country is a major, if not the primary, motive for Pu's embarkation on the visa rescue adventure. One online comment on the Douban website sarcastically summarized the drama's plotline as "a visa officer repeatedly disobeys orders just to realize his promise of issuing a visa to his girl."[19] Another lamented that "what is supposed to be [the spirit of] humanitarianism has been turned into [an issue of] personal love and favor."[20]

As Homi Bhabha (1983) has argued in a different context, racial fetishism involves stereotyping that both demonizes and idolizes the Other. Unlike the heroine of *My Natasha*, Rosa is never sexually available to the male protagonist in *The Last Visa*, being more akin to an object of worship. Pu mistakes her for Helen Michelle from the outset, when in reality Helen has already been murdered by the villainous Hans. In other words, Rosa is nothing more than an illusion. Just like the fetish, for Freud, is the substitute for the maternal phallus,[21] Rosa is the substitute for Helen, who in turn embodies the (lack of) symbolic power associated with national selfhood. Pu's preoccupation with Helen bespeaks not only a will to power over the Other but also a fantasy of masculinizing the self through desiring the Other. He puts up a big poster of Helen's performance in his bedroom and looks at it day and night. To borrow a word that is trendy in Chinese popular culture, Rosa/Helen represents the "goddess" (*nüshen*) type of womanhood, that is, an idealized woman who is worshipped and admired by men from a distance. At the same time, as a pregnant Jewish woman, Rosa is entirely helpless and in her desperation must rely on a Chinese man's protection to survive. This character thus illustrates two paradoxical aspects of the male fantasy about exotic femininity: the exotic female is both a fetishized object of male desire and a symbol of the masculine power associated with race and nationhood. Saving and protecting the white woman renders Pu the pleasure derived from both his confirmed manhood and a feeling of national superiority. In addition, as Slavoj Žižek argues, the fetish is just the other side of the phobic object (1997, 104).[22] The fetishized body of Rosa also constitutes a source of fear. The audience is fully aware that there was never a possibility of any true

Figure 15. Pu Jizhou carrying the pregnant Rosa as they rush to catch the last train leaving Austria. *The Last Visa* (2015).

romance between Rosa and Pu, because, as a pregnant woman, her "contaminated" body can never become part of the "self," but only engenders anxiety and discrimination that eventually lead to abjection.[23]

By contrast, Pu's Chinese wife, Yao Jiali, is supposed to represent the virtues associated with Chinese womanhood: she has a sympathetic heart yet is tough enough to face the enemy and fulfill her responsibilities. She and Pu have been engaged since childhood, as arranged by their parents. Pu, however, is unwilling to be tied down by marriage, and so he runs away from the wedding to become a diplomat in Vienna. Deeply in love with Pu, Yao travels to Vienna alone to look for her husband, only to find a young Caucasian woman, Rosa, living in his apartment. In a storm of jealousy, the two women and one man now stage a melodrama under one roof, a clichéd motif commonly found in Chinese TV dramas. To make Rosa disappear from their life, Yao steals the Consulate General's stamp and forges a visa for her without Pu's knowledge. Hans sees through the fake visa, however, and sends Rosa to a concentration camp. Yao then bravely goes to Hans and assumes responsibility and even risks her own life to rescue Rosa from the camp. Pu realizes

that Yao's actions evince true love for him, and thus that a Chinese wife better suits him than a foreign one.

It seems that humanitarian cosmopolitanism parallels Sinocentric
nationalism in this drama, rather than being in tension with it. Both are elements of and strategies in a congruent system of representation and corre-
late to a new mode of Chineseness. The cosmopolitan spirit has been recon-
structed as an indispensable element of "Chinese culture," exemplified by
the Confucian value of *tui ji ji ren* ("To put oneself in another's position"), as
noted above. Through identification with a cosmopolitan, humanitarian
Chinese man, the drama's audience is expected to react with national pride.
Cosmopolitanism thus serves to strengthen rather than dissolve the Self/
Other binary. At the same time, the ambitious and aggressive version of
nationalism and its global dimension reflect a temporal displacement of
Chineseness, which partially explains Manli Ho's aversion to the drama's
adaptation of her father's story.

CONCLUSION

The past two decades have witnessed growing concern with national soft
power in China. An increasingly self-confident China has begun to feel the
need to offer the world more than just cheaply manufactured commodities
(H. Lee 2014, 244). With growing transnational mobility, the construction
of the Self is increasingly played out in, and through, the inscription of
Otherness.

In this cultural context, more and more images of foreigners—Japanese,
Korean, African, Russian, and a variety of Westerners—are appearing on the
Chinese TV screen. They represent stereotypes of national and cultural Otherness, both "as phobia and fetish" (Bhabha 1983, 19). Comparison of the
three dramas discussed in this chapter lays bare the trajectory of the change
in mentality associated with the narratives of transnational romance and
marriage on Chinese television during the span of a decade or so. In *A Modern Family*, the earliest of the three, the younger Chinese generation, which
has been rendered more modernized and Westernized than the older generation, marry foreigners and migrate to foreign countries, whereas in the later
My Natasha, a sexy, powerful Russian woman becomes a Chinese wife and
willingly submits to the Chinese order (filial piety, wifehood, etc.). If the former represents a desire to embrace the world, the latter displays the fantasy

of taming it. Finally, in *The Last Visa*, a Chinese man becomes a hero who saves the world, with a beautiful but powerless foreign woman depending on him for survival and escape. This superficial and often naïvely fantasized cosmopolitanism actually acts to reinforce Sinocentric and phallocentric nationalist, and sometimes even chauvinist, views of China's self-perceived increasingly dominant positionality in the world.

CHAPTER 6

"Little Fresh Meat" and the Politics of Sissyphobia

AS DISCUSSED AT THE beginning of this book, male actors with feminine beauty appearing on television and in films are today referred to in China as "little fresh meat" (*xiao xian rou*) or, even more insultingly, "sissy pants" (*niangpao*). Notwithstanding the long history of gender fluidity in Chinese performance art, these actors suffer extensive social criticism and a professional blacklist implemented by state media. "Sissyphobia," the fear or hatred of effeminate men, is sweeping China. Yet despite this masculinist backlash, effeminate-looking stars and the androgynous aesthetic they embody are enjoying exponential popularity among high school students and other young people. Stylish men who wear makeup represent a new form of embodied masculinity for young middle-class men in urban China. Through critical readings of recent TV and web dramas featuring this type of male image, this chapter explores the disjuncture between urban youth culture and official attitudes and what the tension between them tells us about gender roles and subjectivity in contemporary China. And through discourse analysis of the media debates triggered by these images, it examines how the effeminate male body is given affective interpretations and significances that differ from those in Western contexts, as well as how the Chinese nation is imagined and articulated through embodied masculinity.

Despite extensive media attention to the subject, dedicated scholarly studies of the portrayal and reception of feminine male beauty in Chinese popular culture are scarce (T. Zheng 2015b). Such beauty is commonly believed to be part of a transnational trend known as "Pan East-Asian soft masculinity" (Jung 2011), reflecting the influence of the *kkonminam* (flower boy) type of male beauty in the Korean Wave and the androgynous *bishōnen* (beautiful boy) aesthetic in the Japanese BL/*Yaoi* subgenre of *shōjo* manga (girls' comics), as well as the idol production system and fandom culture associated with them.

In line with the creation of "desiring subjects" in postsocialist China, an aesthetic dimension has emerged in the country's governance techniques as a form of biopower, and the beauty economy has prospered, becoming the fifth largest consumer market in China (after the real estate, automotive, clothing, and hospitality industries) (J. Yang 2011). The young celebrities who are labeled "little fresh meat"—with a strong implication of (hetero) sexual desirability—are created and promoted by commercial agents and, once they have become successful or even idols, find themselves in high demand among Chinese and foreign companies keen to promote their products to China's vast market of high-tech-savvy and appearance-valuing young millennial consumers. A group of male stars—Lu Han, Wu Yifan (Kris Wu), Yang Yang, Li Yifeng, Xu Weizhou, Wang Junkai, Roy Wang, and Jackson Yee, among others—have been appointed as official brand ambassadors for a host of products and businesses ranging from the high-end cosmetic brands L'Occitane, Lancôme, and L'Oréal Paris to such fast-food outlets as KFC. Their images also appear in men's lifestyle magazines and advertisements for a multitude of products. This type of male image and the market demand for it suggest the dynamics of gender identity/aesthetics and consumer culture (Johansson 2015), the mechanism of celebrity culture and the entertainment industry (Leung, Cheng, and Tse 2017), the production of "desiring subjects" in a cosmopolitan context (Rofel 2007), and the link between queerness, class, and neoliberal subjectivity (Griffins 2007; T. Kong 2019).

The cult of sissiness reflects shifting masculinity in a consumer society (see Song and Lee 2010, 2012). As Laura Miller (2006) argues in discussing young Japanese men's "beautification" practices, these men's "increasing concern with their status as objects of aesthetic and sexual appraisal" indicates that "the ideological sphere of reference of masculinity has widened to include a greater diversity of physical styles" (126). Therefore, Japanese male beauty practices do not constitute the "feminization of men," but rather represent a "shift to[ward] [seeing] beautification as a component of [heterosexual] masculinity" (Miller 2006, 126). Iida (2005) further points out that the "cult of male beauty" is a strategy to distance young men from the conventional masculinity of their fathers and to respond to women's desires.

This last supposition leads to questions about the sexuality of the young men who pursue such an aesthetic. In a small-scale ethnographic study I conducted in March 2019 with young men (aged eighteen to twenty-four) who are self-proclaimed lovers or followers of the aesthetic trend in Guangzhou (n = 10) and Zhuhai (n = 12), around 32 percent cited "to get closer to girls" as the primary reason for their fashion and grooming preferences, reflecting their assumption that this type of male appearance is favored by young women.[1] Only two of the participants (9 percent) admitted to a gay or bisexual identity. This finding is reminiscent of Eva Li's (2017) discussion of the tensions felt by young women in contemporary China who adopt "neutral gender/sex" (zhongxing) practices in everyday life. Although Li's study did not include men, it illuminates a similar ambiguity concerning subjectivities, namely, the coexistence of a desire for individuality and self-expression and a wish to conform to normative trends and practices to fit in.

As gender terminology, "little fresh meat" significantly reverses the traditional "male gaze" on women to portray the men so designated as inexperienced in sex and love ("fresh") and in possession of a young, healthy, and desirable body ("meat"). To a certain extent, it reflects female empowerment and new trends in gender relations in the wake of China's economic growth. Indeed, the popularity of many "little fresh meat" actors in the entertainment industry is attributable not only to the huge market of young female fans but also to the backing of a number of female entrepreneurs for personal or economic considerations.[2] During interviews conducted for the current research, many young women averred that in a relationship they would prefer a man with a weak and fragile body rather than a muscular one, which they appeared to associate with domination, aggression, and violence. In other words, it seems that effeminate men may create among women a sense of an empowered self. As one female informant said, in the past women saw men as protectors and thus desired physically strong, muscular partners. Today, however, women's taste has changed, with some young women treating their boyfriends in a way akin to "keeping a pet." Hence, many prefer frail men who always stay at home.

At the same time, from a national perspective, effeminate male images can be said to be a continuation of the colonial gaze, which views Asian men as the weak Other. To some extent, the view that Chinese men are "aping" the West, and therefore can never reach the Western standard of masculinity (Chua 2000), has been internalized in China. Such internalization explains why "soft" masculinity has become popular in East Asian countries but is unlikely to become the mainstream in Europe or North America.

The discussion of "sissyphobia" in the Western context has been primarily focusing on gay men's performance, under pressure, to conform to heteronormative masculine images and traits in order to "justify and empower their masculinity" (Eguchi 2011, 38; Bergling 2001). I adopt a slightly different, and broader, definition of the term. Premised on a masculine persona of the nation, I use the term to discuss a "fear of castration" on a national scale. The term thus covers a wider scope than homophobia and refers to disdain for and anxiety over male effeminacy. In China, the sissyphobic discourse and its association with anxiety over national virility can be traced back to at least the early 1980s, when intellectuals frustrated by the allegedly "overliberated" women produced by the Mao era began calling for a "search for real men" campaign to remasculinize the nation (Zhong 2000). Thus, although the pressures that gay men experience to be more "appropriately" masculine is without question important for an understanding of antifeminine behaviors and discourse, the case of China demonstrates that sissyphobia also operates in a heterosexual context and sometimes interacts with nationalist ideology and sentiment.

In what follows, I focus on TV programs and web dramas that feature this type of embodied masculinity, as well as the audience reception and media criticism of this male aesthetic trend.

METEOR GARDEN: TRANSNATIONAL MALE BEAUTY

The term "little fresh meat" came into vogue around 2014 when Lu Han and Wu Yifan, two former members of the Korean-Chinese boy band EXO, returned from South Korea to pursue careers as musicians, film actors, and models in the Chinese entertainment industry. The success of Lu Han, whose ubiquitous KFC advertisements are now regarded as a prototype of the "little fresh meat" image (figure 16), best illustrates the influence in China of the aesthetic trend scholars have termed "Pan East-Asian soft masculinity" (Jung 2011).

A salient example of the transnational flow of that image is the multimedia, cross-cultural production and adaptation of the bestselling *shōjo* manga *Boys Over Flowers*. Written and illustrated by Yoko Kamio, the manga was first serialized in *Margaret*, a biweekly magazine published by Shueisha, from October 1992 to September 2003 and then later adapted into anime television series, films, and live-action dramas. It centers on a campus love story between a girl from an ordinary family (Tsukushi Makino) and the imperious

Figure 16. KFC advertisement featuring Lu Han, with the catchphrase "follow your heart and follow your character" at the top.

son of one of Japan's wealthiest families (Tsukasa Domyoji). Makino is forced by her mother to enroll in an expensive elite school, where she is bullied by a gang of four handsome male students known as the F4 (four flower boys), who are worshipped like stars by the school's girls. Makino's resilience in the face of their bullying ultimately causes Domyoji, the gang's leader, to fall in love with her. The F4 have long, stylist-cut hair, soft skin, and a trim physique, take great care of their appearance, wear earrings, and are portrayed enjoying manicures. They are typical representatives of the effeminate male beauty aesthetic.

The F4 gang is arguably associated with "Pan East-Asianness" from the very beginning, with a host of Asian actors of varying nationalities involved.[3] In the TV adaptation *Hana Yori Dango* (2005) and its sequel *Hana Yori Dango Returns* (2007), as well as the film adaptation *Hana Yori Dango Final* (2008), F4 member Akira Mimasaka is played by the Chinese-Japanese actor Tsuyoshi Abe. Abe, whose birth name was Li Zhendong, was born in Heilongjiang Province and moved to Japan at the age of nine. He later returned to China and graduated from the Beijing Academy of Film. Based on Kamio's *Boys Over Flowers*, a Taiwanese television series titled *Meteor Garden* (*Liuxing huayuan*) was aired by the Chinese Television System back in 2001. In *Meteor Garden*, the characters all have Chinese names in accordance with the original *kanji*. For instance, Tsukushi Makino has become Shancai (played by Barbie Shu), and Tsukasa Domyoji is called Daoming Si (played by Jerry Yan). This TV series was followed by a sequel, *Meteor Garden II* (2002), as well as by South Korean (2009), Indian (2014–15), Indonesian (2018), and Thai (2020) remakes. Furthermore, the four Taiwanese actors who portrayed the F4 in *Meteor Garden*, namely, Jerry Yan, Vic Zhou, Vanness Wu, and Ken Chu, established a boy band called F4 in 2001 (disbanded in 2009) after the drama's successful broadcast. The transnational remakes and popularity of *Boys Over Flowers* and the male bodily fashion spurred by it attest to the power of Japanese (queer) modernity in East Asia. At the same time, the backing of these images by major Japanese and Korean companies, and the association of the images with their products, further enhanced the appeal of idols such as those from F4.

In mainland China, *Let's Watch the Meteor Shower* (*Yiqi laikan liuxingyu*), a remake of *Boys Over Flowers* made without permission from the Japanese publisher Shueisha, was produced by Hunan Satellite TV in 2009, with the F4 played by a group of young male stars who had gained fame in *Super Boy*, Hunan Satellite TV's popular singing contest program. *Meteor Shower II* (*Yiqi youkan liuxingyu*), a sequel starring the same cast, was released the next year. Both were well-received by young audiences. In 2018, a mainland version of *Meteor Garden* directed by the Taiwanese original's director, Lin He-lung, was produced and aired by Hunan Satellite TV and its online platform Mango TV. In this series, which is the focus of discussion here, the female protagonist Dong Shancai (the counterpart of Makino Tsukushi in *Boys Over Flowers*) is played by Shen Yue and the F4 members by a group of "post-90s" mainland actors: Dylan Wang (or Wang Hedi) as Daoming Si (the counterpart of Tsukasa Domyoji), Guan Hong as Hua Zelei (the counterpart of Rui Hanazawa), Connor Leong (or Liang Jingkang) as Feng Meizuo (the counterpart of Akira Mimasaka), and Caesar Wu (or Wu Xize) as Ximen Yan (the counterpart of Soujiro Nishikado). Although the characters' names are the same as those in the Taiwanese version, the setting has shifted to mainland China. Also, instead of an elite high school attended by the children of wealthy families, the setting is an ordinary reputable university called Mingde College. This alteration reflects efforts to conform to Chinese norms, that is, to minimize class distinctions and increase the age of dating, as "puppy love" between high school students is prohibited in China. Nevertheless, the "sissy" looks of the F4, now called the "New F4," remains, arousing heated debate over the appropriate standard of masculinity in state and social media, as noted at the beginning of the book.

Compared with the Taiwanese and Japanese series, the images of the F4 in *Meteor Garden* (2018) are notably more feminine, and according to some audience members, they have been dubbed with distinctively "soft" voices (voice actors were used in the drama because the actors' Mandarin pronunciation was not considered sufficiently "standard").[4] In addition, the personality of the male protagonist, Daoming Si, has undergone some significant changes. First, he is depicted as a straight-A student (*xueba*) with a talent for investment, features that are specific to this production. The character may be versatile in other productions, but he is definitely not good at exams. For example, in the Taiwanese production, he uses idioms indiscriminately, and in the Japanese production he does not speak Japanese very well despite being a native speaker. These weaknesses help to create a "man child" image, someone who is a little bit dim and childish but still adorable. In the mainland production, however, academic excellence and a wealthy family background are both reasons for Daoming's arrogance. When he kidnaps Dong Shancai and takes her to his home, he promises her many things in the hope that she will stop fighting him. In the Japanese version, those promises include one billion *yen* and other material comforts, whereas in the Taiwanese version he even offers to buy her the Eiffel Tower. In *Meteor Garden* (2018), however, Daoming tries to tempt Shancai to acquiesce by promising her academic help: "Whenever you have an academic problem, you can come to me!" (episode 1). What is more, unlike the Taiwanese series, in which the F4 are a gang of school bullies, the four young men are now masters of bridge who have formed a bridge club and won many awards for the school. The way they challenge a fellow student is by placing a playing card in his or her locker. Their popularity and hegemony within the school are thus partly based on the intellectual *wen* masculinity, with the fantasy of the luxurious lifestyle of the wealthy minimized. These changes reflect, on the one hand, the fulfillment of the uplifting and aspiring messages required by (self-)censorship in China and, on the other, an elitist emphasis on the quality of superior men in line with the *suzhi* cult, which also explains Daoming's more arrogant and even aggressive attitude toward women in the 2018 production, as elaborated on below.

Second, Daoming is now unbelievably rude and even violent toward women. For example, in episode 1, Daoming deliberately orders take-out food from the small restaurant operated by Shancai's mother to humiliate Shancai. When Shancai arrives, she is provoked by his arrogant attitude and insolence toward the food prepared by her mother and calls him a "parasite on society." A furious Daoming then hits her with the lunchbox, splattering her face, neck, and shirt with greasy food. Inconsistent with her characterization as a brave and tenacious young woman, though, Shancai expresses no anger but acts like a robot after being physically attacked by Daoming. This scene has come in for particular criticism as misogynistic in online comments on the drama. Earlier in the same episode, Daoming pushes Li Zhen, Shancai's best friend and classmate, to the floor when she inadvertently throws a cake at his face. Even more shocking, after discovering that Shancai is interested in Hua Zelei, another member of the F4, a jealous Daoming seizes her by the collar and pushes her up against a wall. He then suddenly kisses the frightened girl as an expression of his love (episode 7). These scenes are reminiscent of the "bossy CEO" leitmotif discussed in the previous chapter.[5] Actually, this seemingly paradoxical characterization of Daoming is not unique to the Chinese version. The similarly patriarchal and violence-prone persona of Daoming in the Taiwanese adaptation has also attracted scholarly attention. The "forced kiss" scene in the Taiwanese version is also presented as a highly desirable expression of romantic passion, as well as an assertion of aggressive masculinity. It is surprising, however, that these male chauvinist elements were not downplayed when the drama was tailored to suit mainland Chinese social conditions. If anything, such patriarchal behavior has even been strengthened. Masculinity, be it derived from intellectual or class superiority or both, appears to justify impolite and even violent behavior toward women.

In contrast to his behavior toward women of his own age, Daoming is cowardly in his interactions with his mother. His father and other male members of the family never appear in the drama. His mother, Daoming Feng, is a powerful woman who strongly opposes his relationship with Shancai because of the young woman's grassroots background. Whereas in the other versions, Daoming protects Shancai from his mother's harassment and insults and does not allow the two women to meet, in the 2018 mainland version he is timid in front of his mother, even obeying her request to bring Shancai home. Once there, the young woman is humiliated by the intimidating mother. Such weakness and obedience toward one's mother reflect recent concerns in Chinese society over the presence of timid *mabao* (mama's boys), as well as the moral obligation of filial piety and a perceived contradiction inherent in the relationship.

The effeminate male beauty aesthetic does not fundamentally challenge traditional gender roles and ideology. Salient examples can also be found in another "youth idol" drama titled *Sweet Combat* (*Tianmi baoji*, 2018), which stars Lu Han, a representative of the controversially effeminate *niangpao* imagery. The plot of this drama is like a reverse version of *Meteor Garden*: the male protagonist Ming Tian comes from a poor family, whereas the female protagonist Fang Yu (Guan Xiaotong) is the daughter of a billionaire. Both are students of boxing at a sports college. Like Daoming Si, Fang is a star student known as the "queen of boxing" in the college. A martial arts fighter of unparalleled ability, she is pretty but haughty in temperament. Ming, by contrast, is humble, gentle, and markedly feminine in appearance. The apparent reversal of traditional gender and power roles is particularly discernible when Fang and her two female friends Cheng Ya'nan (Li Mengmeng) and Song Xiaomi (Shao Yuwei) rescue Ming when he is menaced by gangsters (episode 3).

But, as Stefan Harvey (2019) observes, despite his androgynous looks and soft voice, Ming does not actually transgress traditional gender roles. As the big brother in a single-parent family, he bears the responsibility of looking after his much younger brother and sister and thus plays a paternal role, frequently offering his siblings fatherly guidance. More important, that both Song and Fang fall in love with him and go to considerable lengths to win his affection confirms Ming's heterosexual appeal and ability to command the interest of women. In competing for Ming, the two girls vie with each other to improve their cooking skills. Although Ming carries out domestic chores for his siblings, he eagerly accepts when the girls insist on cooking for his family, and he seems to enjoy the privilege conferred, thereby reinforcing the traditional gendered division of labor (episode 13).

For both the men and women in the drama, the transgression of appearance and codes of dress is contained by a heteronormative binary structure. Fang Yu was called a freak because of her androgynous appearance when she was a child. When she begins dating Ming, however, she readily dresses in the traditional feminine manner, and she always wears feminine outfits when working in the family business. Her best friend Cheng Ya'nan is a typical tomboy, almost exclusively wearing sportswear and keeping her hair short. She even wears a tuxedo to a college dance, garnering praise for looking "handsome" (*shuai*). But she too later takes Fang's advice to wear a feminine outfit when dating, which leads her to win the heart of the man she desires.

These popular youth idol dramas feature a new type of male beauty sparked by a transnational flow of images, promoted by commercial interests, and targeted primarily at young female fans. At the same time, the commercialized cosmopolitan looks of the dramas' characters are contained within domestic concerns over Chineseness. Although the images on display show a tendency toward gender fluidity, and "blurred gender aesthetics feign a liberal attitude to gender, the narrative of the show[s] does little to challenge traditional gender binaries and inequalities, subtly preserving hegemonic masculinities" (Harvey 2019, 1).

THE UNTAMED: BOYS' LOVE OR MALE FRIENDSHIP?

Known as *tanbi* in Japanese,[6] BL is the visual and narrative representation of romantic and sexual relationships between young, good-looking males. It originated from the commercial *shōjo* manga of the early 1970s and spread to other commercial and fan-produced media forms, including *dōjinshi* (fanzines), light novels, anime, drama CDs (audio drama adapted from manga), live action films, collectible figures, video games, and so on. Targeted at adolescent girls and young women, this female-oriented subculture has undergone evolution in recent decades and spread to most East Asian countries.[7] One explanation for the popularity of BL culture in East Asia is that it offers a space for women to imagine an alternative to heteronormativity in societies in which female expressions of sexuality that do not pertain to reproduction are stigmatized or deemed immoral (Y. Li 2020).

In China, BL is known by the Chinese pronunciation of *tanbi*: *danmei*. It has prospered since the late 1990s and "successfully merged with a diverse range of local and global media and celebrity cultures, and developed into a transnational, all-inclusive, and female-dominated meta-fan culture" (Yang and Xu 2017, 3). The primary platform for BL is cyberspace fan creations and serialized online fiction, where explicitly erotic BL content can be found. In TV and film, however, BL is still regarded as a taboo and subject to heavy-handed (self-)censorship, and elements of BL are therefore more ambiguous and more often than not disguised as same-sex friendship regulated by a heteronormative framework.

A recent example of this type of adaptation is the cross-media success of Moxiang Tongchou's (literally, "the smell of ink and coins") online novel *The Grandmaster of Demonic Cultivation* (*Modao zushi*), which was renamed *The Untamed* (*Chenqing ling*, 2019) when adapted into a web drama series. First serialized on the Jinjiang Literature City website between October 2015 and September 2016, *The Grandmaster of Demonic Cultivation* typifies the *xianxia* (fairies and knights-errant) subgenre of online literature, which features a fantasy "world of cultivation." Similar to the *wuxia* (martial arts) world, the *xianxia* world is an imagined space that resembles ancient China but makes no reference to any particular historical period. It is inhabited by adventurers, warriors, and sects who vie with one another for domination and, more importantly, by demons, gods, ghosts, and other supernatural beings. *The Grandmaster of Demonic Cultivation* centers on the adventures of two men, Wei Wuxian, a disciple of the Yunmeng Jiang sect and later founder of the "demonic cultivation" school, and Lan Wangji, the young master of the prestigious Gusu Lan sect. The novel depicts the agonizing love between the two men as they go about the process of learning cultivation skills and investigating a series of plots that could wreak havoc upon the land. They eventually find the mastermind behind the various plots and together defeat him.

The novel is classified as *chun'ai* ("pure love," an alternative term for *danmei*) on the online literature platform to avoid censorship of its BL content, and is also classified as fantasy and *jiakong* (alternate history). Its author, Moxiang, is known for the BL elements in her works. She has published three novels with Jinjiang so far, all of which feature BL romanticism and which have been adapted into other forms of entertainment such as anime and TV dramas. Prior to the release of *The Untamed* in 2019, *The Grandmaster of Demonic Cultivation* had been turned into a radio play, anime, and manga, all of which enjoyed overwhelming popularity. The number of playbacks of the radio play exceeded one billion, and the first (2018) and second (2019) seasons of the anime were rated 8.9/10 and 9/10, respectively, on Douban.

The fifty-episode web drama *The Untamed*, produced by Tencent's Penguin Pictures and Xinpai Media, has been broadcast through Tencent's v. qq.com since June 2019. As of March 2020, it had achieved 7.62 billion playbacks. Two celebrated "little fresh meat" stars of music and film, Xiao Zhan and Wang Yibo, play Wei and Lan, respectively. Both actors started their careers as boy band icons, Wang with the Korean-Chinese group UNIQ and Xiao with the Chinese band X NINE. The drama portrays the duo as soulmates or brothers who regularly pair up to fight evil, and together they investigate a series of murders. There are also scenes showing how the two met and befriended each other as adolescents while studying in the Lan sect's beautiful mountain fortress known as Cloud Recesses, as well as their adventures over the years. In terms of personality, Wei is vivacious and mischievous and is always shown teasing and provoking Lan, whereas Lan is portrayed as righteous and stoic and pretends to be aloof. He also has an aversion to anyone touching his body. The characterization of the two protagonists is very much in line with that commonly found in the heterosexual relationships depicted in many contemporary TV dramas: the relationship between an energetic and passionate woman and a cool, noble man. In fact, although the novel's explicitly homosexual scenes have been removed from the web drama, the latter depicts "palpable sexual tension [between the two men] with microexpressions and lingering eye contact" (figure 17).[8]

Indeed, even before the drama's release, the news that the novel was to be adapted as a TV drama had raised a storm of conjecture among its fans about the possibility of self-censorship of the novel's queerness. One rumor making the rounds was that the emotional bond between Wei and Lan would be replaced by a heterosexual relationship between Wei and Wen Qing, daughter of the head of the evil Wen sect. That rumor prompted such a strong online reaction that the drama's producer took the unusual step of publicly announcing that the audience's views had been heard and would be consid-

Figure 17. Wei Wuxian (left) and Lan Wangji (right) studying together at Cloud Recesses. *The Untamed* (2019).

ered seriously. The end result of this negotiation between commercial drive and official stance was that the emotional link between the two male protagonists was retained in the drama, but in an ambivalent way, being repackaged as brotherhood or friendship rather than romance.[9] Fans of the series have also been careful about not stepping over the red line, avoiding any explicit mention of the show's gay undertones in online chats, but referring to the topic using the misleading but politically charged hashtag "socialist brotherhood" in the hope of avoiding the attention of regulators.

The producer of the drama adeptly capitalized on the novel's established fan base. The defining characteristic of a BL story is the presence of beautiful, young, effeminate-looking men and the conspicuous absence of women. The female characters that do appear in such stories either play minor roles or appear as unsuccessful wooers of one or the other partner in a male pair. None of the male protagonists has a girlfriend or wife. These characteristics are also palpable in *The Untamed*. In fact, the actors who play the male characters, including the two protagonists and the male disciples of the various sects, were carefully selected to cater to the aesthetic standards favored by the BL fandom. The personalities of the two male leads, which are indicative of their active (*gong*) or passive (*shou*) role in a homosexual relationship, also adhere closely to those in the novel. The same adaptation strategy applies to another hit drama adapted from BL fiction: *The Guardian* (*Zhenhun*, 2018).

At the same time, however, a commonly seen strategy for making the male-male relationship less prominent in such dramas is to beef up the role of a female character. In *The Grandmaster of Demonic Cultivation*, Lan has harbored a secret love for Wei ever since their youth and misses three opportunities to confess his affection. When Wei dies, Lan becomes drunk for the first time in his life in an attempt to understand why Wei enjoyed the taste of alcohol, and then, in a fit of drunken grief, he brands his own chest with the iron of the Qishan Wen sect. Thirteen years later, when Wei is resurrected in another person's body, Lan recognizes him and displays jealousy when the resurrected Wei befriends a waiter, causing the waiter to remark that Lan looks as if someone had put his arm around Lan's wife. In *The Untamed*, however, the story has undergone significant modifications. The female warrior Wen Qing (Meng Ziyi) now plays a leading role, and the two men's friendship is much less intense than their relationship in the novel.

As noted in the first chapter of this book, censorship and gender policing in China have rendered queer expressions most discernible in fan activities. As the popular saying goes, "gays through the eyes rot women" (*fuyan kan ren ji*), which is a play on *fujoshi*, or "rotten women," a Japanese term for the female fans of BL content. The implication is that a woman who enjoys fictional gay content is ruined for marriage. These fans are adept at and take pleasure in identifying and inventing male-male romances in mainstream TV shows. Some of them even create videos of their imagined BL couples by professionally editing scenes from the original shows and posting them on such video platforms as bilibili.com and Sina weibo. The jargon for this type of video is "male-male CP (coupling)," a term originating in Japanese ACG culture that is also widely used by fans of Korean pop culture. It originally referred to the practice of imagining nonexistent male-male love in manga or TV dramas by *fujoshi* fans, a practice that has become increasingly popular among TV drama fans in China in recent years, with many male drama characters being "coupled" as gay lovers, sometimes jokingly, by audiences. Some of the female interviewees in this research actually identified themselves as "rotten women," with one attributing her fervent love of BL to her disappointment with "the performing skills of most female stars, such as Angelababy [Yang Ying] and Yang Mi." According to her, female audiences do not accept female leads and thus skip the parts of dramas that feature them to watch male actors alone. Consequently, they would rather imagine a romance between the male lead and a supporting male role in a drama than be "forced" to accept a heterosexual romance between the leading actor and an actress whom they dislike (Ms. Luo, twenty-four-year-old graduate student).

As a subculture targeting young women, *danmei*, or BL, is exerting increasing influence over the aesthetic of the male images in Chinese TV and film. As Zheng Xiqing (2018, 394) points out, however, this booming subculture in China paradoxically relies on the value system of the social mainstream to survive, and thus allows itself to be incorporated into the hierarchical "cultural capital and social capital" of mainstream society. The successful adaptation of BL fiction into mainstream TV or web dramas illustrates such a process of negotiation and containment. BL images and plots are retained out of commercial concerns, but they appear in an ambivalent way, morphing into friendship or brotherhood rather than romance between the male characters. As demonstrated by the foregoing case study of *The Untamed*, despite the popularity of "little fresh meat" images, BL content has to be reduced, regulated, and controlled, because, in the words of Li Yanling (2020), women's obsession with *danmei* is treacherous to both the state and the patriarchy, as it touches upon "all possible taboo[s] in current China": homosexuality, the objectification of men, pornography, and infertility.

LOVE ME, IF YOU DARE: NEGOTIATING "TRANSNATIONAL BUSINESS MASCULINITY"

Considerable changes in audience demographics have taken place in recent years with the rise of web dramas, which are reaching younger, more elite audiences, although they are still confined largely to women. In response to this new viewership, new ideals of manhood are appearing, with a host of transnational male images—including foreigners, returnees from overseas, Chinese students and immigrants living in foreign countries, and white-collar employees of transnational corporations in China—appearing more frequently. The trend demonstrates both a strong desire to see Chinese men depicted in cosmopolitan fashion and a deterritorialized Chinese subjectivity, whether through physical migration or media-inspired imagination.

The 2015 hit drama series *Love Me, If You Dare* (*Ta laile, qing biyan*; literally, "He's coming, please close your eyes"), briefly discussed in chapter 4, puts this new type of masculinity on full display. The twenty-four-episode drama series, a coproduction of the Shandong Film and TV Group and SMG Pictures, is adapted from a popular online novel by Ding Mo and is the first TV drama to successfully expand from an online platform to a traditional TV channel.[10] Series episodes have been simultaneously broadcast on Sohu.com and Dragon TV, a popular Shanghai-based satellite TV station, at 10:00 p.m. every Thursday since October 15, 2015. The program has achieved consistently high ratings and gained exceptional popularity among young audiences with its engaging story lines, creative cinematography, and international ambience (W. Xu 2015). The story line centers on the struggle between a young criminal psychologist named Bo Jinyan (whose English name is Simon), played by Taiwanese actor Wallace Huo, and a dangerous psychopathic killer named Xie Han (Zhang Luyi). Both characters are Chinese men educated in the West. Bo, who is in his late twenties or early thirties, is a professor of criminology at the University of Maryland who moved to the United States with his mother after losing his father at a young age. In the drama, he is depicted as a man with a "high IQ but low EQ." At its outset, he is in China helping the Chinese police to solve a serial murder case. In the process, Bo falls in love with his assistant Jian Yao (whose English name is Jenny and is played by Ma Sichun), a senior university student majoring in English. Together, they gradually come to the realization that all clues point to the killer being Xie, who happens to be an old rival of Bo's. The son of a wealthy family, Xie studied at Princeton University before being expelled because of his "distorted personality." In the second half of the series, which takes place in the United States, Bo, with the help of his close friend Fu Ziyu (Yin Zheng), gains Xie's confidence by making him believe that Bo has a "secondary personality" that desires to be a cold-blooded killer and successfully brings him to justice.

Bo and Fu, who resemble the Holmes and Watson duo, both embody the "tall, rich and handsome" (*gao fu shuai*) ideal, a widely circulated discourse referring to middle- to upper-class men with considerable financial resources and consumer power (see Y. Gong 2016). They also display the aesthetic of feminine male beauty. Wallace Huo is known as a "little fresh meat" star and has a huge female fan base in China, and Fu's appearance is also widely described in online commentary as "feminine" (figure 18). In terms of class background, both men, as well as the evil Xie Han, are returnees from overseas, or *haigui*. The term *haigui*, whose homophonic meaning is "sea turtle," is often half-jokingly used to describe Chinese who have received an education in the West and are thus highly sought after in the job market (see also

Figure 18. Bo Jinyan (left) and Fu Ziyu (right). *Love Me, If You Dare* (2015).

Louie 2015, 73–88). They are a privileged group in terms of knowledge of the world and are considered to be the most cosmopolitan sector of the Chinese population in terms of lifestyle, language, and ways of thinking. In both TV dramas and dating shows, the *haigui* identity always signifies a high level of (heterosexual) desirability. In *Love Me, If You Dare*, Bo and his friend Fu are both graduates of top U.S. universities and can communicate easily with foreigners, such as FBI agent Susan.[11] The term *haigui* is also associated with "cosmopolitan" taste, which is regarded in the popular imagination as superior to and more refined than parochial taste. The elegant European-style villa in which Bo lives and his connoisseurship of coffee and wine serve to illustrate his ample cultural capital and, following Bourdieu (1984), are signs of class distinction and social exclusion.

Strikingly different from the clichéd image of the self-sacrificing policeman, Bo is a workaholic who finds pleasure in fighting perverted killers. Also conspicuously absent is any hint of patriotism in the drama's depiction of the police. As a matter of fact, Bo's work is transnational in nature and demonstrates a cosmopolitan spirit, as it takes the combined effort of cross-national police forces to subdue criminals. He and his assistant and friend are in China one moment and in Hong Kong the next, assisting the Hong Kong police in solving a serial killer case. Then they jet off to the United States to collaborate with their American counterparts. Bo's knowledge and professionalism as a genius and scholar cannot be confined by national borders. Here the obvious influence of *My Love from the Star*, a South Korean TV series that is highly popular among Chinese youths, can be seen. In that series, the male lead is an alien who landed on Earth some four hundred years ago and becomes a professor in modern times. It is clear that the producer of *Love Me, If You Dare* is carefully constructing an image of a cosmopolitan young professional to cater to the tastes and fantasies of young Chinese viewers.

The image of a transnational young male elite conveyed by Bo and his friend Fu is new to the Chinese TV screen. In what follows, I focus on how the bodily rhetoric of "little fresh meat" negotiates with this globally hegemonic form of masculinity. In contemporary gender studies, it is widely acknowledged that rather than a fixed quality, masculinity is inherently historical and that its making and remaking constitute a political process affecting the balance of interests in society and the direction of social change (Connell 2005, 44). As a relational concept, masculinity is always defined in opposition to its others, such as women, racial and sexual minorities, etc., and dominant forms of masculinity are bound up with major forms of social power. Recent studies of masculinities in the West, in particular the work of R. W. Connell, have brought to the fore a form of "hegemonic masculinity" that is associated with global capitalism. Termed "transnational business masculinity," it is represented by globally mobile managers and entrepreneurs (Connell 2005; Connell and Wood 2005). Such men embody the power of transnational capital and "self-consciously manage their bodies and emotions as well as money, and are increasingly detached from older loyalties to nation, business organization, family, and marital partners" (Elias and Beasly 2009, 286).

The cosmopolitan subjectivity of these male images is embodied by the spectacular male body, packaged in a fashionable hairstyle, attire, and appearance closely resembling the style popularized by Korean pop culture. In *Love Me, If You Dare*, Bo is always outfitted in a tight-fitting suit and white shirt, signaling his professionalism and success. He and Fu epitomize the glamor of handsome young professionals with a cosmopolitan vision and tasteful lifestyle. Two aspects of the duo's depiction merit particular attention. The first is the objectification of the male body. Scenes of Bo being tortured by a psycho killer appear repeatedly in the series, with the handsome young psychologist the object of the camera's gaze as it lingers over and closes in on various parts of his seminude body. The second is the homoerotic overtones in the ambiguous relationship between Bo and Fu. Like that between Holmes and Watson, the duo's relationship is akin to master and maid, which to a certain extent is reminiscent of the *yin/yang* hierarchy in same-sex relationships in traditional China (see Song 2004). Fu is so loyal and devoted to Bo that he is concerned with all aspects of Bo's daily life, and he even allows himself to be wounded to protect Bo's girlfriend Jian Yao. Although their friendship is confined within the framework of brotherhood and homosocial bonds within the drama, with no overt suggestion of homosexual love, the pair has become the target of male-male CP fandom recreation through online and simultaneous comments. Both of the aspects singled out above represent trends and imaginaries that are new to the depiction of masculinities on the Chinese TV screen, perhaps validating the point raised by Lisa Rofel in her discussion of the articulation of desires for the purpose of cultural belonging. For her, the meaning of sex and sexuality in a transnational setting "lies at the heart of cultural citizenship" (Rofel 2007, 95). Both the *fujoshi* fad for male-male intimacy and the imagination of gayness as something Western and transnational reflect a passion for "cosmopolitan" desires in the process of subjectification.

But despite the preoccupation with a cosmopolitan subject and lifestyle in *Love Me, If You Dare*, a noteworthy tendency in the drama is its representation of Chinese men as "super brains" to whom men of other races and nationalities cannot hold a candle. The drama's cosmopolitan men represent an image of China and Chineseness worthy of being presented to the world. In this sense, the renegotiation of China's place in the world is being effected not only through consumption but also through an imagined essentialist superiority. The entire series centers on the intellectual combat between two Chinese men (Bo and his nemesis, the psychopathic killer Xie), or, to be more precise, two overseas Chinese men. White men, be they criminals or policemen, appear in the series only as assistants or accomplices. The American policemen appear particularly foolish and stubborn in juxtaposition to the two Chinese men's superior wisdom. This fantasy of superiority is also seen in the episodes in which the trio of Bo, Fu, and Jian assists the local police in Hong Kong, a place that, according to Haiyan Lee, signifies an ambiguous and awkward position in the Self/Other dichotomy and whose people are represented as Chinese who need "to be renationalised" (Lee 2014, 272). When investigating serial killer cases, the Hong Kong police do nothing but follow the instructions of Bo, who appears haughty but is infallibly correct. This handsome man thus represents an idealized version of cosmopolitan masculinity, which is characterized and validated by professionalism, wisdom, knowledge, and, above all, confidence.

SISSYPHOBIA AND THE POLITICS OF NATIONALISM

Although effeminate male images generally do not constitute a threat or challenge to the patriarchal or male-dominated mainstream ideology, they have still generated concerns over unconventional gender expressions in the media, as well as in real life. Although there is a diverse range of opinions regarding the *niangpao* aesthetic, it is noteworthy that many are expressed in nationalistic terms. For instance, in the debate over male effeminacy and its alleged harmfulness to China's next generation sparked by the appearance of the New F4 in CCTV's back-to-school program, the most widely circulated and quoted comment has been "the effeminacy of young men today means an effeminate China tomorrow" (*shaonian niang ze Zhongguo niang*).

This saying first emerged on the Internet when France won the FIFA World Cup championship in July 2018. One sensational online post juxtaposes the macho image of the French football player Kylian Mbappé Lottin with that of the Chinese boy band TFBoys overlaid with the text: "They are both 19 years old. Strong young men promise a strong country, effeminate young men forebode an effeminate country" (figure 19). This comparison of "normal" Western masculinity with effeminate Chinese masculinity reveals long-standing frustration with the failures of the Chinese football team. China has qualified for the World Cup only once, in 2002, and failed to score a single goal in that tournament. Criticism, remorse, and sarcasm fill social media every year in which the World Cup is held, with China's netizens clearly regarding the Chinese team's failures as a source of national shame. Some commentators have attributed those failures to deficiencies in China's education system, which allegedly produces weak men short of stamina and vitality.

Official media outlets have published several articles and editorials in response to the censure of effeminate stars. Although some of them call for greater tolerance toward gender and appearance diversity, most denounce excessive femininity in men for harming the nation and subscribe to a more "uplifting and healthy" masculinity. In an editorial published five days after

图中文字：同样的19岁 少年强、则国强

同样19岁 少年娘、则国娘

Figure 19. Online post juxtaposing the masculine image of French football player Kylian Mbappé Lottin (left) with the feminine image of the Chinese boy band TFBOYS (right).

The First School Class aired in 2018, the official Xinhua News Agency described the aesthetic trend that the New F4 represent as "morbid." The editorial warrants a lengthy quote:

"Sleek hair, creamy face, and an A4 waist; affected manner and orchid fingers." These words describe the staggering image and manners of some of the "little fresh meat" idols who are popular today. While the images, words, and behaviors of these *niangpao* stars flood the screen and attract increasing hype and puffery, some have begun to express their concerns about and reflections on this abnormal phenomenon, which "makes your eyes sting." Unlike "cross-dressing" for the purpose of artistic expression, the *niangpao* trend reflects an affected and distorted persona. These men look androgynous, with delicate makeup and a slim but frail physique and use coquettish language. They not only perform like this in film and TV but also behave in this way in variety shows and in real life.

From being "fresh" to "beautiful" and then to "womanish," the evolution of this morbid aesthetic is thought-provoking. [. . .] It is a new variation of the decadent and grandiose tendency in entertainment circles. With various star-making campaigns, "flower boys" have been propelled into "traffic stars." [. . .] Justified by "appearance is power," some bad actors are being paid lavishly and have become spoiled [celebrities]. With the wrong mindset of "entertainment comes first" and "traffic is the king," some film and TV programs, online platforms, and variety shows meticulously pander to low tastes and make money through displaying weird "freaks," as much as challenging the commonly accepted order and morals. They reek of oddity-hunting, money fetishism, and decadence.

The function of culture is education. The reason the *niangpao* phenomenon has caused public aversion is because its negative impact on adolescents can never be underestimated. Our youth are the future of our nation. [. . .] What the popular culture of a country embraces, resists, and spreads is a matter significant for the future of the country. To cultivate the new generation of our times, who shoulder the mission of national rejuvenation, we need to resist the erosion of bad culture and [embrace] the nutrition of superb culture.[12]

The term "A4 waist" gained traction during a social media trend that began in China in which people, mostly women, post pictures of themselves holding a piece of A4 paper vertically in front of their torso to show that their waist is narrower than the paper's 8.3-inch width. By extension, it has become a symbol of the feminine manner of talking and moving about. "Traffic stars" are celebrities who attract a high volume of digital traffic on social media and, because of their popularity, are highly sought after by both the advertising and entertainment industries.

An article published by the WeChat account of the official *People's Daily* echoes this nationalist concern over "harmful" masculinity and resorts to Chinese soldiers to find an exemplar of the "sunny and robust" manhood needed by the nation. The article also maintains that the inner quality of a man, such as his degree of cultural cultivation and his patriotic sentiment, weighs much more than his appearance, citing the feminine but patriotic Peking Opera actors Mei Lanfang (1894–1961) and Cheng Yanqiu (1904–1958) as examples.[13] The military's *China National Defense Daily* published an editorial on the same day advocating that young men foster true manhood and rid themselves of femininity by serving in the army.[14]

The campaign against effeminate male celebrities was followed by the news, disclosed in social media, that the authorities had issued a directive mandating the blacklisting of all "sissy" actors on the small screen. Although no such directive has so far materialized publicly, it is a fact that scheduled performances by the boy bands TFBoys and NINE PERCENT were never aired and that a number of effeminate-looking male stars have disappeared from TV programs. The news, however, also led to controversy over the definition of *niangpao* and to whom it applies.[15] More recently, in the wake of the arrest of the male star Wu Yifan in July 2021, following an online outcry over sexual assault allegation against him, the government has launched a new and unprecedentedly intensive wave of condemning effeminate celebrities and even ordered to remove effeminate images in games to avoid "feminization" of young men.[16]

The criticisms of *niangpao* in social media have been particularly vitriolic, manifesting anxiety over the effeminacy and weakness of Chinese men compared with an imagined Other, Western, or Japanese men, who embody a strong and intimidating masculinity. For example, one online article asks readers the following: If "Japan cultivates wild wolves, and we cultivate sissies, how can we win a war in the future?" After comparing education in Japan, where the tough training of boys to instill stamina and perseverance starts from kindergarten, with China's exam-oriented education, which produces "frail" men, the article's author attributes the popularity of stars who are "neither men nor women" to the defects of Chinese education.[17] Another critic of the aesthetic under study refers to moments in Chinese history when a weak Chinese civilization was invaded and destroyed by northern tribes to illustrate that "a nation that lacks martial spirit is doomed to decline." This critic goes on to insultingly liken casting the "sissy" actor Lu Han as a masculine boxer in *Sweet Combat* to "hiring a eunuch to be the spokesman for Viagra," noting that such sissies should be eliminated like "the harmful four pests" (namely, rats, bedbugs, flies, and mosquitoes).[18] As noted above, the nationalist sentiments in these comments paradoxically display a tendency toward self-Orientalism, a tendency to regard Western masculinity as the norm and Chinese men as inadequate imitators of their white peers.

The resulting anxiety has also sparked suspicion of the West and even conspiracy theories about the emasculation of Chinese men. One online article asks, for example, "Do you know how hard the CIA works in order to make you a fan of *niangpao*?"[19] According to its author, this type of effeminate imagery originated in postwar Japan, specifically in the male idols created and promoted by Johnny & Associates, the production agency behind numerous popular boy bands in Japan. The agency's founder, Johnny Kitagawa, a U.S.-born and-educated returnee, was a secret CIA agent, as well as a pedophile who liked young, good-looking boys, the author further contends. With funding from the U.S. Army, this ostensible talent manager trained and promoted effeminate male bands, whose popularity effectively reduced the "aggressiveness and revolutionariness" of the Japanese and cultivated among the Japanese people an affinity for American culture. The aesthetic Kitagawa promoted later spread to South Korea and China. As a result, the author concludes, while the younger generation in the United States watches "Captain America, Iron Man, and Spider-Man," the screens in China, Japan, and Korea are occupied by "little fresh meat" idols. In fact, no historical evidence of Kitigawa being a CIA agent can be found. It is likely that the rumor, if not a story fabricated out of thin air, was caused by a misunderstanding of the word "agent," as Kitigawa was the head of a production agency. During my interviews, however, I found this story of political conspiracy to enjoy widespread currency among middle-aged and older people, who discursively link sissiness with abnormality, evil schemes, and a dire threat to national security.

Such sissyphobic comments and government censorship moves have attracted some refutations in social media, with some commentators informed by feminist thought calling for greater tolerance of and respect for individual appearance preferences and diversity in views of masculinity.[20] Interestingly, however, arguments on both sides of the debate are often expressed in nationalist terms. One historical figure that both camps cite to support their argument is Mei Lanfang, the aforementioned Peking Opera master who exclusively played the female *dan* role. Off stage, Mei is renowned for his heroic sporting of a beard during the Japanese Occupation to demonstrate his resolution not to perform for the Japanese. The liberal camp uses him as an example to show that a man with an effeminate appearance can display patriotic spirit. In other words, a man can be soft on the outside but strong and courageous on the inside. The rebuttal from *niangpao* opponents is that today's *niangpao* cannot hold a candle to Mei in terms of moral cultivation, and that it is thus an insult to Mei to be mentioned in the same breath as *niangpao* actors.[21] This example shows how arguments over the *niangpao* phenomenon negotiate interior and exterior qualities at different times, and further explains the entangled interconnection between manhood and nationhood. The vitriolic language used against certain effeminate-looking celebrities and claims to national essence or biological essentialism both highlight anxiety over the need to "get it right" when presenting Chinese men on screen and stage (Harvey 2019).

In a pioneering study on Chinese media reactions to male effeminacy from 2005 to 2012, Tiantian Zheng (2015b, 365) argues that such reactions are a response to "the broad cultural changes produced by market reforms."

Figure 20. Oho Ou as Ye Ting in *The Founding of an Army* (2017) (left) and the actor in a feminine pose (right).

In a globalized age, "distinctive gender roles are considered crucial in safeguarding the security of the nation" and are controlled and monitored through media discourse (T. Zheng 2015b, 365). Such concerns can be seen in the open letter written in August 2017 by Ye Daying, a film director and grandson of late Red Army general Ye Ting, to protest the casting of "little fresh meat" actors as revolutionaries in the blockbuster film *The Founding of an Army (Jianjun daye,* 2017), which commemorated the ninetieth anniversary of the founding of the People's Liberation Army. A particular complaint was that the twenty-four-year-old "effeminate" star Ou Hao (a.k.a. Oho Ou), who plays Ye's grandfather in the film, was not masculine enough for the role and that the casting of so many good-looking, boyish stars as real-life historical figures constituted a distortion of revolutionary history. Referring to a photo of Ou in which the actor leans against a wall with one leg bent backward (figure 20), Ye angrily questions the film's directors: "By appointing this unmanly 'little fresh meat' [actor], who cannot even stand tall, to play Ye Ting, who do you think you are insulting?"[22] Ye's sissyphobic attitude illustrates the tension between the masculinist discourse on revolution and nationalism and commercialized male images.

The diverse range of opinions regarding the reception of "little fresh meat" actors was also reflected in my focus group discussions and interviews with TV audiences. Among the seven subgroups of focus group participants (see chapter 1), retirees were the most averse to such images, and white-collar females were the most sympathetic. A majority of the participating female university students and white-collar employees claimed to be fans of popular actors in this category, including Lu Han, Wu Yifan, Yang Yang, Wang Yibo, Xiao Zhan, and Wang Junkai, and some described themselves as fanatical fans of the BL romance genre.

When discussing why this weak and effeminate type of male beauty is now popular among young women in China, several female informants related the phenomenon to female empowerment rather than to direct influence from Korea or Japan:

> Many of my female friends prefer the "little fresh meat" [type] to the muscular type [of man]. Maybe that's because today's girls are more independent and stronger. They like to be the manipulating party in a relationship. The macho type of man cannot give them a sense of security. On the contrary, [the muscular male body] is sometimes associated with domestic violence and male chauvinism. The "little fresh meat" [type of man], however, makes us feel comfortable and safe. Many of them can be a considerate and thoughtful "warm man" (*nuan nan*) at the same time. They are docile and adorable. (Ms. Li, twenty-one-year-old university student)

Ms. Li's comments echo a point raised at the beginning this chapter, that the "little fresh meat" image represents a reversal of the conventional male gaze and a new direction in gender relations.

While most of the young female informants used the term "little fresh meat" rather than *niangpao*, which indicates excessive femininity, in their comments, the retired group, especially the male members of that group, used the two terms interchangeably. For them, both "little fresh meat" and *niangpao* represented a worrying aesthetic trend for the young men of China.

Echoing the largely disapproving comments in the media, they attributed the popularity of the aesthetic to the malign influence of non-Chinese cultures and, paradoxically, lamented that the men who embrace it "disgrace the Chinese people" (*diu Zhongguoren de lian*). They also agreed that the "neither-men-nor-women" (*bu nan bu nü*) type of image reflects the "profit-before-everything mentality" (*yiqie xiang qian kan*) of the entertainment industry. One informant singled out the character played by Lu Han in *Sweet Combat* for particular criticism, describing it as "most bizarre" (*feiyi suosi*) to cast such a sissy actor as a masculine boxer (Mr. Zhang, sixty-year-old retiree). Another male informant went so far as to say that if Lu were his son, he would "break his legs" for his sissy appearance and manner (Mr. Hu, sixty-five-year-old retiree).

By contrast, the female informants above the age of fifty were less vitriolic and tended to make a distinction between "facial attractiveness" (*yanzhi*) and "sissiness" (*niang*), with the former referring to male beauty within heterosexual parameters and the latter to a disturbing transgression of established gender boundaries. One female retiree commented:

> Many women of my age love "little fresh meat." This is easy to understand: everyone tends to love the beautiful (*aimei zhixin ren jie you zhi*). As society becomes rich, there is nothing wrong with men becoming more delicate (*jingzhi*). However, men must behave like men. When they become too feminine, I believe most women cannot stand it. I, for one, cannot figure out why effeminate *niangpao* stars, with their skinny arms and legs and heavily powdered faces, still have a market. Gay men will like this type, of course, but how about others? What's wrong with them? (Ms. Xue, fifty-three-year-old retiree)

As for the young male informants, their views were mixed and largely determined by such factors as their education level and class background. Generally speaking, university students and middle-class men from larger cities adopted a more open-minded attitude toward the trend, and some of them were even imitators of the "little fresh meat" style in terms of hairstyle and dress. The male migrant worker group, however, showed an obvious aversion and even hostility toward effeminate-looking stars. Calling them "abnormal," one such informant said that he was confused about why so many girls liked that type of man (Mr. Zhuo, twenty-four-year-old supermarket assistant). Another displayed an indifferent attitude, laughingly commenting that both the female fans and male imitators of the "little fresh meat" style are "just rich enough" and "have nothing else to do" (*chi bao le cheng de*) (Mr. Li, twenty-six-year-old factory worker).

CONCLUSION

This chapter situates the prevalence of male effeminacy in contemporary China and the backlash against it in a wider social, cultural, and political context and thus fills an important gap in the study of men and masculinities in contemporary China.[23] The "little fresh meat" story is part of a larger story of growing gender diversity and its dynamic interaction with the commercialized media in postsocialist China. As the product of transnational flows of images and fashions, effeminate male images in Chinese TV and film and the aesthetic trend induced by them effectively mediate between queer masculinities and locally rooted discourse and ideology. The rise and popularity of such "sissy" actors need to be understood within the mechanisms of star making and the entertainment industry. For example, genre development in TV dramas (such as Chinese historical costume dramas featuring romance themes), helped in no small way by existing web romance novels, manga, and animation productions with similar plot lines, has created a massive industry in constant need of finding more "little fresh meat" to fill the roles of stock characters in romance stories.

The "little fresh meat" image represents a significant reversal of the hegemonic male gaze on women through commodification of the male body. Young heterosexual women are the primary target audience for this type of male beauty. Intertwined with the BL subculture, this trend of male effeminacy attests to both the empowerment of women along with China's economic growth and significant changes in female subjectivity and desires. More often than not, the most explicit queer meanings of the male images therein are created and circulated through re-creations and interactive communications among these female fans.

This chapter addresses regional and civilizational differences in queer masculinities by differentiating sissiness in the heterosexual context from effeminacy in the gay context. Media analysis and audience reception studies reveal that manhood and nationhood are closely linked in the severe criticism that this type of "shameful" male aesthetic has attracted, as well as in the anxiety expressed over what an effeminate younger generation will mean for China.

CHAPTER 7

Womanhood and the Many Faces of Chineseness

IMAGES OF WOMEN have long been interwoven with the image of China and reflect contesting imaginations of Chineseness. The Maoist canon notoriously represents asexual, selfless, and brave female soldiers, peasants, and workers, as exemplified by the *Red Detachment of Women*, a ballet performed for U.S. president Richard Nixon during his visit to China in February 1972. Since the late 1970s, the reform period has seen a proliferation of "virtuous wife and good mother" images in literature, film, and TV, a notable example being Liu Huifang in the 1990 TV drama series *Yearnings*, who arguably combines socialist morality with traditional womanhood (Rofel 2007; Wang and Mihelj 2019). Productivist and nationalist values have generated new female images such as the hardworking and self-reliant female employees and peasant women who allegorize the nation, the latter exemplified by the female protagonist in Mo Yan's Red Sorghum series. In recent years, Chinese television has presented an increasingly diverse repertoire of female images, including housewives, white-collar office ladies, domestic helpers, entrepreneurs, and historical figures. Women's changing roles in the family and workplace, along with the new lifestyles and identities associated with them, constitute an important dimension of a modernizing China on the small screen (S. Kong 2008; Y. Huang 2008; L. Li 2011; H. Lee 2014; Cai 2014; Xiao 2014; Wang and Mihelj 2019).

WOMEN, FAMILY, AND MODERNITY

As has been discussed in other Asian contexts, what constitutes an "acceptable" femininity has been a critical issue in the debates surrounding modernity and national identity, inasmuch as "images of modern women have been upheld as a sign of social-economic progression while they have simultaneously been reconfigured to support a distinctive national identity through an 'invented' tradition" (Y. Huang 2008, 104). A salient example is the influential argument in the campaign to "remasculinize" the Chinese nation at the end of the Cultural Revolution that Chinese women had become too strong and no longer looked like women. This supposedly was because of the revolutionary-era Maoist ideology that "men and women are the same," with the result being that Chinese men had suffered mental castration (Zhong 2000; Song 2010). Intellectuals making that argument called for the restoration of such traditional Chinese womanly virtues as selfless motherhood, diligence in housework, obedience to one's husband, and filial piety toward one's in-laws.

Liu Huifang, the female protagonist in *Yearnings*, epitomizes a male fantasy of ideal womanhood. The drama, produced at a time of political crisis after the 1989 Tiananmen Square crackdown, reflects both official sanction for and the popular pursuit of the restoration of traditional values in terms of gender and interpersonal relationships. Liu (Zhang Kaili), an ordinary factory worker, demonstrates kindheartedness and self-sacrifice by marrying a college student with an unfavorable class background during the Cultural Revolution, only to be deserted by him once his situation improves. She also brings up an abandoned disabled child despite her husband's objections, and then returns the girl to her biological parents when they emerge. The drama's unprecedentedly warm reception in the early 1990s, according to Lisa Rofel, was "suffused with reimagined possibilities of national identity" (2007, 33). Reading the story as a political allegory of nation-ness, Rofel argues that it constructs and negotiates a new vision of Chineseness through Chinese femininity inasmuch as "a new emphasis on sexual difference has replaced a Maoist vision of unmarked, nongendered bodies" (Rofel 2007, 62).

A more recent character of a similar type is Qin Huairu, who is featured in *The Courtyard* (*Qingman siheyuan*, 2015), a forty-six-episode TV drama series produced by Yizhao Tianxia Media Company and Beijing Happiness Film and TV Company. The series, which won a China TV Golden Eagle Award in 2018, focuses on the lives of several families living in a traditional courtyard house in Beijing over a thirty-year span beginning in 1966, the first year of the Cultural Revolution. Qin Huairu (Hao Lei) is a female factory worker whose husband died as a result of a workplace accident when she was pregnant with their third child. The widowed Qin leads a tough life looking after three small children and her late husband's mother. She has to please others

to obtain extra food for her children from the factory canteen and is sometimes sexually harassed by her male coworkers. Her neighbor in the courtyard house, a man named He Yuzhu (He Bing), also known as Shazhu (literally, "silly as a pillar"), is a cook in the canteen who often helps her by secretly
bringing food from the canteen to her children. The two eventually develop
a relationship and marry. At the same time, Shazhu is seduced by another
woman living in the courtyard, Lou Xiao'e (Wei Zibing), who later bears his
child. She then migrates to Hong Kong with her family. In the early 1990s,
Lou, now a wealthy businesswoman, returns to Beijing and invites Shazhu to
work as a chef in her restaurant. After a number of conflicts and frustrations,
the magnanimous Qin is eventually reconciled with her love rival, and she
and her husband convert the courtyard house into a nursing home for the
elderly with investment funds from Lou. Under Qin's meticulous care, the
elderly members of several families in the courtyard live happily together in
the new nursing home, which is named Happiness Courtyard.

When asked about characters in TV dramas who embody traditional
womanly virtues, several informants in the retiree group cited Qin Huairu in
unison. What makes Qin an ideal woman, they said, is primarily her consideration for others, whether her husband, son, or mother-in-law, in difficult
circumstances. For example, when she falls in love with Shazhu and the two
plan to get married, her eldest son, a teenager at the time, strongly opposes
the marriage because of courtyard gossip. Out of consideration for her son's
feelings, Qin postpones the marriage for eight years until he finally accepts
Shazhu as his adoptive father. Qin lives with her late husband's elderly
mother and takes care of her for years without complaint despite the woman's selfish and interfering nature. At one point, when the old woman suspects that Qin and Shazhu are having an affair, she even slaps Qin across the
face (episode 16) (figure 21). Nevertheless, Qin remains a filial daughter-in-
law throughout. Another example of Qin's selflessness comes in episode 42.
When her doctor suspects that she may have cancer and suggests a thorough
examination, Qin hides the laboratory test orders because she is reluctant to
spend a cent on herself when the nursing home is in need of money. What is
more, she decides to divorce Shazhu so that he can be with Lou. Her selflessness and forbearance move even her love rival, and the cancer suspicion
turns out to be a false alarm. The informants also praised the virtues of womanhood that Qin displays in taking good care of the courtyard's old people,
behavior reminiscent of the Confucian directive to "care for all aged people
as if they were your own parents."[1]

Figure 21. Qin Huairu after being slapped by her mother-in-law. *The Courtyard* (2015).

One informant observed that the character is "realistic and not perfect": she has to endure verbal insults from the men in her factory for the sake of a little food, and she even deliberately ruins Shazhu's dates with other women on several occasions so as not to lose her "silly pillar." As a weak, widowed woman, she has no other choice. Her "selfishness" is not for herself but for the elderly and children who rely on her to survive. Indeed, this kind of selfishness enhances the richness and verisimilitude of the character, highlighting her powerful survival drive and garnering her understanding and respect (Mr. Yu, sixty-five-year-old retiree). Everything she suffers and sacrifices is for the sake of her family and, by extension, the big family constituted by the courtyard's residents. Women like Qin thus function symbolically as the cornerstone of the "harmonious society" that the state seeks to build.

As an important element in national strengthening through the father, President Xi Jinping has designated the family as the moral foundation of Chinese civilization and, to tremendous domestic media fanfare, emphasized the importance of "the family, family education, and family values" (*zhuzhong jiating, zhuzhong jiajiao, zhuzhong jiafeng*) in building a harmonious society.[2] With the state's open embrace of Confucian values, such as filial piety and traditional gender roles, this imperative articulates "women's familiar obligations to the maintenance of social stability" (Wu and Dong 2019, 478). In response, "family drama," a subgenre of TV drama that focuses on family relationships, in-law relationships in particular, has flourished in recent years. The past two decades have witnessed numerous TV dramas that center on the sometimes difficult relationship between mothers-in-law and daughters-in-law: *The Mother-in-Law* (*Popo*, 2004), *The Spicy Mother-in-Law* (*Mala poxi*, 2006), *The Double-Sided Tape* (*Shuangmian jiao*, 2007), *The Beautiful Time of a Daughter-in-Law* (*Xifu de meihao shidai*, 2009), *The Mother-in-Law Has Come* (*Popo laile*, 2010), *The Cheerful Mother-in-Law and Pretty Daughters-in-Law* (*Huanxi popo qiao xifu*, 2010), *When the Mother-in-Law Meets the Mother* (*Dang popo yushang ma*, 2011), *The Life of Two Cities* (*Shuangcheng shenghuo*, 2011), *How a Daughter-in-Law Is Tempered* (*Xifu shi zenyang liancheng de*, 2012), *The Beautiful Manifesto of a Daughter-in-Law* (*Xifu de meihao xuanyan*, 2012), *The Mother-in-Law Is Also Your Mom* (*Popo ye shi ma*, 2012), *The Mothers and In-Laws of the Only Child* (*Dusheng zinü de popo mama*, 2013), and *Love Is for Happiness* (*Yinwei aiqing you xingfu*, 2016). The large number and popularity of these dramas reflect both the social attention paid to this thorniest of family relationships in a fast-transforming society and the state's agenda to construct the harmonious family as the cornerstone of a stable society. Femininity, as articulated and negotiated in the domestic space in family dramas, is intertwined with and embedded in a variety of tensions and hierarchies in Chinese society, such as the urban-rural divide, cultural competition between southern and northern China, issues arising from the one-child policy, the ever-widening generation gap, and so on. These dramas also convey a paradoxical attitude toward (the imagination of) tradition and modernity. On the one hand, they promote "a [generally] traditional and conservative moral outlook in which harmony and stability prevail" (S. Kong 2008, 83). On the other, they register the frustrations of a younger generation attempting to balance the traditional family structure with their desire for a modern lifestyle.

Another distinctive type of family drama is the "chronicle of ordinary people" through which the history of the PRC is narrated in keeping with the official story (S. Kong 2008, 84). Dramas of this type are particularly well-received by middle-aged and elderly audiences because they evoke nostalgic memories of the old days. Popular examples include *The Years of Burning Passion* (*Jiqing ranshao de suiyue*, 2001), *Golden Marriage* (*Jinhun*, 2007), *Wang Gui and Anna* (*Wang Gui yu Anna*, 2009), *The Romance of Our Parents* (*Fumu aiqing*, 2014), and, more recently, *A Little Woman under the Zhengyang Gate* (*Zhengyangmen xia xiaonüren*, 2018).[3] Following a similar pattern, these dramas all depict evolving historical events through the lens of one or several Chinese families and, without exception, highlight how wealth has dramatically changed the lives and fates of ordinary people since the implementation of China's reform policies. Family narratives thus help to legitimize Deng's contention that "development is the only hard truth." Compared with the "scar literature" of the early 1980s or films such as Zhang Yimou's *To Live* (1994),[4] however, family chronicle TV dramas largely downplay the dark chapters in PRC history, such as the Anti-rightist Movement (1957), Great Leap Forward (1958), and Cultural Revolution (1966–1976), in keeping with President Xi's historical vision: "the Mao era and post-Mao era are an indivisible whole. . . . [T]he Reform period cannot be used to criticise the Mao era, and vice versa" (Lovell 2019, 447). Thus, instead of a catastrophe, the Mao era is portrayed as a period of temporary difficulty or even a memorable experience for some such as the "sent-down" youths.[5]

An indispensable character in family chronicle dramas is the virtuous, forgiving, and capable mother who endures any hardship to provide for her children. The family is thus an allegory of the nation and women a benchmark of social change. A notable example is Xu Huizhen (Jiang Wenli) in *A Little Woman under the Zhengyang Gate*. A native of Beijing, Xu bolsters the family's fortunes by developing a small wine shop given to her by her father-in-law into a giant enterprise. Under her leadership, her taciturn husband and their three daughters all become executives of the company. What remains unchanged throughout, however, is the alleged merits of Chinese womanhood that she embodies, namely kindheartedness, diligence, perseverance, and a strong sense of justice.

Women are not only bound by tradition in Chinese television, but also function as a symbol of modernity or embodiment of the conflict between tradition and modernity. Compared with the "virtuous wife and good mother" type of female image, an increasing number of strong women who outperform men in the workplace while commanding the sexual interest of more than one man are appearing on the small screen. Dramas featuring strong female leads of this type, which are described in the Chinese press and on social media as "supreme heroine (*da nü zhu*) dramas," have brought forth a new possibility of gendered Chineseness. The heroines in these dramas are beautiful, ambitious, and empowered by "intelligence, competence, assertiveness, and willpower" (Bai 2020, 363). Although sometimes victimized by the patriarchal tradition of preferring sons to daughters, through their own efforts they manage to overcome the power of such tradition and gain respect in the male-dominated society. Their stories thus illustrate the self-improvement (*ziqiang*) advocated in the Chinese Dream discourse. Two prominent examples in this regard are Su Mingyu (Yao Chen) in *All Is Well* (*Dou tinghao*, 2018) and Fang Sijin (Sun Li) in *I Will Find You a Better Home* (*Anjia*, 2019). Both are recent hit dramas that have provoked heated public debate on gender issues.

In the forty-six-episode *All Is Well*, which was adapted from a homonymous novel by the female entrepreneur-writer Ah Nai, Su Mingyu impresses the audience as an independent, rebellious, and assertive career woman. She is the youngest child in the Su family and has two older brothers. As she grows up, her mother, a domineering woman who adheres to the traditional mindset of prioritizing boys over girls, allots the family's limited educational resources to her two sons and treats her daughter unfairly. In events that take place before the series begins, Mingyu's parents sell off parts of their residence to send the eldest son to the United States for graduate studies, and they also spend substantial sums on the younger son's wedding and to purchase him an apartment. But they refuse to pay Mingyu's university tuition and forcibly enroll her in an inexpensive teacher training college, even though she is a much better student than either of her brothers and has the potential to enter a top-ranking university. When the aggrieved Mingyu—who left home and stopped relying on her parents economically at the age of eighteen—asks her mother why she has been treated so unfairly, her mother bluntly gives the deeply hurtful response: "You're a girl. How can you compare with your two brothers?" (episode 2). As the series begins, Mingyu is a top-level sales manager who is favored by her wealthy boss. Living in a luxurious apartment that she owns, she is the wealthiest of the three siblings. Despite her mother's mistreatment, she pays all the funeral expenses when her mother dies. As the eldest brother is living in the United States and the second brother has proved to be a loser in both his career and marriage, Mingyu's widowed father moves in with her despite her long-standing agreement with her parents that she would not be responsible for supporting them in their old age because, as a daughter, she would not inherit any family property.

In the final episode of the series, Mingyu's father is diagnosed with Alzheimer's disease. As both of her brothers are now living overseas, she decides to give up her highly paid job to become her father's full-time caregiver. When he becomes lost on the eve of Chinese New Year, an anxious Mingyu eventually finds him near the family's old house clutching a student workbook that he claims he bought for his daughter. Mingyu recognizes it as

Figure 22. Su Mingyu and her father after the two are reconciled at the end of the series. *All Is Well* (2018).

the workbook she had wanted to buy when she was a secondary school student but her mother had not approved. The two walk back home hand in hand. After arriving, they sit on the couch and exchange New Year's greetings remotely with Mingyu's two brothers, with whom she is now reconciled. "It is so good to have a family," Mingyu sighs. The drama ends with a flashback of her mother comforting her when, as a little girl, she has been bullied by her middle brother (episode 46).

This ending was considered unacceptable by many viewers, women in particular. Online comments suggested that it was "contrived" for Mingyu to give up her career and return to the family, even if only temporarily. The character has also been criticized for forgiving her brothers and reconciling with them after all the bullying and mistreatment she has suffered at their hands.[6] One subplot highlighted by some audience members involves the younger brother, Su Mingcheng (Guo Jingfei), who is prone to violence and is shown beating up his adult sister on several occasions. In episode 21, when Mingcheng surmises that Mingyu plans to harm him by deliberately ruining his wife's career, he rushes to his sister's house and punches her when she gets out of her car. Mingyu is so seriously injured that she has to be hospitalized. She is initially angry and swears that she will put her brother in jail, but she is finally persuaded by her family members to withdraw her lawsuit against Mingcheng. Later in the series, she even helps Mingcheng's wife to get a promotion.

Indeed, as many viewers have pointed out, all three men in the Su family are despicable and deserving of heavy criticism from a feminist perspective. The father, Su Daqiang (Ni Dahong), is selfish and appears weak in front of his wife. He never makes any attempt to protect his daughter from bullying or other maltreatment but is ready to take advantage of her and her boyfriend when he is old. The eldest son, Su Mingzhe (Gao Xin), is concerned with face and refuses to let any members of the Su family know when he loses his job. It is only with his sister's secret help that he is able to find a new job. The younger son is emotionally immature as an adult. He is good at currying favor with his mother while she is alive and shamelessly relies on his parents economically. When frustrated with work, he slaps his wife, which eventually leads to their divorce. In a sense, the three men are portrayed as embodiments of the stereotypical weaknesses of Chinese men. They are so disliked by viewers that someone set up a service on the e-commerce site Taobao to allow TV fans to pay to curse them.[7] By contrast, the wives of the two brothers appear to be reasonable and level-headed.[8]

The overwhelming response to the series to some extent reflects grave concerns about gender discrimination in China. Many female audience members have reportedly associated the experiences of Su Mingyu with their own life stories or those of people around them. In defending the ending against online criticism, Yao Chen, the actress who plays Mingyu, commented on Weibo that "Su Daqiang's love for his daughter is only revealed after he loses most of his memory, and Mingyu realizes that she can love her father only when he can't respond to her. It is all about missed love in life."[9] Such a reading has, however, been rebutted by some netizens as "self-deceiving" (ziqi qiren). One young woman in my focus group also commented that the drama's ending attempts to downplay gender discrimination through an "all is well" illusion. To make the audience feel more comfortable with the family's reconciliation, she added, the drama discloses several hidden facts toward the end, such as that Mingyu's mother had had to sacrifice her own career when she found herself accidently pregnant with her third child, Mingyu. This informant, however, found this explanation to be weak justification for her "brutal deprivation of her daughter's opportunities for development" (Ms. Li, twenty-two-year-old university student).

"Except for Mingyu herself, no one believes that her parents, her mother in particular, really loved her and did their best for her," another informant in the same focus group mockingly pointed out (Ms. Lian, twenty-two-year-old university student). Obviously, the focus group had noticed that gender ideology is trumping adequate plot development and character-based story line, and it thus showed resistance to the moral didacticism.

The character Su Mingyu embodies the negotiation between modernity and tradition in terms of womanhood. On the one hand, her rebellion against patriarchal tradition is eulogized and associated with a modern, neoliberal subjectivity characterized by self-improvement and self-determination. On the other, her rebelliousness is significantly contained by tradition. Although Mingyu treats her father with disrespect, her boss, Mr. Meng, has long been regarded by her as a fatherly figure and he thus plays the role of the father. In the end, family and kinship are portrayed as the remedies for female trauma, and filial piety as an indispensable virtue for a good woman. When Mingyu comes to Mr. Meng to bid him farewell, he unexpectedly expresses support for her decision to resign, saying "filial piety will make your life without regrets!" (episode 46). This view was shared by most of the middle-aged and older audience members in the focus group discussions. For them, the drama's "happy ending" illustrates that no matter what conflicts exist between family members, "blood ties are always most important for us Chinese people" (Ms. Wu, sixty-six-year-old retiree).

Another character with a similar life trajectory to Mingyu's is Fang Sijin in *I Will Find You a Better Home.* Based on the 2016 Japanese TV series *Your Home Is My Business!*, albeit with a completely new script, the drama is set in Shanghai. Fang is a shop manager and the star seller of a chain real estate company called Anjia Tianxia. She was born and raised in a small village in a mountainous area. Fang's mother is even more cruel and more unreasonable than the mother in the Su family. She attempts to drown Fang in a well shortly after giving birth to her because she already has three daughters and longs to have a son. The baby girl, who is later named Fang Sijing (meaning "fourth child" and "well"), survives only because her grandfather rescues her. After her mother finally gives birth to a son, she never attempts to hide her partiality, giving all her love and care to her son while treating her fourth daughter like a slave. When Fang gains admission to a renowned university, her mother secretly destroys the letter of admission and phones the university to reject the offer without her daughter's knowledge because she does not want to spend money on her. When Fang finds out, she leaves home in anger and renames herself Fang Sijin (meaning "a glorious future"). When she becomes a successful real estate manager in Shanghai, her mother shamelessly extorts money from her to pay for her brother's new house regardless of the damage caused to Fang's image among her colleagues and neighbors. Unlike Su Mingyu, however, Fang does not forgive her mother in the end because the woman unscrupulously hides news of Fang's grandfather's death from her so she can continue asking for money to cover the grandfather's medical expenses. This deprives Fang of an opportunity to say goodbye to her beloved grandfather.

Compared with Su Mingyu, Fang, who is from the bottom of society, faces both gender and class discrimination in Shanghai, and is thus far more aggressive, even savage, in her career striving. Adopting the motto "there is no house that I cannot sell," which is borrowed from the prototypical Japanese TV series, Fang works energetically every day and stops at nothing to improve her sales performance, even going so far as to steal clients from her colleagues and to purchase a fake university degree certificate. Although the drama ultimately attempts to instill a more "correct" outlook on life through Fang's lover, a Shanghainese man with a more relaxed and caring attitude toward selling real estate, it has been interpreted by most viewers as an "inspirational drama" that sings the praises of "winners" and those who manage to change their fate through continuous self-improvement. Set in Shanghai, a symbol of China's explosive growth, the drama links personal success and value with home ownership as "the quintessential Chinese dream."[10] As a victim of patriarchal tradition, Fang exemplifies a new womanhood that represents, in the words of Haiyan Lee, "not only the displacement of class by cultural and gender dynamics but also the enchantment of womanly virtue as the secret engine of China's march to the neoliberal world order" (H. Lee 2014, 263).

This subgenre of "supreme heroine" drama grows apace and is gaining exponential popularity among urban young females. A notable tendency in recent years has also been the emergence of "group heroine" dramas (nüxing qunxiang ju), in which a group of three or four young women take the leading roles while men are minor characters. Examples include the megahit Ode to Joy (Huanle song, two seasons, 2016–2017) and two warmly received dramas in 2020 that feature women in their twentieth and thirtieth years respectively: Twenty Your Life On (Ershi buhuo, 2020) and Nothing but Thirty (Sanshi eryi, 2020). Through the intertwined life stories of several women, these dramas depict the desires and frustrations of today's young women from various angles and explore women's subjectivity in a powerful way. They are thus likely to enjoy affective resonance with female audiences. Owing to the large base of female viewers and their degree of loyalty, as well as their capacity to contribute to topic discussions on social media, TV platforms, online platforms in particular, have made great efforts to "cultivate" and exploit this market. According to one industry practitioner, around twenty dramas of this subgenre have been produced or begun shooting since 2019, including *Astringent Girls* (*Ai de lixiang shenghuo*, a.k.a. *Se Nülang*, 2021), *Love Yourself* (*Ta qishi meiyou name ai ni*, 2020), *Fighting Youth* (*Zheng qingchun*, 2021) and a new sequel to *Ode to Joy*.[11]

THE FIRST HALF OF MY LIFE: WOMANHOOD AND NEOLIBERAL SUBJECTIVITY

Divorce and extramarital affairs—as well as the array of ethical issues they entail—have long been popular themes in Chinese TV dramas. One common story line is for the female protagonist to start a successful new life after being left by her husband (Xiao 2014). Nevertheless, when *The First Half of My Life* (*Wode qian bansheng*)—a forty-two-episode drama series in which a Shanghai woman bids farewell to the "first half" of her life, a life characterized by dependence and conspicuous consumption—premiered in 2017, it caused quite a stir on social media and generated heated debate over women's role in a rapidly transforming society.

Produced by Xinli TV Culture Company, the series initially aired in July 2017 on Dragon TV and Beijing TV, with numerous reruns in the years since. It is based on a novel of the same name by the Hong Kong writer Yi Shu, with the setting shifted to Shanghai. The female protagonist, Luo Zijun (Ma Yili), is a housewife in her late thirties when the series begins. She enjoys an affluent and happy life with her management consultant husband and eight-year-old son and spends most of her time selecting luxury goods such as designer shoes. She says to her best friend, Tang Jing (Yuan Quan), a high-ranking executive in a consultancy firm, that the only potential threats to her perfect life are her growing wrinkles and the pretty young women in her husband's company (episode 1). She never expects that the woman who will actually end up stealing her husband is a relatively plain, middle-aged working mother, his subordinate Ling Ling (Wu Yue). Tang later states that in a marriage or relationship the party who stagnates is doomed to be abandoned by the one who advances in life (episode 5). As the divide between Zijun and her husband, Chen Junsheng (Lei Jiayin), widens because of the different circles in which they move, Ling avails herself of a chance to win Chen's heart by offering him much-needed understanding and aid in the company. When the bubble of her perfect marriage suddenly bursts, Zijun is forced to face the reality of being a single mother and the challenges of re-entering the workforce after a decade in a career coma. Luckily, Tang remains at her side throughout, and when Tang is sent by her firm to work in Hong Kong for a while, she entrusts Zijun to her boyfriend, He Han (Jin Dong). He, a charming professional, is the most expensive management consultant in the business. He initially dislikes Zijun, regarding her as a simple-minded woman who is capable of nothing other than relying on a man. Beneath his cool, logic-driven exterior, however, he is warm and caring. He offers invaluable advice to Zijun and is always there to help when she is in need. With the aid of He's social network, Zijun is able to embark upon a new life and become a career woman, something she never believed herself capable of. The two eventually fall in love, but Zijun does not want to betray her best friend, and so she chooses to leave Shanghai to work on a business project in Shenzhen. He subsequently quits his job and moves to Shenzhen. The drama ends at this point, leaving the audience to wonder whether the protagonists, now in the same city, will meet again and eventually be together.

The changes made in the TV drama from the original novel reflect desires and fantasies specific to the context of contemporary mainland China. First, in the novel, the female protagonist's (Xu Zijun, the counterpart of Luo Zijun) husband, Shi Juansheng (the counterpart of Chen Junsheng), is a doctor rather than a project manager in a consulting firm. In fact, almost all the main characters, including Tang, He, and Ling, work in the consultancy business, and Zijun later becomes a successful market research professional. The drama sets out to dazzle viewers with the glamorous work life and lifestyle of management consultants, a profession held in high esteem for the high salaries it commands and the qualities associated with the masculine power of the market: rationality, competitiveness, and professionalism. As if to lure in the audience and inspire viewers to achieve success through self-improvement, the drama portrays the characters' luxurious lifestyles, which involve expensive cars, lavish apartments, extravagant watches, fashionable clothes, and high-end food. For example, in one scene, He Han orders sea urchins airlifted from Japan for his girlfriend. In episode 7, to force Zijun to realize the gap between her husband's life and her own, He takes her to his company at night, showing her how the young women in the company work diligently after office hours in a professional and confident manner and then socialize in a bar downstairs after work. A modern, Westernized lifestyle is contrasted with traditional womanhood to educate Zijun and show her how "behind the times" she is. Second, the character He Han, who is of great importance in the drama, does not exist in the novel. A combination of a "warm man" and a "bossy CEO" persona, He embodies the female fantasy of the ideal boyfriend, a wealthy, knowledgeable, humorous, powerful man who always remains calm and is reliable in times of crisis. He displays elegant taste in his dress and home décor and is portrayed as "an omnipotent hero" who can appear at any time to rescue Zijun (Wang and Mihelj 2019, 52). His advice on Zijun's career development is always correct and proves extremely helpful. She finds jobs with the aid of his network, and when faced with problems such as workplace bullying, she turns to him for help. In fact, without He's guidance and help, it is hard to imagine Zijun achieving anything. Above all, the man exhibits an impressive degree of sexual integrity, remaining faithful to Tang throughout their ten years of dating despite being surrounded by young and attractive female admirers.

The characters' names in both the novel and the drama allude to Lu Xun's (1881–1936) classic short story "Regret for the Past" (*Shangshi*). Published in 1925, it tells the tragic story of a young woman named Zijun who, despite the objections of her family, openly cohabits with the man she loves, Juansheng, only to be abandoned by him when she becomes little more than an appendage to him, and she later dies.[12] The story is well-known in China for advocating women's economic independence. By adopting similar names to the story's main characters—Zijun and Junsheng—and showing the female protagonist's successful transformation into a woman with both economic and emotional independence, the drama draws on the time-honored theme of female individualism and implies that the women of today's China are much more fortunate than their predecessors in the 1920s because they have more possibilities for upward mobility. This paean to modernity echoes the neoliberal call for self-transformation and for women to be the agents of their own success or failure (Ringrose and Walkerdine 2008). As He warns Zijun in the drama, "No one else can be a safe harbor in your life; only you can be your own security blanket" (episode 7). At the same time, the neoliberal production of subjects as "entrepreneurs of themselves" (Foucault 2008) also renders women much-needed subjects of the market, as both consumers and producers. In the drama, through perseverance and

Figure 23. Contrasting images of Luo Zijun before and after her divorce, reflecting her transformation from a shallow housewife (left) into an astute career woman (right). *The First Half of My Life* (2017).

self-improvement, Zijun successfully turns herself into a woman with the skills and qualities necessary to succeed in the market economy and thus a model practitioner of the Chinese Dream discourse.

Zijun's transformation is visualized through the sharp contrast in her appearance before and after her divorce. As illustrated in figure 23, Zijun's silly hairstyle and brightly colored clothes connote her shallowness as a full-time housewife who splashes out money on brand names. Once she re-enters the workforce, in contrast, her new, shorter hairstyle and monochrome professional dress convey her new role as a confident, mature career woman. Many of the audience members in the focus group discussions said they did not recognize Ma Yili, the actress who portrays Zijun, in the first few episodes because of her initially frivolous appearance. Through this visual effect, the drama highlights the need for women to cast off their old selves and take on new personae in keeping with a rapidly changing and modernizing society. Zijun's new postdivorce image signifies the new version of ideal femininity she acquires after her transformation.

Although the drama's message concerning the importance of women maintaining economic independence in marriage was well-received by audiences across age groups, many participants, young people in particular, noted that it was difficult to imagine Zijun's success without He's help. In fact, some participants pointed out, she is just another "Mary Sue character," who possesses the power to command men's unreserved service and loyalty. A busy consultant whose time is pricey, He is nevertheless able to be at Zijun's beck and call. He not only takes care of Zijun and her son Ping'er, but her whole family, including her mother, her sister, and her sister's family. To join in the celebration for Ping'er's birthday, He spends a whole day in Hang-zhou, where Zijun happens to be working that day. As a consequence, he misses an important meeting with a vexed colleague and ultimately loses his position as vice president of the company (episode 30). In addition to He, Zijun also has a number of other male admirers. Her ex-husband, Chen, dis-plays obvious regret for their divorce after her transformation into a new woman and does his best to help her succeed in business. Zijun's male coworkers in the two companies she works for also chase after her, with one volunteering to drive her son to school every day and cook for her after work. In one female informant's summation, Zijun's story is that of a woman "being abandoned by a rich man, only to be loved by an even richer man" (Ms. Zhao, twenty-year-old university student). The drama thus adds noth-ing new to the "marry well or work well" dilemma faced by young Chinese women, she added, as it conveys the unmistakable message that a powerful man's help is much more important than one's efforts.

Another character that warrants attention from the perspective of female subjectivity is Zijun's best friend Tang Jing. At the beginning of the series, Tang is presented as something of a role model for Zijun. She is highly inde-pendent, intelligent, and shrewd, and she enjoys a luxurious lifestyle that she earned through her own efforts. She is regarded by all as a perfect match for He. The two began their relationship when Tang was working as an intern at He's company. She learned a lot from him and eventually became his peer in terms of professional capacity. At a certain point, the two even begin pre-paring for their wedding. Tang never expects to be defeated in love by Zijun, a woman whom she pities. As He states at one point, however, he feels relaxed and carefree when he is with Zijun, whereas he feels inadequate and ill-at-ease with Tang because of her outstanding qualities. To some extent, Tang thus embodies the threatening nature of excessive autonomy and individu-alism in women for some men. In the words of one of my informants, Tang is ultimately "punished for being too independent." Whereas Zijun is posi-tioned as a woman who acquires an independent self but remains—albeit sometimes reluctantly—under male protection, Tang goes too far, with the end result that no man will ever be willing to marry her (Ms. Lian, twenty-two-year-old university student). By contrasting these two characters, the drama constructs an ideal femininity that to a certain degree remains "traditional" at the core but is packaged in profeminist thinking and the ambience of cosmopolitan Shanghai. The female characters paradoxically illustrate how a performance of gender strength is underpinned by an acknowledgment of socially prescribed weakness and dependency.

THE STORY OF YANXI PALACE: AN UNWANTED VERSION OF CHINESENESS

Many "supreme heroine dramas" have historical settings, which has given rise to a popular subgenre known as "palace intrigue dramas" (*gongdou ju*). These dramas, most of them set during the Manchu Qing dynasty (1636–1912), feature backstabbing imperial concubines vying for the emperor's favor. One explanation for the genre's popularity is that their distance from reality "makes female power less threatening to the social status quo" (Bai 2020, 364). A government backlash and the banning of such dramas as *The Story of Yanxi Palace*, however, demonstrate the state's disapproval of and concern over the gender ideology in these dramas and its harmful consequences for the propagation of "Chinese culture." Nevertheless, the popularity of the subgenre outside mainland China indicates that there may be an alternative vision of Chineseness to that espoused in official discourse.

Since roughly the late 1990s, TV dramas centering on the stories, both real and fictional, of the Qing dynasty emperors, the storied lives of Kangxi (r. 1661–1772) and Qianlong (r. 1735–1796) in particular, have flourished on the Chinese small screen and enjoyed popularity outside mainland China (see Y. Zhu 2005; Qian 2015).[13] Indeed, some of them have been produced by or in collaboration with Hong Kong and Taiwanese companies and with the significant involvement of directors and actors from the two locales. The rise of palace intrigue dramas, which succeeded "empire fever" in the new millennium, marked a shift in interest from male-dominated (emperors) to female-dominated (empresses and consorts), and is thus regarded by some as a barometer of the "feminist awakening."[14] The Hong Kong TVB series *War and Beauty (Jinzhi yunie,* 2004) was the first TV drama to focus on the power struggles in the imperial harem and is thus taken to mark the beginning of the vogue for palace intrigue dramas. It was followed by such dramas as *Con-*

cubines of the Qing Emperor (Da Qing hougong, 2006), *Beyond the Realm of Conscience (Gongxinji,* 2009, TVB), *Beauty's Rival in the Palace (Meiren xinji,* 2010), *Empresses in the Palace (Zhen Huan zhuan,* 2011), *The Legend of Mi Yue (Mi Yue zhuan,* 2015), and *Ruyi's Royal Love in the Palace (Ruyi zhuan,* 2018). These dramas have been highly successful in terms of ratings, revenue, and influence. *The Story of Yanxi Palace,* which can be said to represent the climax of this subgenre, has generated an unprecedented amount of controversy since it first aired.

The Story of Yanxi Palace is based on a popular web novel of the same title written by Xiaolian Mao (literally, "smiling cat"). Produced by Huanyu Entertainment Company, the seventy-episode drama series premiered on video streaming site iQiyi on July 19, 2018, and was streamed more than fifteen billion times within six weeks. It then aired (in a Cantonese version) on Hong Kong TVB Pearl in August 2018, on Zhejiang Satellite TV in September 2018, and on Taiwan's GTV in November 2018. It quickly took the Chinese-speaking world—and much of the world beyond—by storm, and to date it has been distributed in more than seventy markets worldwide and translated into fourteen languages, including English, Arabic, and Vietnamese.

The drama centers on the life story of a "supreme heroine" named Wei Yingluo (Wu Jinyan). She enters the imperial court as a maid to secretly investigate her sister's death. In the process, she falls in love with the empress's brother, a young imperial guard named Fucha Fuheng (Xu Kai) and becomes the empress's trusted friend and confidant. When the empress is driven to suicide after the mysterious death of her newborn son, Yingluo vows to find the culprit and avenge the late empress. To achieve her goal, she has to give up her romantic feelings for Fuheng and become part of Emperor Qianlong's (Nie Yuan) harem. With the emperor's increasing affection for her, Yingluo topples her rivals one after another and finally punishes Consort Chun, the villainess who is responsible for the late empress's death. In the end, after the evil new empress falls into disgrace following an abortive coup, Yingluo is elevated to the position of Imperial Noble Consort and becomes the most powerful woman in the emperor's inner court.

The prototype for Wei Yingluo is one of Emperor Qianlong's concubines, who became posthumously known as Empress Xiaoyichun, née Weigiya (1727–1775). She was of Han Chinese descent but had a Manchu name because her father joined the Manchus as a bond servant. After her death, her son became the crown prince, and eventually Emperor Jiaqing (r. 1796–1820). Empress Xiaoyichun was therefore the only Qing empress of

Figure 24. Promotional poster for *The Story of Yanxi Palace* (2018) featuring (from left to right) Wei Yingluo, Emperor Qianlong, Empress Fucha (the good empress), and Empress Hoifa-Nara (the evil empress).

Han Chinese ancestry. Most of the story lines in the drama, however, are fictional and reflect the sentiments of modern office politics more than the history of the Qing dynasty. The female protagonist is emotionally strong and indomitable. Many palace intrigue dramas, such as the aforementioned *Empresses in the Palace, The Legend of Mi Yue,* and *Ruyi's Royal Love in the Palace,* follow a similar story arc: the female protagonist appears to be innocent and sweet, and thus ill-suited to the cruelty of palace politics, in the first few episodes, and then morphs into a shrewd woman owing to the ruthless palace environment. Yingluo, in *The Story of Yanxi Palace,* however, is never naïve. From the moment she enters the palace, she has a clear and straightforward mission: to find out who murdered her sister and avenge her death. Regardless of the difficulties and disadvantages she faces, she never gives up that mission. She is depicted as incredibly talented, knowledgeable, and, most impressively given her modest background, eloquent. When bullied by her fellow maids and concubines, she never hesitates to teach them a lesson and let them know that she is not to be trifled with. Her character thus deviates markedly from the features of traditional womanhood, which emphasizes endurance and forbearance, and is more akin to the qualities and strategies needed in a competitive modern business milieu than in an imperial palace setting.

In *The Story of Yanxi Palace*, plot is managed through a particular gendered lens. As a woman, Yingluo achieves her goals by dint of astuteness and resourcefulness instead of power and strength. The subplot concerning her punishment of Grand Consort Yu (one of the late emperor's concubines), the culprit in her sister's murder, is particularly remarkable. Wei Yingluo's sister, Wei Yingning, is raped by Grand Consort Yu's son, Prince He (i.e., Emperor Qianlong's half-brother), when the latter is drunk. To cover up the scandal, Grand Consort Yu sends someone to kill Yingning. When Yingluo discovers that Yu was responsible for her sister's death, she barges into the Grand Consort's residence to boldly expose her misdeeds. Coming out of the house and standing in front of it, Yu vehemently denies the charge and swears that if she is telling a lie, she will be struck by lightning, a common way of swearing an oath in Chinese culture. Everyone is aghast when at that very moment, Yu is struck by lightning and dies! That event was no coincidence, however. After hearing that there would be a thunderstorm that evening, Yingluo secretly hides (conductive) needles in the door curtains of Yu's house. Then, while arguing with her, she entices Yu into the desired position, whereupon the God of Thunder exacts justice on her behalf. Although the emperor knows full well that Yingluo was behind Yu's theatrical death, he has no way to punish her (episode 27).

Of course, it is undeniable that Yingluo's success ultimately depends on men, given the story's setting in premodern China. In fact, she excels at taking advantage of men to achieve her goals, which arguably constitutes the most distinguishable feature of her femininity. In the drama, Emperor Qianlong in many ways resembles the "bossy CEO" character discussed in chapter 4. He is initially bitterly resentful of Yingluo because she dares to defy him and even openly plays tricks on him. But her characteristic audacity and brazenness are what ultimately attract Qianlong: Yingluo is so different from his other concubines. The following conversation, in which the emperor half-jokingly reproaches Yingluo (who is now his favorite concubine) for her presumptuousness, sounds more like a conversation between a permissive top executive and a junior staff member than an interaction between an emperor and concubine.

QIANLONG: You have called yourself a humble slave from day one, but I
never see you really bend your knees in front of me. This makes me
uncomfortable.

YINGLUO: Your Majesty will get accustomed to it one day.

QIANLONG: [smiling] It's always been others who try to get accustomed
to [my way of doing things]; no one else has dared ask me to get
accustomed to them. You are so daring! (episode 49)

The emperor is of a possessive and suspicious nature. He begrudges the love
between Yingluo and Fuheng, and when he discovers that Yingluo (still a
maidservant at the time) is having a rendezvous with Fuheng, he forces
Fuheng to marry Erqing (Su Qing), another maid who waits upon the
empress, threatening him with Yingluo's life (episode 34). At the same time,
however, Qianlong is a constant lover and is deeply attached to Yingluo. He
protects Yingluo with his own body when she falls from her horse, injuring
himself in the process (episode 49). When he finds out that Yingluo is
secretly taking herbal medicine to prevent conception, the emperor is furious, and the now out-of-favor Yingluo decides to accompany his mother to
Yuanming Palace. But Qianlong still loves Yingluo and ostentatiously pam-
pers his new concubine, Concubine Shun, to make Yingluo feel jealous and
insecure. The ploy works, and Yingluo rushes back to the palace to reconcile
with him (episodes 58–60).

Yingluo is a typical "Mary Sue character" who captivates a number of
men who compete with one another for her love. Although Fuheng marries
a woman he does not love to save Yingluo's life, he remains loyal to Yingluo
throughout his life, and dies at the end of the series while desperately seeking an antidote for Yingluo, who has been poisoned (episode 70). Fuheng
also surreptitiously offers help to Yingluo several times, help without which
she would have been hard-pressed to survive the conspiracies against her by
her palace rivals. In addition to Fuheng, a eunuch named Yuan Chunwang
(Wang Maolei), who claims to be the emperor's long-lost half-brother, also
harbors a desire to possess Yingluo and frequently helps her when she is
laboring in the palace sanitation unit. Later, though, Yuan becomes her
enemy, framing her when he thinks she has betrayed him by becoming the
emperor's concubine.

Yingluo's shrewdness and unswerving desire for justice have made her a
target of projection for many female audience members. On social media
platforms, for example, a large number of urban women who are struggling

to obtain better work opportunities have identified with Yingluo's "solo struggle to climb the socioeconomic ladder and negotiate a society structured around wealth-based status and male power and privilege" (Y. Zhou 2018). Yingluo's step-by-step elevation in the imperial concubine system resembles the upward trajectory of an employee in a modern company. She comes from a humble Han Chinese family, and she starts her "career" as a low-ranking seamstress and maid. By triumphing over her enemies and gaining the emperor's affection, she moves up the ladder in the hierarchical consort system until she reaches a position second only to the empress: "palace maid" (*gongnü*) → "Noble Lady" (*guiren*) → "Concubine" (*pin*) → "Consort" (*fei*) → "Noble Consort" (*guifei*) → "Imperial Nobel Consort" (*huang guifei*). The inspirational process of her empowerment is reminiscent of a scene in the film *Go Lala Go!* (*Du Lala shengzhi ji*, literally "Du Lala's Promotion," 2010). Adapted from a popular series of novels written by Li Ke, a former female employee of IBM, the film centers on the upward mobility of an ordinary office worker who ascends the corporate ladder at a fictional Fortune 500 company called DB, rising from secretary to manager of human resources. The film is organized into chapters that mirror Lala's rise. Each time she receives a promotion, Lala is depicted removing her shoes at the company entrance, with her heels growing ever higher over time, mirroring her rise within DB. Like her counterparts in a modern company, Yingluo faces—and bravely defends herself against—jealousy, backstabbing, frame-ups, and vilification by her peers to survive and thrive in the imperial inner court.

Yingluo also displays a marked spirit of independence. As one focus group participant observed, "men are just tools for her to climb to a higher position or seek revenge" (Ms. Wang, twenty-four-year-old postgraduate student). According to this informant, in many TV dramas women suffer miserably because they "cannot let go of an intimate relationship" and therefore have to tolerate men. In *The Story of Yanxi Palace*, in contrast, unlike the other concubines, Yingluo is neither emperor- nor husband-centered. Whether slighted or favored by the emperor, she enjoys her life and has clear goals. She knows how to take advantage of men's weaknesses, such as the emperor's face-saving disposition, to achieve those goals, and she gives up her relationship with Fuheng for a grander purpose. Whereas all the other concubines dream of giving birth to a son, Yingluo takes medicine to prevent conception. In a sense, as one informant put it, she behaves as if the sexes are equal in the palace. She never pins her hopes on men, and does not consider the emperor to be the most important element in her life (Ms. Wang, twenty-four-year-old postgraduate student). Another informant rebutted that point, however, claiming that it is not that Yingluo does not care about the emperor's favor; she is simply playing hard to get. As an example, she cited the scene in which Yingluo immediately rushes back to the emperor's side when she feels her place in his heart is under threat. Furthermore, despite her reluctance to become pregnant, she eventually gives birth to four sons and two daughters for the emperor. Ultimately, her power and status derive from the emperor alone (Ms. Hong, twenty-two-year-old undergraduate student).

With her quasi-modernist selfhood, Yingluo stands in stark contrast to other women in the drama, whose tragedies derive from their inability to extricate themselves from men and from the patriarchal moral order. Notable examples are the two empresses, one good and one evil. The first, Fucha Rongyin, is a gentle and virtuous woman and Yingluo's benefactress. She is beautiful, graceful, kindhearted, and of noble lineage, and she is respected by all as a model of moral rectitude. Although Emperor Qianlong has no complaints about her, Empress Fucha is deeply unhappy because, as the empress, she has to live up to others' expectations and dare not display her talents in dancing and singing for fear of damaging her demure image. When Qianlong asks her why she is so fond of Yingluo and always protects her, Rongyin gives the sentimental reply that she sees her former (true) self in Yingluo, recalling an incident in which, as a newlywed, she was reproached and punished by her mother-in-law for speaking a few more words than her husband had (episode 28). Rongyin's life story is meant to denounce the suffering and shackles associated with traditional Chinese femininity.

The centerpiece of the Confucian discourse on femininity is motherhood, as women's social status is defined primarily in accordance with their reproductive role (Barlow 1991). Rongyin's tragic death is caused by her obsession with motherhood. Her first son died at a very young age. Rongyin misses him terribly and longs to become a mother again. She is also fully aware of the pressure on her to provide the emperor with a male heir. Despite being ill and weak, Rongyin finally becomes pregnant and gives birth to a son. But two of her rivals in the inner court, Consort Chun and Consort Xian, the latter of whom eventually becomes known as the Step Empress, cannot afford to allow the empress to become a mother. Accordingly, they set a fire in the palace that kills the newborn baby (episode 39). His death is a heavy blow for Rongyin, who begins to suffer mental problems and ends her life by throwing herself off the palace roof (episode 40). Her death represents the tragedy of son-centered traditional womanhood: "virtues and ideals die along with the empress. Yingluo replaces them with a powerful sense of individual entitlement" (Y. Zhou 2018).

The Step Empress Hoifa-Nara Shuzhen (formerly Consort Xian) is a treacherous character who is greedy for power and has the means to obtain it. Her Achilles' heel, however, is that she regards the emperor as her husband and is emotionally attached to him. She suffers burns while trying to protect Qianlong from a fire and decides to leave the scars on her body so that he will feel grateful to her whenever he sees them (episode 33). When Yingluo becomes the emperor's favorite concubine, the jealous Shuzhen teams up with the emperor's half-brother, Prince He, who has a crush on Shuzhen, and together they hatch a plot to overthrow the emperor and enthrone Shuzhen's son in his place. But she backs out at the last minute and risks her life to save the emperor (episode 70). After the plot fails, Shuzhen is permanently exiled to a "cold palace"—where out-of-favor concubines reside—although she retains the title of empress. The two empresses depicted in the drama seem to respectively allegorize women's obsession with motherhood and wifehood, two pillars of traditional womanhood, and thus invite interpretations from a contemporary perspective on feminist subjectivity.

As noted, *The Story of Yanxi Palace* became a huge hit, not only in China but in countries around the world. In fact, it was the world's most Googled TV show in 2018, evidence of the significant foreign interest in the series, given that Google is blocked in mainland China.[15] The series was also dubbed into Cantonese and broadcast on Hong Kong's most watched television channel, becoming a smash hit. Furthermore, studies have shown that the growing popularity of Chinese television series like *The Story of Yanxi Palace* have played a role in improving Taiwanese views of the mainland, with many young Taiwanese fans of Japanese and Korean dramas now wanting to watch shows from the mainland.[16] However, despite *The Story of Yanxi Palace*'s phenomenal popularity in China and beyond, the state-run media outlet *Beijing Daily* unexpectedly published an editorial on January 25, 2019, that criticized the genre of palace intrigue drama in general, and *The Story of Yanxi Palace* in particular, for promoting negative values that are "incompatible with the core values of socialism":

[The show] makes the emperor's lifestyle fashionable and something to strive for, pollutes modern society with the concubine's back-stabbing mentality, beautifies imperial China while ignoring the heroes of today, [and] glorifies luxury while attacking thriftiness and hard work.[17]

Days after the editorial's publication, the planned rebroadcast of the show on a number of provincial channels was abruptly canceled. The incident attracted international media attention, with most reports interpreting the backlash as an indicator of the government's tightening of ideological control over the entertainment industry.[18] Some foreign commentators even speculated that *The Story of Yanxi Palace* had been banned because of its insinuation of power struggles at the top level of the CCP. In response to the media fuss, one television practitioner in China responded during an interview that overseas journalists had "overread" the drama's censorship, which, for him, merely reflected the ongoing, and volatile, tension between market tastes and the values of the country's ossified TV censors.[19] In addition to worrying that backstabbing concubines were bad examples for the country's youths, the authorities also found the drama's unexpected overseas popularity embarrassing because it conveyed an unwanted image of China.

China has spent a fortune on attempts to boost its international appeal, investing in such undertakings as the opening of Confucius Institutes around the world and sponsoring the translation and joint publication of Chinese classics in the West. Such efforts center on emphasizing a primordial Chinese tradition characterized by splendid cultural achievements, which helps to justify and provide "positive energy" to fuel China's rise in the modern world. As Xi Jinping, who is eager to promulgate "good Chinese narratives" to the world, remarked at a recent national conference on propaganda and ideology:

> Our outstanding traditional culture is the cultural root of the Chinese nation. Its values, humanistic spirit, and moral standards are not only the intellectual and spiritual kernel of us Chinese people, but are also important for solving the problems faced by all of mankind. We must extract and showcase the spiritual essence of our traditional culture, namely, the elements with contemporary value and world significance. It is necessary to improve the pattern of international communication work, innovate propaganda ideas, innovate operating mechanisms, and gather more resources.[20]

Ironically, in terms of soft power influence, none of the government's efforts has achieved the success of the TV dramas under discussion. The popularity of these dramas in East Asia has arguably given rise to a "Chinese Wave" that has succeeded the Korean Wave. It has even been reported that some foreign fans of these dramas have begun learning Chinese so that they do not have to wait for their translations and can read the web novels on which they are based.[21] The life and culture depicted in these dramas, however, are clearly not in keeping with the "outstanding traditional culture" the government is trying to promote. On the contrary, stories about the brutality of patriarchal politics and fierce, even sinister, womanhood are regarded as awkward because they expose the ugly side of Chinese culture and thus challenge the government's discursive monopoly on Chineseness.

Given that stories about emperors were a popular television subject long before the palace intrigue dramas made their debut and that depictions of scheming politicians and strategists, such as those in the masterpiece *The Romance of Three Kingdoms* (*Sanguo yanyi*), are nothing new, it seems reasonable to infer that it is the images of women in dramas such as *The Story of Yanxi Palace* that have so irked government censors and scholars alike. These images reject the stereotypical labeling of Chinese women, subvert established norms and audience expectations about good and evil, and sometimes evince an anachronistic, feminist-informed subjectivity. The gender transgressions they represent constitute a threat to established "Chinese culture" as a form of social unconscious and cultural capital (Eagleton 2016; A. Louie 2004). They make possible new interpretations and imaginations about gender in traditional China and about Chineseness as such.

In light of the controversy surrounding *The Story of Yanxi Palace*, a more recent TV adaptation of an online historical novel, *Serenade of Peaceful Joy* (*Qingping yue*, 2020), conspicuously shifted the narrative focus from the original romance of a princess to the grand accomplishments of an emperor and a group of male ministers. The protagonist, Emperor Renzong of the Song dynasty (r. 1022–1063), is portrayed as a benevolent ruler with fatherly love for his people. In addition, his empress is notably a woman of integrity and virtue. When the emperor's favorite concubine becomes pregnant, the empress displays no jealousy at all, but instead lavishes her with care. Praising the drama as a faithful representation of history, the history scholar Wu Gou said during an interview:

> [Before *Serenade of Peaceful Joy*], costume dramas were filled with intrigues, trickeries, and schemes. There were few works that displayed the beautiful side of historical culture. *Serenade of Peaceful Joy* enables us to witness the elegant and prosperous culture of that era [i.e., the Northern Song dynasty], and makes possible a pleasant understanding of tradition. I look forward to more historical dramas of this type.[22]

CONCLUSION

From *Yearnings* to *The Story of Yanxi Palace*, the female images in Chinese TV dramas reflect changing ideals of the feminine over a span of three decades. Unlike soap operas in the West, which center primarily around family relations and feature stories that take place in the domestic space, Chinese TV dramas frame their stories within a much broader social space and tend to depict social change and public events (S. Kong 2008). Consequently, they have produced a diverse range of female characters who are portrayed in family, workplace, and even historical settings. Women are constructed as subjects who have benefited from the social change brought forth by the country's reform policies. These characters invite fruitful analysis "through the lens of a clash between tradition and modernity, individualism and collectivism, and nation and globalization" (Wang and Mihelji 2019, 43). With Xi Jinping's promotion of patriarchal family ethics, the women in these dramas are represented as the very embodiment of gendered Chineseness, or as admirable female figures maintaining a harmonious domestic interior through their traditional female virtues while enjoying professional success as model practitioners of the Chinese Dream discourse. The only exception is Wei Yingluo, the strong-headed female protagonist of *The Story of Yanxi Palace*, who projects an unwanted image of gendered "Chineseness," which led to the drama's canceled rebroadcast despite its domestic and overseas popularity.

As diverse as the female images on Chinese TV are, they share a number of patterns as far as gender politics and female subjectivity are concerned. Regardless of whether the setting is contemporary or historical, ideal womanhood is constructed in keeping with the entrepreneurial self, which lies at the core of neoliberal subject making (Bröckling 2015). TV dramas sing the praises of women as autonomous agents who can determine and change their fate through hard work and constant self-improvement in a fast-changing society. Even historical figures such as imperial concubines serve to illustrate the imperative to act like an entrepreneur, as they have to carefully weigh the risks and benefits to succeed in a life-or-death environment. Meanwhile, both government censorship and audience criticism reveal grave concerns about the "proper" womanhood that China presents to the world. Stories of independent, capable women still more or less follow the "bossy CEO" pattern, in which women's success ultimately lies in the hands of men. The "supreme heroines" are without exception "Mary Sue characters," whose power to command men's support and attention is inextricably linked to their female sexuality. Women are still constructed in terms of their bodily existence in many dramas. Through critical readings of the different types of female images in Chinese television, this chapter positions the issue of femininity at the intersection of patriarchal and nationalist politics and reveals the many faces of Chineseness in the twenty-first century.

Epilogue

RISING NATIONALISM and a greater diversity of gender presentations are two of the most prominent features of the social transformation that has taken place in post-Tiananmen-era China, driven by the government's desire to expand the consumer market on the one hand and bolster ideological education on the other. Although much has been written on Chinese nationalism and there is growing scholarship on gender and queerness in Chinese popular culture and media, few studies to date have explored the dynamic interconnections between the two. In filling this research gap, this book bridges new understandings of gender construction and nation building through the lens of recent Chinese television programs. Its various chapters have looked at the relationship between Chinese television production and creative output, the construction of gender in contemporary China, the deployment of gender relations in televisual content, and the way all these phenomena connect the viewer to Chinese subjectivity as preferred by and produced for the state and nation. Through textual readings and audience studies of narrative drama serials, we have seen how television (and web dramas) both reflects and constructs shifting and contested discourses of gendered subjectivity in present-day China and how the nation is imagined and articulated through the meaning of gender.

As we enter the second decade of the twenty-first century, the boundaries between television, film, and video are disappearing, and yet serial narrative, based on the format of TV drama and borrowing film techniques, has emerged as the most robust and popular form of storytelling in China. Its cultural significance can hardly be overestimated. Informed by both China's own rich narrative tradition and Chinese television's exposure to global serial narratives (Y. Zhu 2008, 63), this form of storytelling is prospering as the centerpiece of a fast-growing digital entertainment industry that is gaining overwhelming popularity among the young, as well as growing overseas influence. Watched by the vast majority of the population, TV (and web) drama is also playing an important role in cultural governance in China as a device of the "technology of the self" that mediates effectively between the state and the individual.

Through the prism of gender and nation, the discussions in this book have covered the major subgenres of Chinese TV drama in recent years, including anti-Japanese drama, urban romance drama, youth idol drama, family ethics drama, espionage drama, historical drama, palace intrigue drama, and "supreme heroine" drama. Most of the drama series discussed have generated debate on gender issues in both online commentaries and focus group discussions and thus reflect a variety of social concerns, tendencies, and trends pertaining to gender. Targeting different demographic sections of the Chinese population, these subgenres display a wide range of gender identities and discourses, in keeping with the various affective articulations of Chineseness in postsocialist China. Roughly speaking, however, the heteronormative, patriarchal gender norm premised on a perceived restoration of Chinese traditions remains the mainstream in TV dramas. The hegemonic mode of masculinity—defined by political loyalty to the state, adherence to such Confucian values as homosocial brotherhood, and a repudiation of femininity and queerness—upholds a patriarchy ensconced between the state and people. This gender norm is, however, being increasingly challenged by new gender expressions induced by the quest for a more cosmopolitan identity in the global age. Examples include the severe criticism of toxic masculinity and misogynist postures by female audience members, the emphasis on female agency in adaptations of popular web novels by female writers, and the popularity and imitations of nonconforming gender images among young audiences, to name just a few.

The men and women in Chinese TV dramas are thus products of ongoing negotiations surrounding gender politics and subjectivity in line with television's reproduction of social power relations. Drawing on data collected from online commentaries and gathered in interviews with TV audiences and industry practitioners, the book illustrates how the gender images and imaginaries on television are variously interpreted, negotiated, and manipulated. For instance, the official discourse of patriotic heroism has been commodified and even parodied by entertainment, thereby generating unexpected comedic effects from viewers' perspective. The enthusiastic extolment of "traditional" wifehood, motherhood, and filial piety has been relentlessly attacked and mocked by young informants as a ridiculous example of a patriarchal, sexist ideology. At the same time, however, unconventional gender images have aroused widespread social concern, and dramas featuring an unapproved gender discourse risk a backlash or even being banned by the state. Many gender-related debates and controversies can ultimately be attributed to the paradoxical coexistence of and interplay between nationalism and cosmopolitanism in the Chinese media's mediation between the state and the market.

With Chinese television transforming itself from a "mainstream culture" that endeavors to engage with serious intellectual debates (Zhong 2010) into a digital terrain of entertainment, such themes as depictions of rural life and urban poverty have almost disappeared from the small screen. Instead, Chinese television dramas have become, as Ruoyun Bai succinctly puts it, a "dreamland where fantasies reign" (Bai 2020, 368). As the dramas discussed in the current book reveal, these fantasies typically feature entrepreneurial success and a Cinderella-type romance with a rich and powerful man. The popular "bossy CEO" narrative is one such manifestation of hypergamic fantasies. Targeting the young female audience that has emerged as the primary consumer of drama serials, the "bossy CEO" stories take place in a wide variety of settings, ranging from companies and schools to the harems of imperial China, but are surprisingly similar in their essential constituents, which denote reliance on men and worship of strength or even despotism. In this sense, these stories are in accord with the state agenda to perpetuate both national and male chauvinism. In the same vein, stories following the "Mary Sue" pattern reflect female fantasies about taking advantage of one's body and sexuality to achieve success in a male-dominated society. The images that feature therein are closely related to the "supreme heroine" images that give expression to fantasies about strong, independent women who succeed by dint of hard work, intelligence, and confidence. Imbued with "positive energy," that is, an inspirational and optimistic attitude in the face of challenges, such images embody a new womanhood within the constraints of neoliberalism combined with gendered practices. But as we have discovered through close readings of dramas within these subgenres, stories promoting women's agency as part and parcel of postsocialist modernity may paradoxically end up reinforcing the patriarchal gender order.

Perhaps the most conspicuous fantasy created by Chinese television is that concerning the Chinese nation, which is built on imaginations of its long and continuous history and in contrast to its Others. The preceding chapters build a connection between the male/female binary and national selfhood/otherness. Social concerns about gender issues are usually intertwined with hand wringing over the state of the nation, while images of foreigners help to illustrate an imagination of national strength and increasing dominance in the world. By employing culturally accessible tropes of femininity and masculinity, televisual narratives bolster a China-centered vision of Chineseness and vent the ambition and anxiety associated with China's rise. Chinese television's obsession with a pure, homogeneous "Chineseness," which reinforces cultural essentialism and exceptionalism, exemplifies not only social engineering but also the affective structure of patriotic nation building, if we understand affect as "the power to move and to be moved by others" (Wong 2018, 8).

A number of directions for future research have emerged from this study. In terms of theory, advances in queer studies offer a rich frame of analysis for the increasingly diverse gender expressions seen in Chinese television culture in recent years. In light of new research on queer Asia (see Chiang and Wong 2017), television provides rich texts for culturally saturated, historically specific nuances of Chinese queerness, which promises a new and fruitful arena for studying the global in the local. In addition, Butler's (1990) perception of gender as a performative dimension of social differences based on established, socially recognized norms of super/subordination is a powerful conceptual tool that can be further exploited to investigate the gendered nature of nationalist ideology, inasmuch as it enriches and supplements the Foucauldian approach that understands national identity as mediated forms of subjecthood produced as part of governance. Further research along this line would undoubtedly deepen our understanding of the antifeminine and sometimes racist "mainstream" in Chinese television. Lastly, the intertextuality between TV drama and other forms of popular culture—such as digital games, memes, and other forms of online expression—in the context of increasing media convergence is another promising avenue worthy of further exploration to shed new light on our understanding of narrativity in the digital era.

It is an interesting phenomenon that some Chinese TV dramas, especially those targeting a younger generation of audience, display discernible influence of South Korean dramas by following certain formulars in terms of plot and characterization. For instance, in many romance stories the cold, aloof and arrogant male protagonist is accompanied by a warm and thoughtful male friend. This formulaic "no. 2" male character, such as Zheng Qi in

Boss and Me, Hua Zelei in *Meteor Garden*, and Fu Ziyu in *Love Me, If You Dare*, is so kind and amiable that the female protagonist initially develops a crush on him. But without exception these characters end up as a foil to the male lead in the romance. Another tendency is the recent popularity of dramas featuring love stories between a young man, known as a "little puppy" (*xiao nai gou*) and a woman significantly senior to him in terms of age and status. Such story patterns show traces of copycatting from Korean and Taiwanese dramas. Thus, comparative studies of TV drama production and reception across national borders will help illustrate how transnational flow of popular culture molds and changes gender stereotypes and how Chineseness is imagined and negotiated in the process of localization of motifs and imageries.

At the same time, the Chineseness constructed by Chinese television targets not only viewers within China but also a global audience. As discussed in the book, television programs have become an increasingly important medium for enhancing China's global soft power through affective resonance with the audience. Recent years have witnessed considerable domestic media hype about the popularity of Chinese TV programs overseas, especially in Africa, Australia, and some Southeast Asian countries, including Vietnam. As an essential part of the "going out" project launched under the auspices of the Chinese government, billions of dollars have been spent on translating and promoting government-sponsored TV programs for the overseas market. The transnational circulation of Chinese TV programs necessitates a cultural appraisal of their effectiveness as a soft power agent. A particularly interesting and potentially fruitful perspective would be to explore how the Chineseness constructed by these programs is received and negotiated by non-Chinese audiences. At the same time, the growing ease of accessing mainland Chinese television programs overseas has rendered their consumption by the Chinese diaspora a critical component of the globalization of Chinese entertainment television. According to Wanning Sun (2002b, 9), "media production and consumption in the age of globalization and convergence have created an electronic community of the Chinese nation, consisting of Chinese nationals and former PRC nationals who left China in recent years." Sun argues that the latter inhabit a symbolic space that is "both inside and outside China" and thus possess a "paradiasporic" position in terms of cultural identities and subjectivities (2002b, 92). Transnational mobility and displacement give rise to what Homi Bhabha calls a "third space" of cultural hybridity, the "intervention of the 'beyond' . . . [which] captures something of the estranging sense of the relocation of the home and the world—the unhomeliness—that is the condition of extra-territorial and cross-cultural initiations" (Bhabha 1994, 9). Accordingly, the consumption of Chinese television programs and renegotiation of the transnational imaginary of Chineseness by overseas audiences, as well as the formation of overseas Chinese subjectivities, constitute interesting subjects for future investigation.

In terms of transnationality and soft power, China's cultural engagement with Africa in particular has emerged as a crucial topic in the context of the global response to racial injustice and Afrophobia. This imperative involves inquiries about both how Chinese programs are received by Africans and how images of Africans are imagined and received by Chinese audiences. It is notable that despite the government's trumpeting of Sino-African friendship and the large population of Africans living in China, Africans are seen far less often in Chinese TV dramas than are Asians, Europeans, and Americans.[1] Years ago, a TV commercial for laundry detergent featured a Black man "washed" into an Asian man after being bundled into a washing machine. After going viral, the commercial generated a huge amount of controversy abroad but attracted little attention from domestic viewers or censors.[2] Blacks are also often stigmatized in social media as carriers of infectious diseases and embodiments of hypersexuality, stereotypes that have generated widespread anxiety over Chinese women being "stolen" and contaminated by African men in China. In view of these phenomena, a critical study of the interrelationship between Chineseness and Africanness would deepen our understanding of the multifaceted cultural politics of gender and race in a global context and shed further light on the issues discussed in this book.

The focus group discussions I conducted during research for the book also suggest potential areas for future investigation. Due to space limitations, the book focuses primarily on TV dramas and web dramas. There are, however, other genres of television entertainment that were mentioned by the informants that invite interesting analysis in light of gender and nation. For instance, *If You Are the One* and other dating shows were repeatedly referred to by the informants when discussing ideals of femininity and masculinity. One obvious reason is that, unlike TV dramas, which take place in a fictional or even fantasy sphere, these reality shows are closer to real life and thus connect effectively between discourse and practice in terms of gender. In addition, when asked to name TV programs that promote China's soft power and national pride, *A Bite of China* (*Shejian shang de Zhongguo*, 2012–2018), a documentary TV series on Chinese cuisine and food culture, was unexpectedly cited by many informants. One said that the program made her "feel warm" about being Chinese. Although the program is about food, it "reminds people of the cleverness and creativity of the Chinese in making use of ingredients and preparing food which fits the natural environment," she added. Many informants agreed with her that food is something that the Chinese can show off about to foreigners in a humble yet proud manner without embarrassment. A similar program mentioned by some of the younger informants was *Chef Nic* (*Shi'er dao fengwei*, 2014–2018), an international cuisine program hosted by Hong Kong celebrity Nicholas Tse and simultaneously broadcast by Zhejiang satellite TV and TVB in Hong Kong. These programs are beyond the scope of this book but suggest directions for future research on food as a form of soft power.

The current research also demonstrates that focus group discussions with TV audiences constitute a fruitful interdisciplinary approach to a variety of social issues. For instance, in my focus group discussions, foreigners' participation in dating shows such as *If You Are the One* was taken positively as a reflection of the increasing attractiveness of China and Chinese culture. There was also a sense that China has become a truly international country that attracts foreigners because it provides them with opportunities. Most of the interviewees were open-minded about cross-racial marriage (with the notable exception noted below): "It is a positive sign that foreigners are interested in marrying Chinese, be it a foreigner man or foreigner woman." The idea of hypergamy, however, the idea that men are supposed to marry "down" and women "up," was also readily found. Although Chinese men can easily find wives from less developed countries such as Vietnam, it is "quite something" (*niubi*), in the informants' eyes, when a Chinese man marries a Western woman. An example many cited with amazement and admiration was the marriage of the well-known television host Sa Beining to the Canadian singer Lisa Hoffman. The informants also conveyed the view that it is aspirational for a Chinese woman to want to marry a Western man, but most blatantly stated that they could never accept a Black son-in-law or husband or wife from Africa. These ethnographic data not only enrich our understanding of the reception of and responses to televisual texts but also offer potential value for exploration, from an anthropological or sociological perspective, of the link between representations and lived experiences of interracial marriage.

Last but not least, a phenomenon that warrants more scholarly attention is the increasingly extensive social fury and protests triggered by the patriarchal and sexist ideology in TV programs. As this book is being wrapped up, an officially sponsored TV drama extolling China's battle with Covid-19 has engendered an unexpectedly strong backlash on social media for its stereotypical depiction of women as selfish, cowardly, and family-oriented, and thus for playing down women's contributions to fighting the pandemic. *Heroes in Harm's Way* (*Zuimei nixingzhe*, 2020) is produced by CCTV and consists of seven stand-alone stories. In one scene that takes place in the meeting room of a bus company, a group of male bus drivers eagerly volunteer for an emergency transport team on the eve of the lockdown in Wuhan, something none of the female drivers appears willing to do. When a vexed official asks, "Won't one of our female comrades step up too?" a woman sitting in the back row immediately responds that her family has traveled a long way to visit her for the upcoming Lunar New Year holiday, and so she really can't join the team. The scene irritated many viewers. Pictures of female doctors, nurses, and volunteers engaged in responding to the epidemic were uploaded to and widely shared on social media as a rebuttal to the program's biased portrayal of women. Using the hashtag "Request that *Heroes in Harm's Way* Stop Airing," many users expressed their anger and disappointment. A poll asking whether the show should be canceled received more than 91,000 "yes" votes.[3]

Another subplot that has come in for heavy criticism concerns a reproduction-centered relationship between an elderly woman and her daughter-in-law. In the episode concerned, the two women selfishly sneak out of Wuhan during the lockdown, only to feel moved by the example of volunteers and decide to return in shame. Upon hearing that her son and grandson have not been infected, the older woman sighs in relief, declaring that "as long as your son and my son are safe, we have nothing to worry about."[4] The women's behavior and remarks have been described as "an insult to the audience's intelligence." Online criticism has targeted not only the slight to women but also the CCP's manipulation of the historical narrative and collective memory.[5] Such criticism marks a new wave of recent protests in which Chinese people, mostly the younger generation and educated elite, are challenging the authorities through criticism of patriarchy. Increasing awareness of and sensitivity to gender issues in TV programs have rendered gender politics both an indicator and trigger of deeper-level social dissidence. Progressive gender thinking catalyzes the birth of a civil society. In this sense, television is the beginning but not the end of a larger story of gender-induced tensions, crises, and changes in today's China.

Notes

Chapter 1

1. Kerry Allen, "China Promotes Education Drive to Make Boys More 'Manly,'" *BBC News*, February 4, 2021, https://www.bbc.com/news/world-asia-china-5592 6248 (accessed April 8, 2021).

2. In a series of lectures and articles delivered and written in the later years of his life, Foucault focused on how Western governments retreated from direct intervention in developing good behavior in their populations, who were encouraged to live according to established norms and move up the social ladder through self-improvement, with governments thus being the "conduct of conduct" (see, e.g., Foucault 1991).

3. President Xi made this remark during a speech delivered at the Beijing Forum on Literature and Art on October 15, 2014. See http://news.xinhuanet .com/politics/2015-10/14/c_1116825558.htm (accessed November 11, 2017).

4. See, for instance, Jamie Zhao, "Queer TV China as an Area of Critical Scholarly Inquiry in the 2010s," *Critical Asian Studies* 26 (2019). https://criticalasianstu dies.org/commentary/2019/12/25/201926-jamie-zhao-queer-tv-china-as-an-ar ea-of-critical-scholarly-inquiry-in-the-2010s (accessed August 7, 2020).

5. For a discussion of Li Yuchun and the singing competition *Super Girl* (translated as *Super Voice Girl* in her article) from a queer perspective, see J. Zhao (2018).

Chapter 2

1. On March 21, 2018, as part of efforts to strengthen state propaganda power, CCTV merged with two national radio networks, China National Radio (CNR) and China Radio International (CRI), to become a giant media company—and ministry-level government institution—known as the China Media Group (Zhongyang guangbo dianshi zongtai, literally "Central Radio-Television Station"), with the "Voice of China" adopted as its external name. However, CCTV continues to be used in the logo for the company's TV channels.

2. Beijing Television was established with Soviet aid during the Great Leap Forward (1958–1960), an economic and political campaign mobilized by Mao

Zedong and the CCP leadership to transform China into a modern industrialized country as rapidly as possible, with the overarching ambition of surpassing the most developed countries of the West within as little as a decade (see Hong 1998, 46–49). One concern at Beijing Television's debut was rivalry with Taiwan, which was on the verge of launching its first TV station (Sun and Gorfinkel 2015, 22).

3. Here I borrow Lily Wong's definition of affect as "a politics of emotional mobilization—the power to move and be moved by others" (2018, 8).

4. The "five consecutive championships" are the third Fédération Internationale de Volleyball (FIVB) Women's World Cup in 1981, ninth FIVB Women's World Championship in 1982, 23rd Olympic Games in Los Angeles in 1984, fourth FIVB Women's World Cup in 1985, and tenth FIVB Women's World Championship in 1986. Following the Chinese team's 1981 victory, the official media in China launched a national campaign celebrating the "Spirit of the Women's Volleyball Team" and directing the populace to "Learn from the Women's Volleyball Team, Rejuvenate China." The players became household names thanks to live broadcasts of their games across the country. Viewings were often organized by work units and neighborhood committees.

5. *River Elegy* is a six-part documentary that aired on CCTV in June 1988. It offers a dichotomous contrast between China's isolated land-based civilization, represented by the Great Wall and Yellow River, and the more open and aggressive maritime civilization represented by Western culture. The scriptwriters presented the latter as the future hope of China. After the Tiananmen crackdown, the documentary was condemned by the Chinese government for providing the "theoretical and emotional preparation for the recent turmoil and rebellion" (Nicholas D. Kristof, "China Calls TV Tale Subversive," *New York Times*, October 2, 1989). See also J. Wang (1996, 118–136).

6. Hu Ya, personal communication, August 4, 2017.

7. The long list of reality shows of this type includes an array of "idol" shows such as Dragon TV's *Chinese Idol* (*Zhongguo meng zhi sheng*) and *China's Got Talent* (*Zhongguo daren xiu*) and Zhejiang Satellite TV's *The Voice of China* (*Zhongguo hao shengyin*) and its rebranded version *Sing! China* (*Zhongguo xin shengyin*), both based on *The Voice of Holland*; dating shows such as Hunan Satellite TV's *Women yuehui ba*, cloned from ITV's *Take Me Out* in Britain; talent shows such as Jiangsu Satellite TV's *Super Brain* (*Zuiqiang danao*), copycatted from the German program *Superhirn*; game shows such as Zhejiang Satellite TV's *Running Man* (*Benpaoba, xiongdi*), a program imported from SBS in Korea (the program was renamed *Keep Running* (*Benpaoba*) in 2016 to differentiate it from the Korean version when the Chinese government banned all Korean pop culture following Seoul's decision to deploy a U.S.-developed missile defense system within its borders); and travel programs such as Hunan Satellite's *Where Are We Going Dad?* (*Baba qu na'er?*), originally a Korean TV program produced by the Munhwa Broadcasting Corporation.

8. See, for instance, Gao (2012) on the cultural politics of Cantonese-language television in Guangdong.

9. Although existing scholarship on Chinese television overwhelmingly focuses on the programs on the national channels, there is interesting discussion of local channels, including Bengbu TV in Anhui Province, in Lewis, Martin, and Sun (2016, 68–75). In general, the ground channels' market share is declining, and TV stations at the city/county level, which are at the bottom of the hierarchy, are struggling to survive because of financial constraints (L. Xu 2017, 29). In this book, the focus is on TV programs with national impact, and hence most of the programs discussed herein aired on satellite channels, leaving more locally oriented programming as a potentially interesting topic for a future project on TV and regional identity.

10. According to statistics revealed by the China Netcasting Association, VOD advertising revenue grew by about 40 percent per year from 2013, reaching 462 million yuan in 2017. By July 2017, 565 million people, 75.2 percent of the country's total number of Internet users, were consuming online VOD services in China, 170 million of whom were paid users, purchasing either a premium membership or subscribing to pay-per-view services (Bai 2020, 360).

11. Tengxun chuanmei yanjiuyuan, *Zhongmei shidai: Wenzi, tuxiang yu shengyin de xin shijie zhixu* (*A Time of Multimedia*: A New World Order of Texts, Images and Sounds) (Beijing: China CITIC Press, 2016), pp. 71–72.

12. AGB Nielson ceased its TV audience measurement service in China in 2009, making the joint venture between CCTV and CSM Media Research the only provider of TV audience surveys in the country. Owing to a lack of independent data gatherers, TV ratings are generally taken with a grain of salt in China. It is common practice to alter or even "purchase" ratings to make the figures attractive for advertisers. See "False Ratings an Unwanted link in TV Profit Chain," *China Daily*, January 11, 2017, http://www.chinadaily.com.cn/opinion/2017-01/11/content_27918956.htm (accessed September 5, 2017).

13. Chen Yuying, personal communication, November 20, 2019.

14. See "Tai fengkuang! Chenqing ling gaobie yanchanghui menpiao zuigao bei chaodao 15 wan yizhang" (Crazy! Tickets of *The Untamed* Concerts Sold at ¥150,000!), 163.com, October 12, 2019, https://money.163.com/19/1012/20/ERAKR56600259DLP.html (accessed August 26, 2020).

15. According to James Poniewozik (2014), writing in *TIME*: "'TV'—actual, mainstream, desirable TV content—is now no longer something you necessarily watch on a television set or receive through a cable or satellite company's pipes. It can be, as with Netflix and Amazon, a library of archival and original programming you get over the Internet. . . . It can be, as with HBO, a service you contract for separately. It can be, as with Simpsons World, an online entity in which a show becomes a 'channel,' a destination." For further discussion of media convergence and the redefinition of "television" in the postbroadcast era, see Spigel and Olsson (2004), Jenkins (2006), Turner and Tay (2009), Kackman et al. (2011), and Newman and Levine (2012).

16. When discussing "privatization" in the postsocialist era, Lisa Rofel (2019, 133) contends that "[i]n contemporary China, the line between public and pri-

vate, or state-owned and independently owned, is much less precise than one would assume from an analysis based on a supposed modal type of capitalism. There exists a range of situations along the spectrum from fully private to hybrid public/private to completely ambiguous and blurred statuses. [. . .] This blurring of the distinction is a deliberate strategy." This is an apt description of the situation of ownership in the TV production industry.

17. The name of the state agency in charge of radio and television changed several times as a result of government restructuring in China during the past four decades. From 1982 to 1998, it was known as the Ministry of Radio and Television (renamed the Ministry of Radio, Film and Television in 1986). In March 1998, due to government streamlining, the ministry was downsized to the State Administration of Radio, Film and Television (SARFT). Then, from 2013 to 2018, it was the State Administration of Press, Publication, Radio, Film and Television (SAPPRFT). During the latest government overhaul in March 2018, the radio and television sections of SAPPRFT morphed into a new agency known as the National Radio and Television Administration (NRTA). What has remained unchanged over the years, however, is the direct leadership of the CCP Publicity Department. In fact, the director of the NRTA also serves as deputy director of the Publicity Department of the CCP Central Committee.

18. Jimmy Yardley, "An Unlikely Pop Icon Worries China," *International Herald Tribune*, September 5, 2005.

19. An anecdotal case of self-censorship that I heard from an industry practitioner who prefers not to reveal his name concerns the 2017 hit drama *Nothing Gold Can Stay (Na'nian huakai yue zheng yuan)*. Apparently, the term *chongxi* was erased from the characters' conversations due to political concerns (episode 6). *Chongxi* (to exorcise [evil spirits] through joyous events) is the superstitious belief that joyous events such as weddings and birthday celebrations can cure the seriously ill by exorcizing the evil spirits occupying their bodies. The term has become sensitive because it sounds like *chong Xi*, with *chong* referring to the feng shui term for flooding a person with negative energy and Xi being paramount leader Xi Jinping, and can thus be understood as "doing something harmful to Xi."

20. See Charlie Campbell, "Chinese Censors Have Taken a Popular Gay Drama Offline and Viewers Aren't Happy," *TIME*, February 25, 2016, http://time.com/42 36864/china-gay-drama-homosexuality/ (accessed March 10, 2018).

21. See Lee Wei Lin, "Disgraced Chinese Star Zheng Shuang Reportedly Owes Fertility Clinic S$90K; Past Awards Rescinded After Surrogacy Scandal," *Today*, January 22, 2021, https://www.todayonline.com/8days/sceneandheard/entertai nment/disgraced-chinese-star-zheng-shuang-reportedly-owes-fertility (accessed April 19, 2021).

Chapter 3

1. *Wolf Warrior II (Zhanlang II)*, an action-packed blockbuster directed by martial artist Wu Jing, who also cowrote the film and plays the lead role, is the

highest-grossing Chinese film ever and has been widely discussed in China and beyond since its premiere in the summer of 2017. A Hollywood-style action-adventure featuring a former Chinese special-ops soldier's rescue operations in a war-torn African country, the film combines commercial spectacularism with the "main melody" propaganda of patriotism and tells us a lot about the cultural imaginaries on China's rise and its engagement with the wider world. The leit-motif of "Chinese men rescuing the world" is also echoed in other blockbuster films, including 2018's *Operation Red Sea (Honghai xingdong)*, directed by Dante Lam. A collection of essays discussing the gender and sexual politics of *Wolf Warrior II* was presented at a forum on "China in the Global South: The Central Role of Gender and Sexuality" convened by Lisa Rofel and Huang Yingying in Beijing from September 15 to 17, 2017. These essays are available at http://u.osu.edu/mclc /online-series/liu-rofel/ (accessed August 3, 2018).

2. The official term for the war in China is the War of Resistance against Japan (*Kang Ri zhanzheng*). It is also known as the Second Sino-Japanese War in some non-Chinese history books.

3. For the Chinese government's concern over the proliferation of "crude and shoddily produced" anti-Japanese dramas, see "Staged Warfare, Bashing Japan," *The Economist*, June 1, 2013, http://search.proquest.com/docview/1357534085 ?accountid=14548 (accessed February 9, 2015); see also Zhang Yang, "Shazhu kang Ri ju "leiren" zhi feng xu duofang "geili" (Concerted efforts are needed to put an end to absurdity in Anti-Japanese dramas), http://comment.scol.com.cn /html/2013/04/011010_1096930.shtml (accessed February 9, 2015); and Ernest Kao, "State Broadcaster CCTV Slams Anti-Japanese War Dramas," *South China Morning Post*, April 11, 2013, http://www.scmp.com/news/china/article/1212279 /state-broadcaster-cctv-slams-anti-japanese-war-dramas (accessed February 9, 2015).

4. See Philip J. Cunningham, "China's TV War Machine," *New York Times*, September 12, 2014, http://www.nytimes.com/2014/09/12/opinion/china-tv -war-on-japan.html (accessed September 28, 2020); Philip J. Cunningham, "The Yasukuni Shuffle: China and Japan Duke It Out via TV Serials on the Wrongs of WWII," *Informed Comment*, http://www.juancole.com/2014/10/yasukuni-televis ion-serials.html (accessed April 24, 2021); and Kathy Guo "Anti-Japanese Dramas to Flood Chinese TV Screens Next Month," *South China Morning Post*, August 28, 2014, http://www.scmp.com/news/china/article/1581474/anti-japanese-dram as-flood-chinese-tv-screens-next-month (accessed September 28, 2020).

5. The seven listed companies are Huayi Brothers, Huace Film and TV, Enlight Media Group, Beijing Hualu Baina Film and TV Company, Shanghai New Culture Media Group, China Television Media, and Zhejiang Great Wall Film and TV Company (Yang 2014, 56).

6. Hu Ya, personal communication, August 4, 2017.

7. Matthias Niedenführ (2013, 106) contends that "the lack of reliable rules and the intentional ambiguity of the censorship process result in a high degree of self-censorship." He also quotes Chinese TV drama producer Zhang Jizhong, who

says that producers tend to jump on the bandwagon of successful formats, which leads to the overproduction of TV dramas in a market already oversaturated with that genre. The government's interventions are thus merely a move to alleviate the industry's concerns.

8. Anticorruption drama had remained a taboo for more than a decade since 2004, when a directive from SARFT banned "excessive" violence in dramas with gangster and anticorruption themes. It was not until 2017, when *In the Name of the People* (*Renmin de mingyi*) hit the screens, that the depiction of government corruption on the TV screen was allowed again. *In the Name of the People*, commissioned and financed by China's national prosecutor's office, the Supreme People's Procuratorate, is regarded as propaganda for Xi's antigraft campaign and thus obtained special approval from high-profile government officials. In view of the societal shock engendered by the drama's airing, however, industry insiders predict that dramas exposing the dark side of Chinese officialdom on such a large scale are unlikely to appear again in the near future (Li Xueping, personal communication, August 4, 2017).

9. Depictions of the Korean War on the TV screen remained a taboo for many years until 2015, when a series entitled *The 38th Parallel* (*Sanba xian*) was allowed to air. Read as an indicator of international relations, the airing of the series is believed to reflect China's tougher stance toward the United States and is in line with President Xi's advocacy of growing "confidence" when facing the world.

10. Yang Ji, personal communication, July 20, 2015

11. "Kangzhan ju: Zhongguoren jiu ai yiyin qiangguo" (Anti-Japanese dramas: Chinese people are prone to strengthen their nation in fantasy), ifeng.com, April 11, 2013, http://news.ifeng.com/opinion/special/kangzhanju/ (accessed July 18, 2015).

12. The play was banned from satellite airing by SARFT after being briefly broadcast by some ground channels of local stations in 2015, allegedly due to audience complaints about its vulgar and obscene plot and dialogue, the "grenade in crotch" scene in particular. See "Yiqi da guizi zao jinbo, leiren taici jingdai wangyou" (*Together Let's Kill the Devils* was banned, netizens were shocked by its ridiculous lines). People.cn, May 20, 2015, http://culture.people.com.cn/n/20 15/0520/c22219-27027759.html (accessed December 14, 2018).

13. The absurdity of these anti-Japanese dramas has also attracted the attention of the media in Japan. A Japanese man named Iwata Takanori, who finds the dramas highly entertaining, has compiled a comprehensive book on the genre that has been widely reported by the media. The book, titled *The Chinese Anti-Japanese Drama Reader: The Unexpected Anti-Japanese Patriotic Comedy* (Tokyo: Publib, 2018), covers the images, plots, and language in twenty-one dramas of this type and points out their historical errors. See Chris Cheng, "Patriotic Comedies? Japanese Author Compiles an Encyclopaedia of Chinese Anti-Japan Dramas," *Hong Kong Free Press*, May 6, 2018, https://www.hongkongfp.com/2018/05/06/pa triotic-comedies-japanese-author-compiles-encyclopaedia-chinese-anti-japan -dramas/ (accessed August 22, 2018). For an introduction to the book in Japanese, see http://publibjp.com/20180411 (accessed August 22, 2018).

14. Since the dying days of the Qing empire, Chinese men have engaged in a struggle to cast off China's label as the "sick man of Asia": the early and mid-twentieth century saw the denigration of the Confucian aesthete and adoption of national self-strengthening philosophies embodied in nationalist, revolutionary renderings of manhood, and in the past two decades the white-collar man has emerged as the workhorse of the new Chinese dream of individual material success and national resurgence (Song and Hird 2014, 256).

15. A pronounced example is the infamous tirade launched by Peking University professor Kong Qingdong against the people of Hong Kong. He accused them of being "dogs of the British imperialists . . . not humans" during a webcast interview in January 2012, provoking bitter controversy. See Jonathan Watts, "Chinese Professor Calls Hong Kong Residents 'Dogs of British Imperialists,'" *The Guardian* (International Edition), January 24, 2012, http://www.theguardian .com/world/2012/jan/24/chinese-professor-hong-kong-dogs (accessed November 21, 2013).

16. Both the beggars' sect and the dog-beating staff—the chieftain's totem— are imaginaries borrowed from martial arts novels such as Jin Yong's (Louis Cha) *The Legend of the Condor Heroes* (*Shediao yingxiong zhuan*) and its sequel *The Return of the Condor Heroes* (*Shendiao xialü*). The beggars' sect is a fictional underground organization formed by beggars and vagrants at the margins of cities that appears in a number of *wuxia* novels and even films such as *King of Beggars* (*Wu zhuangyuan Su qier*, 1992). The wooden sticks in the hands of beggars are both a membership emblem of the sect and a weapon, and thus in Jin Yong's novels the sect is called *ganzi bang* (literally, "the sect of sticks"), a name that has been appropriated by the TV drama under discussion.

17. Kam Louie (2002, 14) lists the seven virtues defining *wu* masculinity (in the past tense): "suppressed violence, gathered in arms, protected what was great, established merit, gave peace to the people, harmonized the masses and propagated wealth."

18. The nationalist discourse on masculinity has arguably become the hegemonic masculinity of today's China in the sense that it is assumptive, widely held, and has the quality of appearing to be "natural" (Morgan 1992; Donaldson 1993).

19. This plotline was obviously influenced by the online condemnation by ultranationalist netizens of *dailu dang,* a term that can be roughly translated as "the Quislings Party." It is widely used to refer to those labeled as "traitors" to the Chinese nation, who lead the way for the enemies invading their homeland.

20. Baili Jingqi, "Jiedu xiaorenwu Bai Jingui" (Reading the small man Bai Jingui), http://blog.sina.com.cn/s/blog_63dce2be0101h5rt.html (accessed June 21, 2014).

21. Excessive emotional links with one's immediate family have long been construed as hampering true masculinity/heroism, as can be seen in Xin Qiji's (1140–1207) *ci* poem "Water Dragon's Chant": "I'd be ashamed to see the patriot, Should I retire to seek for land and cot" (Xu Yuan-zhong, trans. *300 Song Lyrics* [Changsha: Hunan chubanshe, 1996], p. 416).

22. When he is young, he is nicknamed "Second Daughter" (*er yatou*), which implies a transgender identity. When he is older and becomes the head of the bandit gang at Cockscomb Mountain, his men call him "Old Second Aunt" (*lao ershen*), a common name for a middle-aged woman in rural China.

23. *Weiniang* (fake women), a term originating from the Japanese, is used to refer to men with a woman's appearance. It has become a vogue word in online discussions and even singing contests in recent years, reflecting the trend among urban youths in China of engaging in transgender cosplay. For more details, see http://socialmediauppsala.wordpress.com/2013/10/31/a-puzzle-of-gender-a-un ique-culture-generated-by-a-weiniang-forum/ (accessed June 21, 2014).

24. "Dagou gun Anhui weishi rebo, nanrenbang chengjiu chuanqi daxi" (A gang of men make The Dog-Beating Staff a masterpiece), http://tieba.baidu.com /p/2665320727 (accessed June 22, 2014). "Orchid fingers" refers to a hand gesture in traditional Chinese operas, in which the fingers are positioned to resemble the petals of an orchid to indicate a character's femininity.

25. See "Yu Yi Dagou gun yan Er yatou, beicheng Zhongguo hao Gay me" (Yu Yi is called a good gay friend for his performance of Old Second Aunt in *The Dog-Beating Staff*), http://ent.163.com/13/1025/11/9C1DESDH00031GVS.html (accessed June 22, 2014).

26. *Farewell My Concubine*, a canonical play in the Peking Opera tradition, is based on the historical story of the last battle between Xiang Yu (232–202 BC), the self-styled "Hegemon-King of Western Chu," and his rival Liu Bang (256–195 BC), founder of the Han dynasty. In the play, Xiang is surrounded by Liu's forces and commits suicide on the banks of the Wu River after his loyal concubine Consort Yu kills herself in front of him using Xiang's sword.

27. "Yanzhi yaoyan jianhuo quanfen, Fanpai Su Xiaoding: wo shi chun yemen'er" (Paying a sexy bitch in *Rookie Agent Rouge*, Su Xiaoding: I am a 100% straight man!), http://ent.qq.com/a/20161020/027449.htm (accessed November 2, 2016).

28. A well-known example is that in Lao She's 1946 novel *Four Generations* (*Sishi tongtang*), in which an old man asserts that the Japanese invaded China because they wanted to steal the stone lions engraved on the Marco Polo Bridge in Beijing.

29. Chris Cheng, "Patriotic Comedies?" (accessed August 22, 2018).

30. For details of the life story of and narratives on Kawashima Yoshiko (Aisin Giorro Xianyu), see chapter 5 of L. Edwards (2016).

31. This widely circulated story appears in Chinese school textbooks and propaganda paintings, films, and TV programs. In October 1938, eight female soldiers of the communist-led Northeast Anti-Japanese United Army, who were aged between thirteen and twenty-three, were cornered by Japanese troops at the Wusihun River when covering the retreat of the main forces. Having run out of ammunition, they put an end to their lives by jumping into the river. They were later declared martyrs by the CCP.

32. For discussions on gender and the female body in Maoist revolutionary culture, see Roberts (2010) and Z. Wang (2016).

33. "Aiguozhe shouguan, Liu Zhihan yan huo xifu lixiangxing" (In *Patriots*, Liu Zhihan brings an ideal wife to life), People.com, July 6, 2018, http://ent.people.com.cn/n1/2018/0706/c1012-30131634.html (accessed November 2, 2018).

34. A recent TV drama called *POWs* (*Fulu bing*) has attracted media attention because of the lines of bitter rebuke to the Communist Party put into the mouths of the program's villains. In one scene, for example, a group of high-ranking Guomindang officials are letting off steam at a military meeting when one of them says, "Unless the communists are rooted out, there will be no chance of realizing the rejuvenation of our nation and peace in the world." Another says, "The Communist Party? I don't give a damn about what it says!" These supposedly villainous lines found an unexpectedly strong echo among netizens on the mainland after the drama aired. They jokingly exclaimed at how true these statements were, even giving voice to suspicions that they constituted an intentional expression of the true feelings of the director. See http://hk.apple.nextmedia.com/realtime/china/20150706/53937525 (accessed July 8, 2015).

35. I benefited from MacLachlan and Chua (2004) in the design of the audience research.

36. See http://bbs.hupu.com/10730738.html (accessed April 11, 2015).

37. For a discussion of the politics of using local dialects in recent Chinese TV programs, see Liu (2013, 59–81). Many of the characters in *Red* speak Shanghainese or Mandarin with a Shanghainese accent.

38. L. Chen (2018) provides a good reference on the tensions and negotiations between patriotic education and the growing popularity of Japanese popular culture among young people in China.

39. See http://tv.brtn.cn/20140917/ARTI1410941139798392.shtml (accessed April 11, 2015).

Chapter 4

1. See Kerry Allen and Patrick Evans, "China Tycoon Yu Minhong Caught Up in Sexism Row," BBC News, November 19, 2018, https://www.bbc.com/news/blogs-trending-46261469 (accessed November 29, 2018).

2. See "Zhinan'ai shi zenyang de zhengzhuang? qi dian fuhe daibiao ni yi aizheng moqi" (What are the symptoms of Straight-man Cancer?), *ETToday.net*, http://www.ettoday.net/dalemon/post/13327 (accessed January 12, 2017).

3. See chapter 4 of Xiao (2014) for a reading of *Chinese-Style Divorce* from the perspective of female subjectivity.

4. Wang Baoqiang, known as a "grassroots star" in China, was born and raised in a poor family in rural China and became a celebrated actor by playing the roles of peasants and migrant workers in several movies and TV dramas. In 2016, Wang

exposed on microblogging platform Sina Weibo an illicit affair between his wife Ma Rong, a young model, and his manager Song Zhe. Ma and Wang's divorce and a series of subsequent events have remained headline events ever since, with the case being dubbed "China's most discussed love triangle." The majority of people expressing their opinions in social media have sympathized with Wang and been angry about Song's cuckoldry of him. See https://www.whatsonweibo.com/chin as-discussed-love-triangle-wang-baoqiang-ma-rong-song-zhe/ (accessed January 29, 2019).

5. See Song (2004, 157–91) for a discussion of the dynamic link between masculinity and the self-mastery of sexual desire and immunity to the temptation of female charms in premodern Chinese literature.

6. See "A Foreigner Quit Drug Addiction by Indulging in Chinese Web Fiction," ChinaDaily.com.cn, http://www.chinadaily.com.cn/interface/yidian/113 9302/2017-03-24/cd_28643531.html (accessed January 23, 2019).

7. Hu Hao, "Zhang Yiwu: Badao zongcai wen yeshi wangluo wenhua chuanbo de yizhong fangshi" (Zhang Yiwu: The bossy CEO fiction is a channel for cultural spread), *Zhejiang jishi bao*, December 18, 2015, http://zjnews.zjol.com.cn/system /2015/12/18/020957758.shtml (accessed November 28, 2018).

8. See "Yige jiao badao zongcai de wenhua guaitai" (A cultural freak called "the bossy CEO"), *Shaonian Zhongguo pinglun*, October 13, 2016, https://archive.is /Mqfyd (accessed February 19, 2019).

9. A mode of operation called "4+x" was in force before 2015, whereby approximately four satellite channels, together with some local ground channels, would create an alliance to share the costs of TV drama purchase and simultaneously air the premiere of the dramas. This, however, was changed with a new policy by SARFT in 2015, which stipulates that "there must not be more than two channels playing the same drama during the 'golden slot' [i.e. 7:30 to 9:30 p.m.] and no more than two episodes of the same drama could be aired on satellite channels each night." This new policy, known as "one drama, two satellite [channels]" (*yiju liangxing*), has had a dramatic impact, not only on provincial TV stations but also on the production companies of television dramas, by significantly increasing the budget needed to purchase dramas. As a result, CCTV and some larger provincial stations such as Hunan and Jiangsu TV began to monopolize the market, outcompeting smaller production companies and channels at the second or third tiers. Some of the latter turned to so-called "IP dramas" to survive.

10. See https://kknews.cc/zh-hk/entertainment/knqlkgb.html (accessed June 7, 2019).

11. See Cao Yu, *Thunderstorm*, trans. Wang Tso-liang and A. C. Barnes (Beijing: Foreign Languages Press, 1964), 44–46.

12. "Zhe Shijian, weiyou mengxiang yu hao guniang buke gufu" (Only dreams and good girls in this world deserve our loyalty). *Douban dianying*, July 27, 2014, https://movie.douban.com/review/6764705/ (accessed May 25, 2019).

13. "Zhe Shijian, weiyou mengxiang yu hao guniang buke gufu" (accessed May 25, 2019).

14. Matchmaking events (*xiangqin*) are common in China. In many big cities, anxious parents gather spontaneously in city parks on the weekends to search for future spouses for their children. With young people's personal information strung up on trees and notice boards, these events look very much like a marriage market.

15. See Li You, "Chinese Reality Show Slammed for Reinforcing Gender Stereotypes," *Sixth Tone*, January 30, 2019, https://www.sixthtone.com/news/1003521/chinese-reality-show-slammed-for-reinforcing-gender-stereotypes (accessed July 25, 2019).

16. See http://www.haijiangzx.com/2018/1017/1996661.shtml (accessed February 25, 2019).

17. Originally published in *Xinmin congbao* (*New Citizen Journal*) between 1902 and 1905, *Discourse on the New Citizen* is a twenty-article series that delineates Liang's diagnosis of China's political and social problems and his advocacy for making a new citizenry as the key to transforming the old imperial state into a robust modern nation-state (see T. Lee 2007).

18. Liang says, "Victor Hugo, a famous western novelist, once said, 'A woman is weak, but she becomes strong after being a mother.' Why can a weak woman turn into a strong mother? The only answer lies in her sincere love of her kids. Though she may be so weak as being unable to bear the clothes she wears and behaves like a bird, she dares to trudge up a thousand mountains alone, not fearing roaring tigers and wolves or tedious ghosts. How great is this love! The power of love is so great that it can easily change a person that way." See Liang Qichao, "Lun Shangwu" (On Martial Spirit), chapter 17 of *Xinmin shuo* (Discourse on the New Citizen), https://ctext.org/wiki.pl?if=gb&res=900281(accessed November 20, 2019).

19. *The Handmaid's Tale* refers to the 2017 TV adaptation of Canadian author Margaret Atwood's 1985 novel of the same name. The novel, a dystopian sci-fi fable, is well known for its exploration of the theme of subjugated women in a patriarchal society. The popularity of the TV series is believed to reflect concerns over women's position in Trump's America.

20. Luo Yansu, "Guochan qibaju, gesong nüde que chengle shoushi guanjun" (A sloppy domestic drama, a eulogy of feudal female virtues becomes a ratings champion), https://mp.weixin.qq.com/s/qNhdSKfOvORN_3dGpgL61A (accessed November 20, 2019).

21. According to Ruoyun Bai (2020, 363), a "Mary Sue drama" "typically features a perfectly beautiful and virtuous heroine whose enchanting power is such that she causes practically all males who set eyes upon her to [fall] in love, to unconditionally serve as stepping stones for her ascendency in the social or power hierarchy, and even to die for her. As such she is absolutely hated by her jealous female arch-enemies, whose sole objective is no less than to destroy her, an objective forever thwarted. . . . [Such a character] is mockingly referred to as [a] 'Mary Sue,' a nod from Chinese popular culture to Paula Smith's 1973 'A Trekkie's Tale' and its seemingly perfect character Mary Sue."

Chapter 5

1. Personal communication, March 19, 2018.

2. Liu Xuesong, personal communication, March 26, 2018.

3. See Yang Meiju and Wang Shuang, "'Guizi zhuanyehu' Shiye Haoer: wo ai Zhongguo!" (A Professional "Japanese Devil"—Koji Yano: I Love China!). *Guoji xianqu daobao*, August 2, 2012, http://ihl.cankaoxiaoxi.com/2012/0802/69348.shtml (accessed October 26, 2012).

4. According to Hu Ya, a renowned TV writer, at least 70 percent of TV dramas categorized as "urban love story plays" include at least a couple of scenes shot in a foreign country, most likely somewhere in Europe or North America (personal communication, April 8, 2018).

5. During the focus group discussion, several informants commented that the linkage between modernity and transnational romance and marriage is rather "naïve" and "outdated" (personal communication, August 14, 2017).

6. The stereotype of the "neighborhood committee aunt" is a common one on Chinese TV. It refers to the older women who actively serve on one of the neighborhood committees (*juweihui*) common in Chinese cities, especially Beijing. Such women are presented as warm-hearted but often very nosy.

7. The slogan "to connect track with the world" (*yu shijie jiegui*) or "to connect track with international practices" (*yu guoji jiegui*) first appeared in the Chinese media around 2001, when China successfully joined the World Trade Organization, reflecting the government's commitment to opening up its market and acting in conformity with international standards. The catchphrase is now widely used by Chinese people to refer to the integration and globalizing processes of not only many industries but also aspects of daily life, such as etiquette and education. A search of the China Core Newspaper Full-Text Database identifies 605 articles published since 2000 in major Chinese newspapers that contain the phrase "to connect track with the world/international practices" in their headlines, with its peak appearance in the 2000–2003 period.

8. The poem was written in June 1956 and describes Mao's swimming across the Yangtze River in Wuhan in the previous month. "Chu" is the name of an ancient state during the Warring States period (475–221 BC). Its territory includes most of the present-day provinces of Hubei (of which Wuhan is the capital) and Hunan. See Mao Zedong, *Nineteen Poems* (Beijing: Foreign Languages Press, 1958), pp. 28–29.

9. For a comprehensive discussion of the role played by *go* in Chinese masculinity, see Moskowitz (2013).

10. At his son's wedding in Seoul, Mr. Xiao gives a lengthy speech that includes the following.

> When we were young, we seldom went beyond our native county, city, or province for work and study. The same was true when we looked for a husband or wife. But today my son has come to Korea, a distant country. He has found not only a job here but also his beloved. I really feel happy about

that. The earth has become smaller due to the development of technology. The new century will be a more open one, with freer and more frequent interactions between people of different countries. The marriage between our two families today marks the everlasting friendship between our two nations. (episode 10)

II. The "Cave of Silken Web" (*Pansi dong*) is a fictional place in the sixteenth-century Chinese novel *Journey to the West* (*Xiyou ji*) where sensual but dangerous sirens live.

12. See "Wode Natasha rebo, Gao Mantang: gushi zhenshi cunzai" (Gao Mantang: The hit drama *My Natasha* is based on real stories). *Beijing chenbao*, January 7, 2012, http://ent.qq.com/a/20120107/000067.htm (accessed December 13, 2013).

13. The historical prototype of the Japanese Germ Factory is the infamous Unit 731 (*Nana-san-ichi butai* in Japanese), a secret bacteriological research unit of the Japanese army stationed in Harbin in northeast China during the Sino-Japanese War. Its criminal activities, which were exposed after the war, included experimenting with bacteriological weapons on live humans. Most of the victims were Chinese and other Allied POWs.

14. In Jiang Wen's 1995 film *In the Heat of the Sun* (*Yangguang canlan de rizi*), set during the Cultural Revolution, children are so familiar with *Lenin in 1918* that they have memorized every line in the film and imitate its characters.

15. Johansson (1999) also notes the Chinese media's tendency to present Western women as being "active, productive and strong" (380), and even as the embodiment of "an animalistic sexuality," in contrast to Chinese women's cultivated virtues of civilization (384).

16. "Zuihou yizhang qianzheng shaqing, dazao 2016nian gaopinzhi fanzhanju" (*The Last Visa* promises a high-calibre antiwar drama in 2016). Sohu. com, January 11, 2016, http://yule.sohu.com/20160111/n434108744.shtml (accessed May 4, 2018).

17. Raymond Zhou, "Depiction of Chinese Schindler Falls Short," *China Daily USA*, February 9, 2017, http://usa.chinadaily.com.cn/a/201702/09/WS5a31d3f8a3108bc8c6732eb5.html (accessed May 4, 2018).

18. Personal communication, August 16, 2017.

19. Douban, https://movie.douban.com/review/8281128/ (accessed May 7, 2018).

20. Aijuqing, https://www.ijq.tv/yingshi/14423934351869.html (accessed August 6, 2018).

21. In his essay "Fetishism" (1927), Freud argues that the fetish is a substitute for the woman's (i.e., the mother's) penis that the little boy once believed in. In refusing to recognize his mother's lack of a penis, the boy disavows what he sees, thus resulting in both a belief and nonbelief in the maternal phallus. This compromise (produced by the conflict between perception and counter-wish) results in a substitute (i.e., the fetish): "It remains a token of triumph over the threat of castration

and a protection against it." See Sigmund Freud, "Fetishism," https://cpb-us-w2.wpmucdn.com/portfolio.newschool.edu/dist/9/3921/files/2015/03/Freud-Fetishism-1927-2b52v1u.pdf (accessed December 20, 2018).

22. In discussing the relationship between the fetish and the phobic object, Žižek (1997, 104) maintains that "[t]he phobic object is . . . a kind of reflection-into-self of the fetish: in it, the fetish as the substitute for the lacking (maternal) phallus, turns into the harbinger of this very lack. . . . The point not to be missed is that we are dealing with *one and the same* object" (emphasis in the original).

23. For a psychoanalytical discussion of abjection, see Kristeva (1982).

Chapter 6

1. The study's informants were recruited through a survey company based in Zhuhai. The study took the form of simple questionnaires and focus group discussions. When asked why they preferred a more "neutral" (*zhongxing*) style of appearance, "to look different from other [men]" (41 percent), to be an "iconoclast" (27 percent), and "the influence of pop culture" (23 percent) were among the other top answers, revealing the paradoxical interplay between the desire for individualist performance and herd mentality in a consumer culture.

2. Fan Xiaoping, personal interview, January 30, 2020.

3. For a critical discussion of "how queer matters for Asia and vice versa" in light of the complexity of "Asia" as a geopolitical and ideological signifier, see Chiang and Wong (2017) and the special issue edited by them on "Queer Asian as Critique," published by *Culture, Theory and Critique* 58, no. 2 (2017).

4. Inna Chou and Leah Lee, "Xinban liuxing huayuan peiyin shi yinwei zhege? . . . jingdian fanpai ni bu zhidao de jijian shi" (The new adaptation of *Meteor Garden* uses voice actors for this reason? . . . What you don't know about the remake of the classic). *Elle*, July 17, 2018, https://www.elle.com/tw/entertainment/drama/g22154587/meteor-garden-2018-drama/ (accessed February 16, 2020).

5. For online criticism of these scenes, see https://www.bilibili.com/read/cv712549/ (accessed February 22, 2020).

6. The word *tanbi*, which means "the pursuit of beauty," was first used to refer to a style of modern Japanese literature that focused on conveying pure enjoyment of beauty to readers. Since the 1970s, however, the term has gradually deviated from its original meaning to become another term for BL, and it thus now refers exclusively to a genre depicting romance between two good-looking young men (see X. Zheng 2018).

7. The Japanese word *shonen ai* (love between adolescents) was first employed by the Year 24 Group, a group of talented female manga authors who were born in and around the 24th year of the Showa era (1949), in their depictions of melancholic same-sex feelings between young boys. In the 1970s, the magazine *JUNE* became known for its publication of *shonen ai* manga works whose hallmark image is beautiful effeminate young men. In 1979, the word *yaoi*, which was

coined by combining the first characters of *yama nashi, ochi nashi*, and *imi nashi* (no climax, no resolution, and no meaning), first appeared in fanzines and was used to refer to explicit sex scenes between young men in fan-created works. By the 1990s, the English term "Boys' Love," or BL, first coined by a magazine called *b-Boy* published by BIBLOS, was being widely used, and the BL genre soon spread to other forms of media and culture and has been imitated and reproduced in a variety of East Asian countries, including Korea, Hong Kong, Taiwan, and China, as well as in several Southeast Asian countries (see Lavin, Yang, and Zhao 2017).

8. "'The Untamed': Chinese Boy Love Drama We Can't Stop Watching," *Film Daily*, https://filmdaily.co/news/the-untamed/ (accessed March 2, 2020).

9. "The Untamed." See also "Chenqing ling shi danmei ma?" (Is *The Untamed* a BL story?). Sougou.com, August 15, 2019, https://ld.sogou.com/article/i56224 66.htm?ch=lds.pc.sh.media.all (accessed March 2, 2020).

10. Before 2017, TV drama series were first aired by a satellite TV channel, and then several hours later became available for streaming on such online platforms as Sohu, LeTV, Youku, Tudou, and iQiyi, with their secondary copyright purchased by the video-streaming sites. *Love Me, If You Dare*, however, marked a new broadcast mode at a time of rapid cross-platform development. Its copyright was successfully sold back to the traditional TV sector. See chapter 6 of Keane (2015).

11. In the drama, Bo and the other Chinese characters speak Chinese when talking with the foreign characters, who answer in English. The audience is made to believe that they are communicating in English.

12. Xin Shiping, "Niangpao zhi feng dang xiu yi" (It is time to put an end to the trend of *niangpao*), Xinhuanet.com, September 6, 2018, http://www.xinhuanet .com/politics/2018-09/06/c_1123391309.htm (accessed March 13, 2020).

13. Gui Conglu, "Shenme shi jintian gaiyou de nanxing qizhi?" (What is the masculinity we need today?), Sina Weibo, September 7, 2018, https://www.weibo .com/ttarticle/p/show?id=2309404281529374237719 (accessed March 16, 2020).

14. Qian Zongyang, "Zhongguo shaonian, yanggang zhiqi buke xiao" (Manliness needed for Chinese youth), *Zhongguo guofang bao*, September 7, 2018, http:// www.81.cn/gfbmap/content/2018-09/07/content_215278.htm (accessed March 17, 2020).

15. See, for instance, "Yangshi xianniangling zhengshi shishi, daitou fengsha niangpao" (CCTV officially implements a policy to ban sissy actors), *Meiri toutiao*, October 8, 2018, https://kknews.cc/zh-hk/entertainment/ye54bqn.html (accessed March 17, 2020).

16. See, for instance, AFP, "China Orders Gaming Giants to Cut 'Effeminate' Gender Imagery," Yahoo! News, September 9, 2021, https://news.yahoo.com/chi na-orders-gaming-giants-cut-052311000.html?guccounter=1 (accessed September 19, 2021).

17. "Riben peiyang yelang, women peiyang niangpao, weilai zhanzheng women na shenme daying?" (Japan cultivates wild wolves, we cultivate sissies, how can we win a war in the future?), *Meiri weixiaoshuo*, September 24, 2018,

https://www.wenzhangba.com/yuanchuangwenzhang/201809/402401.html (accessed March 18, 2020).

18. Changsha Moli, "Ba zhexie niangpaomen dangcheng sihai chuleba" (Please eliminate these sissies as pests), Baidu.com, September 30, 2018, http://baijiahao.baidu.com/s?id=1613001359500701830 (accessed March 18, 2020).

19. Wang Xiaowei, "Weile rang ni xihuan niangpao, ni zhidao CIA you duo nuli ma?" (To make you love *niangpao*, do you know how hard the CIA worked?), Sohu.com, October 20, 2019, https://www.sohu.com/a/348291009_570238 (accessed March 20, 2020).

20. See, for instance, Xiao Meili, "Xiaomie niang neng jiu Zhongguo ma?" (Can we really save China by eliminating sissies?), Zhihu.com, September 8, 2018, https://zhuanlan.zhihu.com/p/44008074 (accessed March 18, 2020).

21. "Bie na niangpao he Mei Lanfang xiangti binglun, tamen hai bu pei" (Don't mention *niangpao* [actors] in the same breath as Mei Lanfang, they do not deserve it), Sohu.com, November 19, 2018, https://www.sohu.com/a/276342779_804333 (accessed March 23, 2020).

22. "Ye Ting zhi sun nu pi Jianjun Daye xiaoxianrou naiqi tai nong" (The grandson of Ye Ting criticizes *The Founding of an Army* for the effeminacy of the "little fresh meat" actors), *Media Club*, July 28, 2017, www.mediaclub.cc/News/infos/id/8689 (accessed March 23, 2020).

23. Engaging with critical studies of men and masculinities in the West (Kimmel, Hearn, and Connell 2005; Connell 2005), Chinese masculinity studies have emerged as a burgeoning field in the past two decades. A growing body of work has addressed various aspects of men and masculinities in China from a range of disciplines. Some of these studies attempt to bring Chinese-specific cultural frameworks—such as *yin/yang* and *wen/wu*—into conversation with Western gender theory (Louie 2002; Song 2004); some focus on the reconstruction of masculine discourse in literature and history (Zhong 2000; M. Huang 2006; Hinsch 2013; Vitiello 2013); some examine men and masculinities through the prisms of class (Osburg 2013; Lin 2013; Choi and Peng 2016), ethnicity (Dautcher 2009), and leisure (Moskowitz 2013); and some delve into the hybridity of Chinese masculinity in a global age (Louie 2015; Hird and Song 2018). Youth masculinity, however, remains an understudied area. Although youths have been involved in studies of the "new rich" (Osburg 2013), middle-class white-collar employees (Song and Hird 2014), migrant workers (Lin 2013; Choi and Peng 2016), and male sex workers and homosexual men (Kong 2011; T. Zheng 2015a), generational masculinities of the male body and transnational links remain a lacuna to be filled.

Chapter 7

1. The original is from chapter 1 (King Hui of Liang, Part One) of *Mencius*: "Extend your respect and care for your aged parents to all the aged, and extend your love for your own children to all children."

2. See Xi Jinping's speech at a meeting with representatives of the first National Congress on Civilized Values in the Family, December 12, 2016, http://

theory.people.com.cn/n1/2018/0103/c416126-29743636.html (accessed May 11, 2020).

3. See Ho (2015, 75–93) for a discussion of *Golden Marriage* and the discourse on a harmonious society.

4. Named after Lu Xinhua's 1978 short story "The Scar," "Scar literature" refers to a group of literary works published in the late 1970s and early 1980s that severely denounce the Maoist line of class struggle and sentimentally portray people's sufferings, especially those of cadres and intellectuals, during the Cultural Revolution.

5. In a popular family chronicle drama, *The Romance of Our Parents*, the narrator's mother, An Jie (Mei Ting), comes from a bourgeois family in Shanghai and marries a PLA naval officer, Jiang Defu (Guo Tao), who is from the countryside. An's sister and her husband, Ouyang Yi (Liu Yijun), a returnee from overseas, originally look down on Jiang because of his background. Ouyang shows off his dexterous use of a knife and fork in front of Jiang at the dinner table. But when Ouyang is later labeled a "rightist" and the whole family is sent to a labor camp, it is Jiang, who happens to be stationed nearby, who helps them at considerable risk to himself. The conceited Ouyang learns his lesson and becomes good friends with Jiang after his rehabilitation.

6. See Lu Feiran, "Popular Drama about Family Life Perturbs Viewers," SHINE, April 15, 2019. https://www.shine.cn/feature/entertainment/1904153030/ (accessed May 21, 2020).

7. One seller on Taobao, China's eBay, set up a service called "cursing the Su family father and sons." For a fee of 0.5 yuan per curse, the seller would open up a chat window, pretending to be one of the despised characters by displaying his photo and name, and let the client vent his or her anger. The seller also displayed a counter to show how many times each character had been cursed by customers. See Manya Koetse, "Catharsis on Taobao? Chinese 'All is Well' TV Drama Fans Are Paying Up to Scold the 'Su Family Villains,'" *What's on Weibo*, March 23, 2019, https://www.whatsonweibo.com/chinese-all-is-well-tv-drama-fans-are-paying -up-to-scold-soap-opera-villains/ (accessed May 21, 2020).

8. Yin Yiyun, "TV Drama Highlights Gender Discrimination in Chinese Families," *Sixth Tone*, March 11, 2019. https://www.sixthtone.com/news/1003660/tv -drama-highlights-gender-discrimination-in-chinese-families (accessed May 21, 2020).

9. Lu Feiran, "Popular Drama about Family Life Perturbs Viewers."

10. Elaine Yau, "Chinese TV Series about the Gritty Realities of Buying a Home Clocks Up 4 Billion Online Views," *South China Morning Post*, March 23, 2020, https://www.scmp.com/lifestyle/entertainment/article/3076416/chinese-tv-ser ies-about-gritty-realities-buying-home-clocks (accessed June 4, 2020).

11. Wang Jun, personal communication, May 8, 2021.

12. For an English translation of Lu Xun's "Regret for the Past," see https:// www.marxists.org/archive/lu-xun/1925/10/21.htm (accessed June 17, 2020).

13. The craze for portrayals of the Qing emperors on the small screen began with the tongue-in-cheek historical drama *The Hunchback Prime Minister* (*Zai-*

xiang Liu Luoguo, 1997). Among the most popular dramas in this category are *Kangxi's Incognito Travels* (1997–2003) and *The Eloquent Ji Xiaolan* (*Tiechi tongya Ji Xiaolan*, 2001–2008) and the entertaining *Princess Pearl* (*Huanzhu Gege*, 1998, 1999) series, which has been tremendously popular in Hong Kong and Taiwan and in overseas Chinese communities. There are also more serious historical depictions of the most accomplished Qing emperors, including *The Granaries under Heaven* (*Tianxia liangcang*, 2002), *The Dynasty of Yongzheng* (*Yongzheng Wangchao*, 1999), *The Dynasty of Kangxi* (*Kangxi wangchao*, 2001), *The Dynasty of Qianlong* (*Qianlong wangchao*, 2003), and *Li Wei the Magistrate* (*Li Wei dangguan*, 2002–2004) and its sequel *Li Wei Resigns from Office* (*Li Wei ci guan*, 2006).

14. See Yi Weiguan, "Cong nüxing yu nüquan zhuyi jiaodu tan gongdou ju" (On palace intrigue dramas from the perspective of women and feminism), Baidu.com, December 31, 2019, http://baijiahao.baidu.com/s?id=165443868205 6999133 (accessed June 22, 2020).

15. See "A Chinese Drama Is the Most Googled TV Show of 2018," SBS News, December 28, 2018, https://www.sbs.com.au/news/a-chinese-drama-is-the-most -googled-tv-show-of-2018 (accessed June 26, 2020).

16. Michelle Wong, "If Period Drama *Yanxi Palace* Is Gone, What's the Story for Chinese Soft Power?" *South China Morning Post*, January 29, 2019, https://www.sc mp.com/news/china/society/article/2184169/if-period-drama-yanxi-palace-go ne-whats-story-chinese-soft-power?utm_campaign=contentexchange&utm _medium=partner&utm_source=mediacorp (accessed June 27, 2020).

17. Eduardo Baptista, "Will China's Hit Period Drama 'Yanxi Palace' Face Censorship?" Channel3000.com, February 3, 2019, https://www.channel3000.com /will-chinas-hit-period-drama-yanxi-palace-face-censorship/ (accessed June 26, 2020).

18. See "Gongdouju xiaoshi: Zhou Xun Ruyi zhuan, Wu Jinyan Yanxi gonglue fen xiajia; dalu chushou jiaqiang guanzhi" (The palace intrigue dramas have disappeared: *Ruyi's Royal Love in the Palace* and *The Story of Yanxi Palace* have been put off air; control tightened on the mainland), *Apple Daily*, September 28, 2020, https://hk.appledaily.com/entertainment/20200928/OSN4BFAO7NFYLDFKSR NSEKTGDQ/ (accessed September 28, 2020).

19. Li Yang, personal communication via WeChat, July 24, 2020.

20. "Xi Jinping chuxi quanguo xuanchuan sixiang gongzuo huiyi bing fabiao zhongyao jianghua" (Xi Jinping delivered an important speech at the national conference on propaganda ideology), Gov.cn, August 22, 2018, http://www.gov .cn/xinwen/2018-08/22/content_5315723.htm (accessed July 28, 2020).

21. "China Focus: Chinese Web Novels Create Reading Frenzy among Foreigners," Xinhuanet.com, April 17, 2017, http://www.xinhuanet.com//english/2017 -04/17/c_136215918.htm (accessed July 27, 2020).

22. "Qingping yue li Wang Kai yan de Song Renzong fuhe lishi ma? Zhuanjia zheyang shuo" (Is the emperor played by Wang Kai in *Serenade of Peaceful Joy* faithful to the historical facts?), *Shangguan xinwen*, April 12, 2020, http://ent.163 .com/20/0412/08/FA0FJ2PL00038FO9.html (accessed July 29, 2020).

Epilogue

1. Africans appear more frequently in dating shows, singing contests, and reality shows than in drama serials. One African American image in a recent TV drama is a Black American soldier named Elvin who appears in *The 38th Parallel*, which is set during the Korean War. Elvin is bullied by White fellow soldiers in a POW camp and later becomes sympathetic toward the Chinese after being inspired by the doctors and nurses of the Chinese People's Volunteer Army.

2. See Emma Graham-Harrison, "Black Man Is Washed Whiter in China's Racist Detergent Advert," *The Guardian*, May 28, 2016, https://www.theguardian .com/world/2016/may/28/china-racist-detergent-advert-outrage (accessed May 16, 2020).

3. Vivian Wang, "A TV Drama on China's Fight with Covid-19 Draws Ire over Its Depiction of Women," *The New York Times*, September 20, 2020, https://www .nytimes.com/2020/09/20/world/asia/china-tv-women-coronavirus.html (accessed September 21, 2020).

4. Nü Quan, "Zuimei nixingzhe: Nüxing kangyi zai meiti chengxian de quan-mian kuitui" (*Heroes in Harm's Way*: The retreat of women in media representa-tions of fighting the pandemic), https://mp.weixin.qq.com/s/5A60Vl1a3tIMRdv 9ezSQ_Q (accessed September 24, 2020). For online commentaries on the sexist messages in the drama, see http://weibointl.api.weibo.com/share/173467143.ht ml?weibo_id=4551000591184130 (accessed September 24, 2020).

5. Vivian Wang, "A TV Drama on China's Fight with Covid-19 Draws Ire over Its Depiction of Women."

Bibliography

Ang, Ien. 1991. *Desperately Seeking the Audience*. London: Routledge.

Ang, Ien. 1996. *Living Room Wars: Rethinking Media Audiences for a Postmodern World*. London: Routledge.

Ang, Ien. 2004. "The Cultural Intimacy of TV Drama." In *Feeling Asian Modernities: Transnational Consumption of Japanese TV Dramas*, edited by Koichi Iwabuchi, 303–9. Hong Kong: Hong Kong University Press.

Ang, Ien. 2007. "Television Fictions Around the World: Melodrama and Irony in Global Perspective." *Critical Studies in Television* 2, no. 2: 18–30.

Appiah, Kwame Anthony. 2006. *Cosmopolitanism: Ethics in a World of Strangers*. New York: W. W. Norton.

Bai, Ruoyun. 2014. *Staging Corruption: Chinese Television and Politics*. Vancouver: University of British Columbia Press.

Bai, Ruoyun. 2020. "Refashioning Chinese Television through Digital Fun." In *The Routledge Companion to Global Television*, edited by Shawn Shimpach, 359–70. London: Routledge.

Bai, Ruoyun, and Geng Song, eds. 2015. *Chinese Television in the Twenty-First Century: Entertaining the Nation*. London: Routledge.

Barlow, Tani E. 1991. "Theorizing Woman: *Funü, Guojia, Jiating* (Chinese Women, Chinese State, Chinese Family)." *Genders* 10: 132–60.

Barlow, Tani E., ed. 1997. *Formations of Colonial Modernity in East Asia*. Durham, NC: Duke University Press.

Barmé, Geremie. 1995. "To Screw Foreigners Is Patriotic: China's Avant-garde Nationalists." *The China Journal* 34: 209–34.

Bergling, Tim. 2001. *Sissyphobia: Gay Men and Effeminate Behavior*. New York: Harrington Park Press.

Bhabha, Homi K. 1983. "The Other Question: Difference, Discrimination and the Discourses of Colonialism." *Screen* 24, no. 6: 18–36.

Bhabha, Homi K. 1994. *The Location of Culture*. London: Routledge.

Bourdieu, Pierre. 1984. *Distinction: A Social Critique of the Judgement of Taste*. Translated by Richard Nice. London: Routledge.

Bröckling, Ulrich. 2015. *The Entrepreneurial Self: Fabricating a New Type of Subject*. London: SAGE.

Butler, Judith. 1990. *Gender Trouble: Feminism and the Subversion of Identity*. London: Routledge.

Cai, Shenshen. 2014. "Rhetoric and Politics of the Female Body and Sex in Two Contemporary Chinese TV Drama Series: *The Place Where Dreams Start* and *Blow the North Wind*." *Journal of International Women's Studies* 15, no. 1: 151–66.

Cai, Shenshen. 2016. *State Propaganda in China's Entertainment Industry*. London: Routledge.

Callahan, William A. 2006. "History, Identity, and Security: Producing and Consuming Nationalism in China." *Critical Asian Studies* 38, no. 2: 179–208.

Chang, Maria Hsia. 2001. *Return of the Dragon: China's Wounded Nationalism*. Boulder, CO: Westview Press.

Chen, Lu. 2018. *Chinese Fans of Japanese and Korean Pop Culture: Nationalistic Narratives and International Fandom*. London: Routledge.

Chen, Xiaomei. 1995. *Occidentalism: A Theory of Counter-Discourse in Post-Mao China*. New York: Oxford University Press.

Chiang, Howard, and Alvin K. Wong. 2017. "Asia Is Burning: Queer Asia as Critique." *Culture, Theory and Critique* 58, no. 2: 121–26.

Choi, Susanne Yuk-Ping, and Yinni Peng. 2016. *Masculine Compromise: Migration, Family, and Gender in China*. Berkeley: University of California Press.

Chow, Rey. 1991. "Violence in the Other Country: China as Crisis, Spectacle, and Woman." In *Third World Women and the Politics of Feminism*, edited by Chandra Talpade Monhanty, Ann Rosso, and Lourdes Torres, 81–100. Bloomington: Indiana University Press.

Chow, Rey. 2000. "Introduction: On Chineseness as a Theoretical Problem." In *Modern Chinese Literary and Cultural Studies in the Age of Theory: Re-imagining a Field*, edited by Rey Chow, 1–25. Durham, NC: Duke University Press.

Chua, Beng Huat. 2000. "Consuming Asians: Ideas and Issues." In *Consumption in Asia: Lifestyles and Identities*, edited by Beng Huat Chua, 1–34. London: Routledge.

Chun, Allen. 1996. "Fuck Chineseness: On the Ambiguities of Ethnicity as Culture as Identity." *boundary 2* 23, no. 2: 111–38.

Cohen, Stephen. 2004. "'No Assembly but Horn-Beast': The Politics of Cuckoldry in Shakespeare's Romantic Comedies." *Journal for Early Modern Cultural Studies* 4, no. 2: 5–34.

Connell, R. W. 2005. *Masculinities*. 2nd ed. Berkeley: University of California Press.

Connell, R. W. 2007. *Southern Theory: The Global Dynamics of Knowledge in Social Science*. Cambridge: Polity Press.

Connell, R. W., and Julian Wood. 2005. "Globalization and Business Masculinities." *Men and Masculinities* 7, no. 4: 347–64.

Curtin, Michael. 2009. "Matrix Media." In *Television Studies After TV*, edited by Graeme Turner and Jinna Tay, 9–19. Abingdon: Routledge.

Dautcher, Jay. 2009. *Down a Narrow Road: Identity and Masculinity in a Uyghur Community in Xinjiang China*. Cambridge, MA: Harvard University Press.

Delanty, Gerard. 2012. *Routledge Handbook of Cosmopolitanism Studies*. London: Routledge.

DeWoskin, Rachel. 2005. *Foreign Babes in Beijing: Behind the Scenes of a New China*. New York: W. W. Norton.

Donald, Stephanie Hemelryk, Micheal Keane, and Yin Hong, eds. 2002. *Media in China: Consumption, Content and Crisis*. London: RoutledgeCurzon.

Donaldson, Mike. 1993. "What Is Hegemonic Masculinity?" *Theory and Society* 22: 643–57.

Eagleton, Terry. 2016. *Culture*. New Haven, CT: Yale University Press.

Edwards, Louise. 2016. *Women Warriors and Wartime Spies of China*. Cambridge: Cambridge University Press.

Edwards, Tim. 2006. *Cultures of Masculinity*. London: Routledge.

Eguchi, Shinsuke. 2011. "Negotiating Sissyphobia: A Critical/Interpretive Analysis of One 'Femme' Gay Asian Body in the Heteronormative World." *Journal of Men's Studies* 19, no. 1: 37–56.

Elias, Juanita, and Christine Beasley. 2009. "Hegemonic Masculinity and Globalization: 'Transnational Business Masculinities' and Beyond." *Globalizations* 6, no. 2: 281–96.

Enloe, Cynthia. 1990. *Bananas, Beaches, and Bases: Making Feminist Sense of International Politics*. Berkeley: University of California Press.

Erwin, Kathleen. 1999. "White Women, Male Desires: A Televisual Fantasy of the Transnational Chinese Family." In *Spaces of Their Own: Women's Public Sphere in Transnational China*, edited by Mayfair M.-H. Yang, 232–55. Minneapolis: University of Minnesota Press.

Feng, Pengzhi. 2016. "Cong 'sange zixin' dao 'sige zixin'—Lun Xi Jinping zongshuji dui Zhongguo tese shehuizhuyi de wenhua jiangou" (From "three confidences" to "four confidences": On General Secretary Xi Jinping's cultural construction of socialism with Chinese characteristics). http://theory.pe ople.com.cn/n1/2016/0707/c49150-28532466.html.

Foucault, Michel. 1980a. *Power-Knowledge: Selected Interviews and Other Writings 1972–1977*. Edited by Colin Gordon. New York: Harvester Wheatsheaf.

Foucault, Michel. 1980b. "What Is an Author?" In *Language, Counter-memory, Practice: Selected Essays and Interviews by Michel Foucault*, edited by Donald F. Bouchard. Ithaca, NY: Cornell University Press.

Foucault, Michel. (1978) 1991. "Governmentality." In *The Foucault Effect: Studies in Governmentality*, edited by Graham Burchell, Colin Gordon, and Peter Miller, 87–104. Chicago: University of Chicago Press.

Foucault, Michel. 2008. *The Birth of Biopolitics: Lectures at the Collège de France, 1978–79*. Translated by Graham Burchell. New York: Palgrave Macmillan.

Gao, Helen. 2019. "'Little Fresh Meat' and the Changing Face of Masculinity in China." *New York Times*, June 12. https://www.nytimes.com/2019/06/12/opi nion/little-fresh-meat-china.html.

Gao, Xuesong. 2012. "'Cantonese Is Not a Dialect': Chinese Netizens' Defence of Cantonese as a Regional Lingua Franca." *Journal of Multilingual and Multicultural Development* 33, no. 5: 449–64.

Gong, Qian. 2021. *Remaking Red Classics in Post-Mao China: TV Drama as Popular Media*. Lanham, MD: Rowman & Littlefield.

Gong, Yuan. 2016. "Online Discourse of Masculinities in Transnational Football Fandom: Chinese Arsenal Fans' Talk around '*gaofushuai*' and '*diaosi*.'" *Discourse & Society* 27, no. 1: 20–37.

Gorfinkel, Lauren. 2018. *Chinese Television and National Identity Construction: The Cultural Politics of Music-Entertainment Programmes*. London: Routledge.

Gorfinkel, Lauren, and Andrew Chubb. 2015. "When Foreigners Perform the Chinese Nation: Televised Global Chinese Language Competitions." In *Chinese Television in the Twenty-First Century*, edited by Ruoyun Bai and Geng Song, 121–40. London: Routledge.

Greenblatt, Stephen. 1988. *Shakespearean Negotiations*. Oxford: Clarendon Press.

Gries, Peter Hays. 2004. *China's New Nationalism: Pride Politics and Diplomacy*. Berkeley: University of California Press.

Griffins, Penny. 2007. "Sexing the Economy in a Neo-liberal World Order: Neo-liberal Discourse and the (Re)Production of Heteronormative Heterosexuality." *British Journal of Politics and International Relations* 9, no. 2: 220–38.

Guo, Yingjie. 2004. *Cultural Nationalism in Contemporary China*. London: RoutledgeCurzon.

Harrell, Stevan, and Gonçalo Santos. 2017. "Introduction." In *Transforming Patriarchy: Chinese Families in the Twenty-first Century*, edited by Gonçalo Santos and Stevan Harrell, 3–36. Seattle: University of Washington Press.

Hartsock, Nancy. 1985. *Money, Sex, and Power: Toward a Feminist Historical Materialism*. Boston: Northeastern University Press.

Harvey, Stefan. 2019. "'Sissies Weaken the Nation?': Mapping the Discourse Surrounding *Niangpao* and Reading Gender Performance in the TV Drama *Sweet Combat*." MA dissertation., Shanghai Theatre Academy.

Heningsen, Lena. 2011. "Coffee, Fast Food and the Desire for Romantic Love in Contemporary China: Branding and Marketing Trends in Popular Chinese-language Literature." *Transcultural Studies* 2: 232–70.

Hesse-Biber, Sharlene. 2006. *The Cult of Thinness*. Oxford: Oxford University Press.

Hinsch, Bret. 2013. *Masculinities in Chinese History*. Lanham, MD: Rowman & Littlefield.

Hird, Derek, and Geng Song, eds. 2018. *The Cosmopolitan Dream: Transnational Chinese Masculinities in a Global Age*. Hong Kong: Hong Kong University Press.

Ho, Wing Shan. 2015. *Screening Post-1989 China: Critical Analysis of Chinese Film and Television*. New York: Palgrave Macmillan.

Hong, Juntao. 1998. *The Internationalization of Television in China: The Evolution of Ideology, Society, and Media since the Reform*. New York: Praeger.

Huang, Martin W. 2006. *Negotiating Masculinities in Late Imperial China*. Honolulu: University of Hawai`i Press.

Huang, Ya-chien. 2008. "Pink Dramas: Reconciling Consumer Modernity and Confucian Womanhood." In *TV Drama in China*, edited by Ying Zhu, Michael Keane, and Ruoyun Bai, 103–14. Hong Kong: Hong Kong University Press.

Hughes, Christopher R. 2006. *Chinese Nationalism in the Global Era*. London: Routledge.

Iida, Yumiko. 2005. "Beyond the 'Feminization of Masculinity': Transforming Patriarchy with the 'Feminine' in Contemporary Japanese Youth Culture." *Inter-Asia Cultural Studies* 6, no. 1: 56–74.

Jeffreys, Elaine, ed. 2010. *China's Governmentalities: Governing Change, Changing Government*. London: Routledge.

Jeffreys, Elaine, and Gary Sigley. 2010. "Governmentality, Governance and China." In *China's Governmentalities: Governing Change, Changing Government*, edited by Elaine Jeffreys, 1–23. London: Routledge.

Jenkins, Henry. 2006. *Convergence Culture: Where Old and New Media Collide*. New York: New York University Press.

Johansson, Perry. 1999. "Consuming the Other: The Fetish of the Western Woman in Chinese Advertising and Popular Culture." *Postcolonial Studies* 2, no. 3: 377–88.

Johansson, Perry. 2015. *The Libidinal Economy of China: Gender, Nationalism, and Consumer Culture*. Lanham, MD: Lexington Books.

Jung, Sun. 2011. *Korean Masculinities and Transcultural Consumption: Yonsama, Rain, Oldboy, K-Pop Idols*. Hong Kong: Hong Kong University Press.

Jurriëns, Edwin, and Jeroen de Kloet. 2007. *Cosmopatriots: On Distant Belongings and Close Encounters*. Amsterdam: Rodopi.

Kackman, Michael, Marnie Binfield, Matthew Thomas Payne, Allison Perlman, and Bryan Sebok, eds. 2011. *Flow TV: Television in the Age of Media Convergence*. London: Routledge.

Kahn, Coppélia. 1981. *Man's Estate: Masculine Identity in Shakespeare*. Los Angeles: University of California Press.

Keane, Michael. 2007. *Created in China: The Great Leap Forward*. London: Routledge.

Keane, Michael. 2015. *The Chinese Television Industry*. London: Palgrave.

Keane, Michael. 2016. "Disconnecting, Connecting, and Reconnecting: How Chinese Television Found Its Way Out of the Box." *International Journal of Communication* 10: 5426–43.

Keane, Michael, Anthony Y. H. Fung, and Albert Moran. 2007. *New Television, Globalization, and the East Asian Cultural Imagination*. Hong Kong: Hong Kong University Press.

Kimmel, Michael S., Jeff Hearn, and R. W. Connell, eds. 2005. *Handbook of Studies on Men and Masculinities*. London: SAGE.

Kong, Shuyu. 2008. "Family Matters: Reconstructing the Family on the Chinese Television Screen." In *TV Drama in China*, edited by Ying Zhu, Michael Keane, and Ruoyun Bai, 75–88. Hong Kong: Hong Kong University Press.

Kong, Shuyu. 2014. *Popular Media, Social Emotion and Public Discourse in Contemporary China*. London: Routledge.

Kong, Travis. 2011. *Chinese Male Homosexuals: Memba, Tongzhi and Golden Boy*. London: Routledge.

Kong, Travis. 2019. "The Pursuit of Masculinity by Young Gay Men in Neoliberal Hong Kong and Shanghai." *Journal of Youth Studies*, https://doi.org/10.1080/13676261.2019.1646893.

Kristeva, Julia. 1982. *The Powers of Horror: An Essay on Abjection*. Translated by Leon S. Roudiez. New York: Columbia University Press.

Lavin, Maud, Ling Yang, and Jing Jamie Zhao, eds. 2017. *Boy's Love, Cosplay, and Androgynous Idols: Queer Fan Cultures in Mainland China, Hong Kong, and Taiwan*. Hong Kong: Hong Kong University Press.

Laws and Regulations Department of the State Administration of Radio, Film and Television. 2013. *The Radio, Film and Television Laws and Regulations of the People's Republic of China*. Beijing: China Legal Publishing House.

Lee, Haiyan. 2014. *The Stranger and the Chinese Moral Imagination*. Stanford, CA: Stanford University Press.

Lee, Teresa Man Ling. 2007. "Liang Qichao and the Meaning of Citizenship: Then and Now." *History of Political Thought* 28, no. 2: 305–27.

Leung, Vivienne, Kimmy Cheng, and Tommy Tse. 2017. *Celebrity Culture and the Entertainment Industry in Asia*. Bristol: Intellect.

Lewis, Tania, Fran Martin, and Wanning Sun. 2016. *Telemodernities: Television and Transforming Lives in Asia*. Durham, NC: Duke University Press.

Li, Eva Cheuk-Yin. 2017. "Querying Gender: The Everyday Practice of Zhongxing (Neutral Gender/Sex) among Chinese Women." PhD dissertation, King's College London.

Li, Li. 2011. "The Television Play, Melodramatic Imagination and Envisioning the 'Harmonious Society' in Post-1989 China." *Journal of Contemporary China* 20, no. 69: 327–41.

Li, Yanling. 2020. "'We Are All Guilty': Censorship of Danmei in China." Paper presented at the Association for Asian Studies (AAS) Annual Conference, Boston, March 19–22. http://www.asianstudies.org/wp-content/uploads/2020-AC-Program-FINAL.pdf.

Liang, Yi. 2015. "Lun badao zongcai qingjie muti cong wenxue dao dianshiju lingyu de liudong" (On the evolution of the bossy CEO motif from literature to TV drama). *Dongnan chuanbo* 6: 108–11.

Lin, Xiaodong. 2013. *Gender, Modernity and Male Migrant Workers in China: Becoming a "Modern" Man*. London: Routledge.

Liu, Jin. 2013. *Signifying the Local: Media Productions Rendered in Local Languages in Mainland China in the New Millennium*. Leiden: Brill.

Liu, Kang. 2004. *Globalization and Cultural Trends in China*. Honolulu: University of Hawai`i Press.

Liu, Petrus. 2018. "Women and Children First—Jingoism, Ambivalence, and Crisis of Masculinity in *Wolf Warrior II*." In *Wolf Warrior II: The Rise of China and Gender/Sexual Politics*, compiled and edited by Petrus Liu and Lisa Rofel. MCLC Resource Center Publication. http://u.osu.edu/mclc/online-series/liu-rofel/.

Lodziak, Conrad. 1986. *The Power of Television: A Critical Appraisal*. New York: St. Martin's Press.

Louie, Andrea. 2004. *Chineseness across Borders: Renegotiating Chinese Identities in China and the United States*. Durham, NC: Duke University Press.

Louie, Kam. 2002. *Theorising Chinese Masculinity: Society and Gender in China*. Cambridge: Cambridge University Press.

Louie, Kam. 2015. *Chinese Masculinities in a Globalizing World*. London: Routledge.

Lovell, Julia. 2019. *Maoism: A Global History*. London: Bodley Head.

Lu, Sheldon. 2000. "Soap Opera in China: The Transnational Politics of Visuality, Sexuality, and Masculinity." *Cinema Journal* 40, no. 1: 25–47.

Lull, James. 1991. *China Turned On: Television, Reform, and Resistance*. New York: Routledge.

MacLachlan, Elizabeth, and Geok-lian Chua. 2004. "Defining Asian Femininity: Chinese Viewers of Japanese TV Dramas in Singapore." In *Feeling Asian Modernity: Transnational Consumption of Japanese TV Dramas*, edited by Koichi Iwabuchi, 155–75. Hong Kong: Hong Kong University Press.

Malvey, Laura. 1975. "Visual Pleasure and Narrative Cinema." *Screen* 16, no. 3: 6–18.

Martin, Fran, and Tania Lewis. 2016. "Lifestyle Media in Asia: Consumption, Aspiration and Identity." In *Lifestyle Media in Asia: Consumption, Aspiration and Identity*, edited by Fran Martin and Tania Lewis, 13–31. London: Routledge.

Miller, Laura. 2006. *Beauty Up: Exploring Contemporary Japanese Body Aesthetics*. Berkeley: University of California Press.

Moran, Albert, and Michael Keane, eds. 2004. *Television across Asia: Television Industries, Programme Formats and Globalization*. London: Routledge.

Morgan, David. 1992. *Discovering Men*. London: Routledge.

Morley, David. 1992. *Television, Audiences and Cultural Studies*. London: Routledge.

Morley, David. 1993. "Active Audience Theory: Pendulums and Pitfalls." *Journal of Communication* 43: 13–19.

Moskowitz, Marc L. 2013. *Go Nation: Chinese Masculinities and the Game of Weiqi in China*. Berkeley: University of California Press.

Mulvey, Laura. 2009. *Visual and Other Pleasures*. New York: Palgrave Macmillan.

Muñoz, José Esteban. 1999. *Disidentifications: Queers of Color and the Performance of Politics*. Minneapolis: University of Minnesota Press.

Murong, Xuecun. 2014. "China's Television War on Japan." *New York Times*, February 9. http://www.nytimes.com/2014/02/10/opinion/murong-chinas-television-war-on-japan.html?_r=0.

Nagel, Joane. 1998. "Masculinity and Nationalism: Gender and Sexuality in the Making of Nations." *Ethnic and Racial Studies* 21, no. 2: 242–69.

Newman, Michael, and Elana Levine. 2012. *Legitimating Television: Media Convergence and Cultural Status*. London: Routledge.

Ng, How Wee. 2015. "Rethinking Censorship in China: The Case of *Snail House*." In *Chinese Television in the Twenty-First Century*, edited by Ruoyun Bai and Geng Song, 87–103. London: Routledge.

Niedenführ, Matthias. 2013. "The Tug-of-War between Regulatory Interventions and Market Demands in the Chinese Television Industry." *Political Economy of Communication* 1, no. 1: 90–110.

Nyíri, Pál, and Juan Zhang. 2010. "China's Cosmopolitan Nationalists: 'Heroes' and 'Traitors' of the 2008 Olympics." *The China Journal* 63: 25–55.

Ong, Aihwa, and Zhang Li. 2008. "Introduction: Privatizing China: Powers of the Self, Socialism from Afar." In *Privatizing China: Socialism from Afar*, edited by Li Zhang and Aihwa Ong, 1–20. Ithaca, NY: Cornell University Press.

Ong, Aihwa, and Donald Nonini, eds. 1997. *Ungrounded Empires: The Cultural Politics of Modern Chinese Transnationalism*. London: Routledge.

Osburg, John. 2013. *Anxious Wealth: Money and Morality among China's New Rich*. Stanford, CA: Stanford University Press.

Peterson, V. Spike. 1999. "Sexing Political Identities/Nationalism as Heterosexism." *International Feminist Journal of Politics* 1, no. 1: 34–65.

Poniewozik, James. 2014. "The Post-Television TV Era Has Begun." *TIME*, October 30. http://time.com/3547960/simpsons-world-hbo-streaming-tv/.

Qian, Kun. 2015. "*Tianxia* Revisited: Family and Empire on the Television Screen." In *Chinese Television in the Twenty-First Century*, edited by Ruoyun Bai and Geng Song, 175–91. London: Routledge.

Qiu, Zitong. 2013. "Cuteness as a Subtle Strategy: Urban Female Youth and the Online Feizhuliu Culture in Contemporary China." *Cultural Studies* 27, no. 2: 225–41.

Reeser, Todd W. 2010. *Masculinities in Theory: An Introduction*. Chichester: Wiley-Blackwell.

Ringrose, Jessica, and Valerie Walkerdine. 2008. "Regulating the Abject." *Feminist Media Studies* 8, no. 3: 227–46.

Roberts, Rosemary. 2010. *Maoist Model Theatre: The Semiotics of Gender and Sexuality in the Chinese Cultural Revolution (1966-1976)*. Leiden: Brill.

Rofel, Lisa. 2007. *Desiring China: Experiments in Neoliberalism, Sexuality, and Public Culture*. Durham, NC: Duke University Press.

Rofel, Lisa. 2019. "The (Re-)Emergence of Entrepreneurialism in Postsocialist China." In *Fabricating Transnational Capitalism: A Collaborative Ethnography of Italian-Chinese Global Fashion*, edited by Lisa Rofel and Sylvia J. Yanagisako, 119–60. Durham, NC: Duke University Press.

Schneider, Florian. 2012. *Visual Political Communication in Popular Chinese Television Series*. Leiden: Brill.

Sedgwick, Eve Kosofsky. 1985. *Between Men: English Literature and Male Homosocial Desire*. New York: Columbia University Press.

Sigley, Gary. 2006. "Chinese Governmentalities: Government, Governance and the Socialist Market Economy." *Economy and Society* 35, no. 4: 487–508.

Sigley, Gary. 2009. "*Suzhi*, the Body, and the Fortunes of Technoscientific Reasoning in Contemporary China." *positions* 17, no. 3: 537–66.

Silverstone, Roger. 1994. *Television and Everyday Life*. London: Routledge.

Song, Geng. 2004. *The Fragile Scholar: Power and Masculinity in Chinese Culture*. Hong Kong: Hong Kong University Press.

Song, Geng. 2010. "Chinese Masculinities Revisited: Male Images in Contemporary Television Drama Serials." *Modern China* 36: 404–34.

Song, Geng, and Derek Hird. 2014. *Men and Masculinities in Contemporary China.* Leiden: Brill.

Song, Geng, and Tracy K. Lee. 2010. "Consumption, Class Formation, and Sexuality: Reading Men's Lifestyle Magazines in China." *The China Journal* 64: 159–77.

Song, Geng, and Tracy K. Lee. 2012. "'New Man' and 'New Lad' with Chinese Characteristics? Cosmopolitanism, Cultural Hybridity and Men's Lifestyle Magazines in China." *Asian Studies Review* 36, no. 3: 345–67.

Spigel, Lynn, and Jan Olsson, eds. 2004. *Television After TV: Essays on a Medium in Transition.* Durham, NC: Duke University Press.

Strathern, Andrew, and Pamela J. Stewart. 2010. "Shifting Centres, Tense Peripheries: Indigenous Cosmopolitanisms." In *United in Discontent: Local Responses to Cosmopolitanism and Globalization,* edited by Dimitrios Theodossopoulos and Elisabeth Kirtsoglou, 20–44. New York: Berghahn Books.

Sun, Wanning. 2002a. "Semiotic Over-determination or 'Indoctritainment': Television, Citizenship, and Olympic Games." In *Media in China,* edited by Stephanie Hemelryk Donald, Michael Keane, and Yin Hong, 116–27. London: RoutledgeCurzon.

Sun, Wanning. 2002b. *Leaving China: Media, Migration, and Transnational Imagination.* Lanham, MD: Rowman & Littlefield.

Sun, Wanning, and Lauren Gorfinkel. 2015. "Scale and Place-Identity in the PRC: Provincial, National and Global Influences from 1958–2013." In *Television Histories in Asia: Issues and Contexts,* edited by Jinna Tay and Graeme Turner, 19–37. London: Routledge.

Theodossopoulos, Dimitrios, and Elisabeth Kirtsoglou, eds. 2010. *United in Discontent: Local Responses to Cosmopolitanism and Globalization.* New York: Berghahn Books.

Turner, Graeme, and Jinna Tay, eds. 2009. *Television Studies after TV: Understanding Television in the Post-Broadcast Era.* London: Routledge.

Unger, Jonathan, ed. 1996. *Chinese Nationalism.* Armonk, NY: M. E. Sharpe.

Vitiello, Giovanni. 2013. *The Libertine's Friend: Homosexuality and Masculinity in Late Imperial China.* Chicago: University of Chicago Press.

Wallis, Cara. 2013a. "Technology and/as Governmentality: The Production of Young Rural Women as Low-Tech Laboring Subjects in China." *Communication and Critical/Cultural Studies* 10, no. 4: 341–58.

Wallis, Cara. 2013b. *Technomobility in China: Young Migrant Women and Mobile Phones.* New York: New York University Press.

Wang, Chih-ming. 2018. "New China in New Times." In *Wolf Warrior II: The Rise of China and Gender/Sexual Politics,* compiled and edited by Petrus Liu and Lisa Rofel. MCLC Resource Center Publication. http://u.osu.edu/mclc/onli ne-series/liu-rofel/.

Wang, Hui, and Minghui Hu. 2016. "Why Culture: The Great War and Du Yaquan's Civilizational Discourse." In *Cosmopolitanism in China, 1600–1950,* edited by Minghui Hu and Johan Elverskog, 263–307. Amherst, NY: Cambria Press.

Wang, Jing. 1996. *High Culture Fever: Politics, Aesthetics, and Ideology in Deng's China*. Berkeley: University of California Press.

Wang, Pan. 2015. *Love and Marriage in Globalizing China*. London: Routledge.

Wang, Qin. 2018. "Niangdao de zhengyi he shouzhong de liangge shijie" (The controversy over *Mother's Life* and the two worlds of audience). *Zhongguo funü bao*, October 25, 5.

Wang, Yingzi, and Sabina Mihelj. 2019. "A Socialist Superwoman for the New Era: Chinese Television and the Changing Ideals of Femininity." *Feminist Media Histories* 5, no. 3: 36–59.

Wang, Zheng. 2016. *Finding Women in the State: A Socialist Feminist Revolution in the People's Republic of China, 1949–1964*. Berkeley: University of California Press.

Wen, Huike. 2015. *Television and the Modernization Ideal in 1980s China: Dazzling the Eyes*. Lanham, MD: Lexington Books.

Wong, Lily. 2018. *Transpacific Attachments: Sex Work, Media Networks, and Affective Histories of Chineseness*. New York: Columbia University Press.

Wu, Hung. 2008. "Television in Contemporary Chinese Art." *October* 125: 65–90.

Wu, Jingsi Christina. 2017. *Entertainment and Politics in Contemporary China*. New York: Palgrave MacMillan.

Wu, Xiao Angela, and Yige Dong. 2019. "What Is 'Made-in-China Feminism(s)'? Gender Discontent and Class Friction in Post-socialist China." *Critical Asian Studies* 51, no. 4: 471–92.

Xiao, Hui Faye. 2014. *Family Revolution: Marital Strife in Contemporary Chinese Literature and Visual Culture*. Seattle: University of Washington Press.

Xu, Lijun, ed. 2017. *Zhongguo dianshi shoushi nianjian 2017* (China TV rating yearbook 2017). Beijing: Zhongguo chuanmei daxue chubanshe.

Xu, Wei. 2015. "TV Thrillers Take Cue from Online Novels." *Shanghai Daily*, November 7. http://www.shanghaidaily.com/feature/TV-thrillers-take-cue-from-hit-online-novels/shdaily.shtml.

Yan, Grace, and Carla Almeida Santos. 2009. "'China, Forever': Tourism Discourse and Self-Orientalism." *Annals of Tourism Research* 36, no. 2: 295–315.

Yang, Fan. 2016. "Rethinking Commercial Nationalism: The 'Chinese Dream' in Neoliberal Globalization." In *Commercial Nationalism: Selling the Nation and Nationalizing the Sell*, edited by Zala Volcic and Mark Andrejevic, 65–85. London: Palgrave Macmillan.

Yang, Jie. 2011. "Nennu and Shunu: Gender, Body Politics, and the Beauty Economy in China." *Signs: Journal of Women in Culture and Society* 36, no. 2: 333–57.

Yang, Ling, and Yanrui Xu. 2017. "Chinese Danmei Fandom and Cultural Globalization from Below." In *Boy's Love, Cosplay, and Androgynous Idols: Queer Fan Cultures in Mainland China, Hong Kong, and Taiwan*, edited by Maud Lavin,

Ling Yang, and Jing Jamie Zhao, 3–19. Hong Kong: Hong Kong University Press.

Yang, Mayfair Mei-hui. 1999. *Spaces of Their Own: Women's Public Sphere in Transnational China*. Minneapolis: University of Minnesota Press.

Yang, Mingpin, ed. 2011. *Zhongguo dianshiju chanye fazhan yanjiubaogao* (A research report on the development of the TV drama industry in China). Beijing: Zhongguo guanbo dianshi chubanshe.

Yang, Mingpin, ed. 2014. *Zhongguo guangbo dianying dianshi fazhan baogao (2014)* (The report on the development of broadcasting, film and television in China (2014)). Beijing: Shehui kexue wenxian chubanshe.

Yau, Kinnia Shuk-ting. 2013. "Meaning of the Imagined Friends: Good-Japanese in Chinese War Films." In *Imagining Japan in Post-war East Asia*, edited by Paul Morris, Naoko Shimazu, and Edward Vickers, 68–84. London: Routledge.

Yu, Haiqing. 2009. *Media and Cultural Transformation in China*. London: Routledge.

Zhang, Xudong. 2008. *Postsocialism and Cultural Politics: China in the Last Decade of the Twentieth Century*. Durham, NC: Duke University Press.

Zhao, Jamie J. 2017. "Queering the Post-*L Word* Shane in the 'Garden of Eden': Chinese Fans' Gossip about Katherine Moenning." In *Boy's Love, Cosplay, and Androgynous Idols: Queer Fan Cultures in Mainland China, Hong Kong, and Taiwan*, edited by Maud Lavin, Ling Yang, and Jing Jamie Zhao, 63–90. Hong Kong: Hong Kong University Press.

Zhao, Jamie J. 2018. "Queer, Yet Never Lesbian: A Ten-Year Look Back at the Reality TV Singing Competition Show *Super Voice Girl*." *Celebrity Studies* 9, no. 4: 470–86.

Zhao, Suisheng. 2004. *A Nation-State by Construction: Dynamics of Modern Chinese Nationalism*. Stanford, CA: Stanford University Press.

Zheng, Jiawen. 2018. "Why It's Silly for Chinese to Worry about 'Sissy' Young Men." *Sixth Tone*, September 19. http://www.sixthtone.com/news/1002942/why-its-silly-for-chinese-to-worry-about-sissy-young-men.

Zheng, Tiantian. 2015a. *Tongzhi Living: Men Attracted to Men in Postsocialist China*. Minneapolis: University of Minnesota Press.

Zheng, Tiantian. 2015b. "Masculinity in Crisis: Effeminate Men, Loss of Manhood, and the Nation-State in Postsocialist China." *Etnográfica* 19, no. 2: 347–65.

Zheng, Xiqing. 2018. "Xiangxiang danmei: Wufa pobi de yawenhua ziben he danmei yawenhua de hefaxing beilun" (Imagining the danmei: The cultural capital of a subculture and the legitimacy of the danmei subculture). *Dialogue Transculturel* 39: 390–411.

Zheng, Yongnian. 1999. *Discovering Chinese Nationalism in China: Modernization, Identity and International Relations*. Cambridge: Cambridge University Press.

Zhong, Xueping. 2000. *Masculinity Besieged?: Issues of Modernity and Male Subjectivity in Chinese Literature of the Late Twentieth Century*. Durham, NC: Duke University Press.

Zhong, Xueping. 2010. *Mainstream Culture Refocused: Television Drama, Society, and the Production of Meaning in Reform-Era China*. Honolulu: University of Hawai`i Press.

Zhou, Laura. 2018. "Rights Group Urges Respect after Boy Band Called 'Sissies.'" *South China Morning Post*, September 11, A7.

Zhou, Raymond. 2017. "Depiction of Chinese Schindler Falls Short." *China Daily USA*, February 9. http://usa.chinadaily.com.cn/epaper/2017-02/09/content_28149689.htm.

Zhou, Yun. 2018. "The Story of Yanxi Palace." *The China Story 2018*. https://www.thechinastory.org/yearbooks/yearbook-2018-power/forum-power-and-the-patriarchy/the-story-of-yanxi-palace/.

Zhu, Ping. 2015. *Gender and Subjectivities in Early Twentieth-Century Chinese Literature and Culture*. New York: Palgrave.

Zhu, Ying. 2005. "Yongzheng Dynasty and Chinese Primetime Television Drama." *Cinema Journal* 44, no. 4: 3–17.

Zhu, Ying. 2008. *Television in Post-Reform China*. London: Routledge.

Zhu, Ying. 2012. *Two Billion Eyes: The Story of China Central Television*. New York: New Press.

Zhu, Ying, and Chris Berry, eds. 2009. *TV China*. Bloomington: Indiana University Press.

Zhu, Ying, Michael Keane, and Ruoyun Bai, eds. 2008. *TV Drama in China*. Hong Kong: Hong Kong University Press.

Žižek, Slavoj. 1997. *The Plague of Fantasies*. London: Verso.

Glossary

Ai de lixiang shenghuo	爱的理想生活
Aiguo zhe	爱国者
Anjia	安家
badao zongcai	霸道总裁
Bailu yuan	白鹿原
baofahu	暴发户
baojia, weiguo xingbang	保家、卫国、兴邦
Beijingren zai Niuyue	北京人在纽约
Biele, Wengehua	别了，温哥华
Chaoji nüsheng	超级女声
Chenqing ling	陈情令
chun yemen'er	纯爷们儿
chunjie lianhuan wanhui (chunwan)	春节联欢晚会（春晚）
cong yi er zhong	从一而终
da nü zhu	大女主
Da Qing hougong	大清后宫
Da zhangmen	大掌门
Dagou gun	打狗棍
Dahe ernü	大河儿女
Dai Tianli	戴天理
dailu dang	带路党
daimeng	呆萌
dama	大妈
Dang popo yushang ma	当婆婆遇上妈

danmei	耽美
danmu	弹幕
Dongya bingfu	东亚病夫
Dou tinghao	都挺好
Du Lala shengzhi ji	杜拉拉升职记
Dusheng zinü de popo mama	独生子女的婆婆妈妈
dushi qinggan ju	都市情感剧
e'gao	恶搞
Ershi buhuo	二十不惑
Fei	妃
Feicheng wurao	非诚勿扰
Feicui fenghuang	翡翠凤凰
feizhuliu	非主流
Fenghuo shuangxiong	烽火双雄
fenqing	愤青
fujoshi	腐女子
Fumu aiqing	父母爱情
fuyan kan ren ji	腐眼看人基
fuzeren daguo	负责任大国
ganzi bang	杆子帮
gao fu shuai	高富帅
gong	攻
gongdou ju	宫斗剧
gongnü	宫女
Gongxinji	宫心计
guifei	贵妃
Guiqu lai	归去来
guiren	贵人
guizi zhuanyehu	鬼子专业户
Guo Jingyu	郭靖宇
haigui	海归
hanjian	汉奸
he gu	河姑
Heping fandian	和平饭店

Heshang	河殇
Heyi shengxiaomo	何以笙箫默
hongge	红歌
Hongse	红色
Hua qiangu	花千骨
huang guifei	皇贵妃
Huanle song	欢乐颂
Huanxi popo qiao xifu	欢喜婆婆俏媳妇
Jianjun daye	建军大业
Jianzai xianshang	箭在弦上
Jin Xing	金星
Jinhun	金婚
Jinzhi yunie	金枝欲孽
Jiqing ranshao de suiyue	激情燃烧的岁月
Kaede Sendo	仙道枫
Kang-Ri qixia	抗日奇侠
Kang-Ri shenju	抗日神剧
Kenichi Miura	三浦研一
Kewang	渴望
Koji Yano	矢野浩二
Kuaile nüsheng	快乐女声
Lao er shen	老二婶
Li Yuchun	李宇春
Liang jian	亮剑
Leiyu	雷雨
Lian'ai xiansheng	恋爱先生
Lin shifu zai Shouer	林师傅在首尔
lixiang	立项
Liuxing huayuan	流星花园
lizhi	励志
Lu Han	鹿晗
Luolongzhen nüren	罗龙镇女人
mabao	妈宝
Mala poxi	麻辣婆媳

Mama Mia	妈妈咪呀
Meiren xinji	美人心计
meng	萌
Mi Yue zhuan	芈月传
minzu dayi	民族大义
Mishi Luoshanji	迷失洛杉矶
Modao zushi	魔道祖师
Modeng jiating	摩登家庭
Na Tulu	那图鲁
nan zhu wai, nü zhu nei	男主外，女主内
Na'nian huakai yue zheng yuan	那年花开月正圆
Nansheng nüsheng xiang qian chong	男生女生向前冲
niangpao	娘炮
nuannan	暖男
nü hanzi	女汉子
Nüren de kangzhan	女人的抗战
nüshen	女神
nüxing qunxiang ju	女性群像剧
nüzi ben ruo, wei mu ze gang	女子本弱，为母则刚
Oshin	阿信
Ou Hao	欧豪
Paomo zhi xia	泡沫之夏
pin	嫔
Popo	婆婆
Popo laile	婆婆来了
Popo ye shi ma	婆婆也是妈
Qingman siheyuan	情满四合院
Qingping yue	清平乐
Qingxian Basailuona	情陷巴塞罗那
qingyi	情义
Qiong baba, fu baba	穷爸爸，富爸爸
Qiong Yao	琼瑶

Renmin de mingyi	人民的名义
Ruyi zhuan	如懿传
Sanba xian	三八线
sanguan	三观
Sanshi eryi	三十而已
Se Nülang	涩女郎
sha bai tian	傻白甜
Shanghairen zai Dongjing	上海人在东京
Shangshi	伤逝
Shangyin	上瘾
Shanshan laichi 杉杉来吃	
Shanshan laile 杉杉来了	
shaonian niang ze Zhongguo niang	少年娘则中国娘
Shejian shang de Zhongguo	舌尖上的中国
Shewai baomu	涉外保姆
Shi'er dao fengwei	十二道锋味
shou	受
Shuangcheng shenghuo	双城生活
Shuangmian jiao	双面胶
suzhi	素质
Ta laile, qing biyan	他来了，请闭眼
Ta qishi meiyou name ai ni	他其实没有那么爱你
Taizifei shengzhiji	太子妃升职记
Tenma Shibuya	涩谷天马
Tianmi baoji	甜蜜暴击
tui ji ji ren	推己及人
Wang Gui yu Anna	王贵与安娜
Weizhuangzhe	伪装者
Wode Natasha	我的娜塔莎
Wode qian bansheng	我的前半生
Wu Yifan	吴亦凡
Xi Juan	席绢
xianxia	仙侠
Xiao liuxuesheng	小留学生

xiao nai gou	小奶狗
xiao saozi	小嫂子
Xiao Shenyang	小沈阳
xiao xian rou	小鲜肉
Xifu de meihao shidai	媳妇的美好时代
Xifu de meihao xuanyan	媳妇的美好宣言
Xifu shi zenyang liancheng de	媳妇是怎样炼成的
xinyi	信义
xiongdi shao	兄弟哨
Xiucai yudao bing	秀才遇到兵
xueba	学霸
xuexing	血性
Yangniu zai Beijing	洋妞在北京
yangpian	样片
Yanxi gonglue	延禧攻略
yaoqi	妖气
Yi Shu	亦舒
Yingsu de qingren	罂粟的情人
Yinwei aiqing you xingfu	因为爱情有幸福
Yiqi da guizi	一起打鬼子
Yiqi laikan liuxingyu	一起来看流星雨
Yiqi youkan liuxingyu	一起又看流星雨
Yonggan de xin	勇敢的心
Yu Minhong	俞敏洪
Zai Xini deng wo	在悉尼等我
zhainan	宅男
Zhang Luyi	张鲁一
Zhen Huan zhuan	甄嬛传
Zhenhun	镇魂
zheng nengliang	正能量
Zheng qingchun	正青春
Zheng Shuang	郑爽
zhengfu	政府
Zhengyangmen xia xiaonüren	正阳门下小女人
zhili	治理
zhinan ai	直男癌

Zhongguo shi guanxi	中国式关系
zhongxing	中性
zhuzhong jiating, zhuzhong jiajiao, zhuzhong jiafeng	注重家庭，注重家教，注重家风
ziqiang	自强
zizun zixin	自尊自信
Zuihou yizhang qianzheng	最后一张签证
Zuimei nixingzhe	最美逆行者

Index

Note: Page numbers in italics refer to the illustrations.